UTOPIAS

Social Ideals and Communal Experiments

Edited by

Peyton E. Richter

Professor of Humanities
Boston University

Holbrook Press, Inc. / Boston

TO GLENN R. NEGLEY

For he, Adeimantus, whose mind is fixed upon true being, has surely no time to look down upon the affairs of earth, or to be filled with malice and envy, contending against men; his eye is ever directed towards things fixed and immutable, which he sees neither injuring nor injured by one another, but all in order moving according to reason; these he imitates, and to these he will, as far as he can, conform himself. Can a man help imitating that with which he holds reverential converse?

Socrates

Contents

III. CONTRA UTOPIA

IV. UTOPIAN REJOINDERS

Preface

Today's students need little professorial prodding to ask many of the questions which have always interested social and moral philosophers. What is the best kind of life? How can it be achieved? How can society be reformed to meet better the needs of man? Is a utopia or a perfect society possible? If it is, is it desirable? Fortunately, such questions are no longer thought to be strictly academic. To the contrary, they are increasingly being considered essential to survival and happiness in light of the shocking but still not widely enough recognized fact that man's natural and social environments are rapidly deteriorating. Many would agree that Lord Beveridge's remark to a group of students at the beginning of the Second World War is more apropos today: "The choice is no longer between Utopia and the pleasant ordered world that our fathers knew. The choice is between Utopia and Hell."

So first of all, the content of this book, with its focus on utopian speculation and planning, should promote further discussion of some of the big social issues of our time and shed some light on several of the major problems of social philosophy—for example, the nature of an ideal social order, the relation of human nature to social institutions, and the problem of freedom and control. The study of utopias is not intended to encourage students to escape from unpleasant social realities or merely to build castles in the air, but rather to help them to develop standards by which to judge actual society and to improve the quality of life in the present-day world.

A second aim has been to provide a source book in utopian thinking and action which would help satisfy (as well as increase) the interest which many readers have in intentional communities or utopian experiments and in social planning and prognostication. With one exception (Morning Star), the experiments included are "classical" or "paradigm" utopias—for example, the Shakers, Brook Farm, and Oneida. The assumption underlying this editorial decision is that the new student of intentional communities should attain some knowledge of what has already succeeded and failed before studying the variety of contemporary communes or perhaps embarking on communal experiments of his own. In this connection, the questions and reading lists included at the end of each part may provide an aid to the student who wants to attain new perspectives and to make discoveries throughout the whole realm of utopian construction in imagination or in fact.

A third and final aim of *Utopias* is to provoke critical discussion of the characteristics, advantages, and disadvantages of utopian thinking and planning. Even when utopias exist nowhere except in their creators' imaginations, they certainly can evoke passionate loyalty and vehement criticism. As one reads Aristotle's attacks on Plato's *Republic*, Spencer's and Huxley's attacks on the sort of regimented utopia advocated by Bellamy, or Krutch's attack on Skinner's *Walden Two*, and later reads the rejoinders of the utopian authors, one will find oneself inevitably weighing arguments and taking sides. Until then a person may not realize how much of a utopian or an anti-utopian he really is. Perhaps this book can help its readers in accomplishing one of the original and chief goals of philosophical reflection, self-knowledge.

While the content of *Utopias* places it within the domain of philosophy and should therefore make it appropriate for use in courses in social and political philosophy, it may also be used as an adjunct text which can provide new perspectives and fresh material for general education courses in the humanities and the social sciences. And wherever a discussion of utopian thought might be desirable—in particular courses in religion, literature, history, sociology, economics, and human relations, for example—the book may serve a variety of purposes.

Let me conclude by thanking all those who in one way or other have helped me in bringing this book to completion. My colleagues in the Humanities Division at Boston University College of Basic Studies, Professor James A. Fisher, Chairman, and Professors Doris Hunter and Pat Cole, were kind enough to read the entire manuscript and to give me the benefit of their penetrating criticisms and comments. Professor Harry Crosby and Joseph Jurich, both of Boston University, and Professor Joseph H. Wellbank of Northeastern University, also helped me by giving me their expert advice on several matters pertaining to the form and content of the manuscript. I am especially grateful to Professor Walter L. Fogg, Chairman of the Department of Philosophy and Religion at Northeastern University, for reading the Introduction and making a number of valuable suggestions for improving it. For whatever shortcomings the book may have I of course assume sole responsibility.

Because they helped me either directly or indirectly in increasing my knowledge of American utopian communities, I want to thank the following persons: Sisters Lillian Phelps and Bertha Lindsay of the Canterbury (New Hampshire) Shakers; Mr. Charles ("Bud") Thompson, Curator of the Canterbury Shaker Museum; Mr. and Mrs. Al Coons of West Copake, New York; Mr. Daniel B. Reibel, Curator, and Mrs. Evelyn P. Matter of Old Economy, Ambridge, Pennsylvania; Mr. William Henry Harrison, Director of Fruitlands Museums, Harvard, Massachusetts; Professor Howard Hunter of Tufts University; Mrs. Jane B. Owen of New Harmony, Indiana; Miss Wessie Connell and Mrs. Barbara Williams of the Roddenbery Memorial Library (Cairo, Georgia); and Dean Horatio LaFauci of Boston University College of Basic Studies. Also, out of the hundreds of former students who have inspired this book on utopias by their stimulating dialogue, I cannot fail to mention a number who have been especially helpful to me in widening my knowledge of utopian thinking and experimentation: Mike Bonacorso, Dick Burke, Ollie and Alex Chanler, John Donovan, Ann Edwards, George McDonough, John Richardson, Pat Sherman, and Steve Serota.

Finally, the dedication page attests to my greatest debt of gratitude, that to Glenn R. Negley, Professor of Philosophy at Duke University, who evoked in me, while I was his graduate assistant years ago, a keen and continuing interest in the quest for utopia.

Peyton E. Richter

Introduction

I. UTOPIA: THE LURE OF THE IDEAL

The ideal of utopia, the perfect society, has long exerted a powerful influence upon the thinking, feeling, and action of human beings. Some of the most influential movements in history—Judaism, Christianity, Confucianism, Islam, communism, democratic socialism—have developed from a utopian vision and been sustained by a commitment of masses of people to the achievement of a utopian goal.[1] Utopian thinkers have claimed that the major advances in civilization would not have taken place without utopian aspirations and aims. H. G. Wells said that "the human mind has always accomplished progress by its construction of Utopias."[2] This is of course debatable.[3] But whether utopia has been conceived of as a paradisial garden from which man has been expelled; or as a promised land of milk and honey into which, after trial and testing, a chosen people would someday enter; or as a kingdom of God which promised salvation from sin and suffering to the elect; or as a classless society in which the state had withered away and the governance of persons had been replaced by the administration of things; or as a land of freedom and equality in which each person would be seeking his own greatest happiness; or as a unified and peaceful world controlled by an international government—no matter how it has been conceived, the ideal of utopia has retained a central place in the hopes, desires, fantasies, and spiritual aspirations of humanity. To dismiss utopia as a foolish and discredited notion without relevance to the world today would be to dismiss an ideal which has an irresistible attraction for large numbers of people and which helps to explain behavior that otherwise would seem incomprehensible.[4]

[1] The Western utopian tradition, with its roots in Greek, Judaic, and Christian cultures, is surveyed in Joyce O. Hertzler, *The History of Utopian Thought* (New York: Macmillan, 1923). For a recent survey of the less well known Eastern utopian tradition, see Jean Chesneaux, "Egalitarian and Utopian Traditions in the East," *Diogenes* 62 (Summer 1968): 76–102.

[2] Quoted by Mulford Q. Sibley, "Apology for Utopia: II Utopia and Politics," *The Journal of Politics* 2 (May 1940): 165.

[3] See Georg G. Iggers, "The Idea of Progress: A Critical Reassessment," *The American Historical Review* 71 (October 1965): 1–17.

[4] For example, several of the problems confronting the United States today—the hostility of a monolithic communist power in China, the presence of a Marxist

Depending upon how it is conceived, utopia can appeal to the most base and the most elevated aspects of human nature. An ideal society is naturally expected to guarantee food, shelter, and clothing, as well as protection against fear and insecurity. It can hold out the promise of perpetual contentment. It can insure against frustration and boredom by providing in their proper proportion tranquility and adventure. For many the dream of utopia can offer a change which cannot help but be for the better. For the enraged, it offers an outlet; for the alienated, a hope of reconciliation; for the exhausted, a hope of renewal; for the simple-minded a panacea; for the fanatical, an only solution. For men who live lives of quiet desperation, the utopian vision can give assurance that their puny lives have a higher significance; that more harmonious relationships with their fellowmen are desirable and feasible; and that cooperative effort and continuous sacrifice are worthwhile for the noblest of human purposes, the building of heaven on earth. Through the quest for utopia, saints have found their salvation, sinners their satiety, men of genius and charisma a faith to live and lead by and a cause to die for, the self-deluded a following to share delusions with, and hucksters "a fast buck."

The lure of utopia is certainly evident today. Young people are forming communes in various parts of the world.[5] Space engineers and scientists are designing utopian moon colonies and dreaming of settlements in outer space. Politicians and city planners are envisaging a number of model cities which will provide an ideal way of life for their inhabitants. A variety of scientists and prognosticators are speculating about conditions in the forthcoming century. Some are even predicting the advent of a world utopia.[6] And a host of computer-minded planners seem to be emerging as "the new utopians" who expect to succeed where other men have failed in designing and building the perfect society.[7] While "utopian" is still used by some as a derogatory epithet in contrast to "practical," ours is an age of luxuriant utopian speculation.

---

experiment at her doorstep in Cuba, the conflicting demands made by the Israelis and Arabs—cannot be understood fully without taking into account the powerful emotional, moral, and intellectual appeals of a utopian ideal.

[5] For example, see "The Commune Comes to America," *Life* 67, 18 July 1969, pp. 16–23; Ralph Blumenthal, "A Berlin Commune is a Big Happy Family (Sometimes)," *New York Times Magazine*, 1 December 1968, pp. 52–174; Robert Houriet, "Life and Death of a Commune Called Oz," *New York Times Magazine*, 16 February 1969, pp. 30–103; and Richard Todd, "Walden Two: Three? Many More?," *New York Times Magazine*, 15 March 1970, pp. 24–126. The quarterly *The Modern Utopian* gives accounts of current intentional communities.

[6] See "Toward the Year 2000: Work in Progress," *Daedalus* 96 (Summer 1967); Herman Kahn and Anthony J. Wiener, *The Year 2000: A Framework for Speculation on the Next Thirty-Three Years* (New York: Macmillan, 1967); and Andrew Shonfield, "Thinking About the Future," *Encounter* 32 (February 1969): 15–26.

[7] See Robert Boguslaw, *The New Utopians, A Study of System Design and Social Change* (Englewood Cliffs, N. J.: Prentice-Hall, 1965).

II. THREE ROLES FOR UTOPIAN THINKERS

UTOPIAN DESIGNER

Three kinds of roles have been assumed traditionally by those who are concerned with utopian ideals.[8] The first may be called that of utopian designer. In this role, the utopian thinker is an architect of an ideal society. He draws up a blueprint according to which a utopia can be built. In doing this, he depends not just on observation of actual society or upon reflection on past and present social problems; he also engages in philosophical speculation, envisaging ideal social ends and the means by which they may best be achieved. Although the utopian designer may not be a philosopher *per se*, he is, like the philosopher, concerned not primarily with what *is* but with what ought to be; that is to say, he is concerned with the norms, the ideal standards of human conduct.[9]

Usually the utopian designer believes that the ideal scheme he envisages, or the social reconstruction he proposes, can or will come about. Robert Owen, Charles Fourier, Saint-Simon, for example, presented in some detail utopian designs in which they had great confidence and which they hoped to see put into effect. Few could match the enthusiastic confidence of J. A. Etzler, an obscure German utopian designer who is remembered today mainly because Henry David Thoreau reviewed his book *The Paradise Within the Reach of All Men* (1841).[10] Here is a typical passage from this work.

> Fellowmen! I promise to show the means of creating a paradise within ten years, where everything desirable for human life may be had by every man in superabundance, without labor, and without pay; where the whole face of nature shall be changed into the most beautiful forms, and man may live in the most magnificent palaces, in all imaginable refinement of luxury, and in the most delightful gardens; where he may accomplish, without labor, in one year, more than hitherto could be done in thousands of years; may level mountains, sink valleys, create lakes, drain lakes and swamps, and intersect the land everywhere with beautiful canals, and roads for transporting heavy loads of many thousand tons, and for traveling one thousand miles in twenty-four hours; may cover the ocean with floating islands moveable in any desired direction with immense power and celerity, in perfect security, and with all comforts and luxuries, bearing gardens and palaces, with thousands of families, and provided with rivulets of sweet water; may explore the interior of the globe, and travel from pole to pole in a fortnight; provide himself with

---

[8] The roles are to be distinguished rather sharply in this section for sake of clarity of delineation. In actuality they are often merged in one and the same thinker.

[9] Among modern philosophers who were also utopian designers (at least in some of their works) are Jean Jacques Rousseau, Auguste Comte, John Stuart Mill, and John Dewey.

[10] See "Paradise (To Be) Regained" in *The Writings of Henry David Thoreau* (Boston: Houghton Mifflin and Co., 1893), vol. 4 (Cape Cod and Miscellanies), pp. 280–305.

means, unheard of yet, for increasing his knowledge of the world, and so his intelligence; lead a life of continual happiness, of enjoyments yet unknown; free himself from almost all the evils that afflict mankind, except death, and even put death beyond the common period of human life, and finally render it less afflicting. Mankind may thus live in and enjoy a new world, far superior to the present, and raise themselves far higher in the scale of being.[11]

Although the utopian designer may indulge in such high-flying rhetoric in attempting to persuade his readers of the desirability and feasibility of his proposed utopian design, he presents it—usually in straightforward expository prose—not as a work of art or as a utopian vision, but as a plan for partial or overall institutional and social reconstruction.

UTOPIAN ARTIST

When the designer of a utopia chooses to present his plan in a fictional form, embodying it in a literary work, he assumes the role of utopian artist. The utopian artist may present his utopian proposals as the main content of a short story, a dialogue, a drama, or, more usually, a novel. He may do this to avoid responsibility for his views, to disguise social criticism, or to make his proposals easier to grasp. Usually he chooses this form for a more practical reason. Instead of writing in the abstract of what ought to be, or presenting in expository prose his views of an ideal society as the social philosopher and the utopian designer might do, the utopian artist shows how his views would work out in practice. By presenting his utopian vision through a work of art, he hopes to make it clearer, more coherent, and more realistic. Also he believes that his ideals in fictional form will appeal at once to imagination, feeling, and intellect. He knows that utopias can be, in the words of an American philosopher, "the most efficacious instrumentalities available to the social reformer."[12]

UTOPIAN ORGANIZER

The third kind of utopian role involves more than formulating and presenting a utopian design or writing a literary utopia. This utopian thinker may be capable of doing both, but his primary interest lies in putting utopian ideals into actual practice. Accepting Thoreau's challenge, he puts foundations under his castles in the air and shows that they are feasible rather than fantastic. He assumes the role of utopian organizer. The utopian organizer stands in relation to the utopian designer and utopian artist as an engineer or builder stands to an architect. Following a plan which he sometimes has to modify in light of actual conditions and unexpected obstacles, he proceeds to create a set of social relationships and build a system of institutions which will bring into existence, at least temporarily, the exemplification of a utopian scheme.

[11] Ibid., pp. 280–81.

[12] Mulford Q. Sibley, "Apology for Utopia: II Utopia and Politics," *The Journal of Politics* 2 (May 1940): 172.

To do this requires not only a great deal of knowledge and skill, patience and perseverance on the part of the leader, and a strong belief in his ability, a continuous support of his efforts, and a willingness to cooperate with the leader and with one another on the part of the followers. It also requires that the leader have personal charisma. For example, whatever one might think of Fidel Castro's plans and efforts to transform Cuba according to a utopian Marxist design, there can be little doubt that he has most of the qualities of a successful utopian organizer, including considerable charisma. As a recent critic Richard Fagen puts it:

> For an understanding of political mobilization and social transformation in Cuba, the most important attribute of Castro is his charisma. Strictly speaking, this is not a characteristic of the man himself, but of his relationship with the masses. Following the well-known formulation by Max Weber, charisma involves much more than popularity. The charismatic leader is perceived by his followers as being endowed with superhuman or at least exceptional powers or qualities. And he perceives himself as "elected" from above to fulfill a mission. Both of these requirements were met in Cuba.[13]

What Fagen says of Castro could also be said of other successful utopian organizers. Ann Lee of the Shakers, George Rapp of the Harmonists, John Humphrey Noyes of the Oneida Perfectionists, Robert Owen of the Utopian Socialists, to mention only a few of the outstanding organizers of American utopian communities of the last century, all had remarkable charisma along with other qualities necessary to make them superior utopian organizers. They had a dedication to their cause and a conviction of its righteousness which placed it, to them and their followers, far above the level of ordinary human undertakings and made it eminently real rather than utopian. The communities they founded, whether they called them utopian or not, were certainly attempts to transform the actual in accord with an ideal of perfection. The success of these leaders was due to a large extent to the fact that they made a powerful appeal to religious aspiration. They assured their followers that by joining together into an ideal community they were relating harmoniously not just to one another but also to a supernatural being.

The leaders of utopian communities have often claimed supernatural sanction for the establishment of their communities. They have gained followers by making promises such as to help true believers to follow the will of God, achieve forgiveness for sins, and win happiness and eternal life. Often such a promise has been given particular urgency by the leader's claim that the millennium, or the second coming to earth of Jesus Christ, is about to occur, and that those who do not want to be condemned eternally at the last judgment must seek refuge in the utopian creed and community. Fear of punishment as well as hope for reward have thus played an important role in some of the most successful communities organized by utopian reformers. A student of American utopian communities and a member of one of them, William A. Hinds, concluded that:

[13] Richard R. Fagen, "Revolution—For Internal Consumption Only," *Transaction* 6 (April 1969): 13.

The promised Second Coming of our Lord has doubtless given birth to a greater number of religious sects and to more social experiments than any other event, actual or anticipated, in the world's history, save his first coming, and especially fruitful has this promised event been in organizations claiming to be the practical beginning and embodiment of the kingdom of heaven on the earth.[14]

Utopian organizers who have rejected religious supernaturalism have had to make other appeals in order to attract a following and to succeed in the pursuit of their often self-appointed missions. The range of these appeals has been suggested in the first section of this introduction and will be discussed further in Parts 1 and 4 of this book. Because of the intensity of belief and involvement necessary to establish and sustain a utopian experiment, it is not surprising that utopian organizers and their followers have often appeared to be fanatical and eccentric people. While some have been shining exemplars of the purest altruism, the keenest insight, and the most genuine humility imaginable, others have been pitiful victims of their own delusions of grandeur, extravagant superstitions, and insatiable lust for power. But as a defender of utopian thinkers, H. J. N. Horsburgh, points out:

> The utopian, as an eccentric, fool or man of genius, has quite different doctrinal interests from those which predominate in the community; and this intellectual isolation is a perpetual challenge, forcing him to the limit of his capacity in the effort to justify his unusual conclusions. It sometimes requires an extremist to attain the clarity of thought concerning a neglected aspect of a problem. Such a man is usually sand-blind; but what he sees between the sightless patches is of savage interest to him, sometimes conferring on his vision a special, if selective acuity. Utopian simple-mindedness often serves society in a similar fashion, breaking through the conspiracies of silence and piercing the capacities of common-place reflection.[15]

III. VARIOUS APPROACHES TO THE STUDY OF UTOPIANISM

THE LITERARY CRITIC'S APPROACH

The study of utopian literature and experimentation may be approached in a variety of ways depending upon the interest and orientation of the person undertaking the study. The literary critic, for example, with his interest in the nature and function of works of literary art, will be concerned with the medium through which the creator of a literary utopia expresses his message; with his use of symbolism, myth, and imagery; with his skill in creating character and constructing plot; and with other such matters.[16]

---

[14] William A. Hinds, *American Communities and Cooperative Colonies*, 2nd rev. ed. (Chicago: Charles H. Kerr, 1908), p. 563.

[15] H. J. N. Horsburgh, "The Relevance of the Utopian," *Ethics* 67 (1957): 134–35. Copyright 1957 by the University of Chicago. Reprinted by permission of the University of Chicago Press.

[16] See, for example, David Lodge, "Utopia and Criticism: the Radical Longing for Paradise," *Encounter* 32 (April 1969): 65–75.

He may trace the origin and influence of various literary utopias, comparing them as to purpose, period, style, and so on.[17] Or he may attempt to relate works of literature to actual utopian experiments or movements, as for example, Hawthorne's *Blithedale Romance* to Hawthorne's views on utopian socialism and his experiences as a member of the Brook Farm experiment.[18]

THE SOCIAL REFORMER'S APPROACH

The social reformer, on the other hand, will have little or no interest in the aesthetic aspects of literary utopias. He will read them as he reads reports on utopian communities from a predominantly practical point of view. His interest will be in garnering insights, suggestions, and approaches to the solutions of problems which will help him in undertaking successfully the reforms to which he is committed. He will be apt to transform a utopian vision into a program for action or to relate it to an ideology in such a way that it lends support to his own or his party's envisaged reforms. The communist Friedrich Engels' treatment of the utopian socialists in his *Socialism: Utopian and Scientific* is a good case in point. (See Part 1).

THE SOCIAL SCIENCES AND UTOPIANISM

Another of the most important approaches to the study of utopias is from the viewpoint of one or more of the social sciences. These theoretical disciplines undertake to study critically and systematically social phenomena and processes and attempt to analyze, describe, and explain them so as to make possible predictions or projections based on observation and experimentation. The social scientist—whether psychologist, sociologist, anthropologist, historian, or economist—attempts to apply scientific methods to gather facts in the area of his interest, to construct and test hypotheses upon the basis of these facts, and to reach conclusions which will be subject to later revision should new evidence be forthcoming. In this way, he clarifies and interprets some aspect of human and social experience. As a result of the joint and cumulative efforts of social scientists, new specialized knowledge is acquired and new insights are reached which increase our understanding of the nature of man as a social being.

The Historian's Viewpoint

Why should a study of utopian literature (the products of utopian designers and artists) and of utopian experimentation (the products of utopian organizers and their followers) be of interest to social scientists? First, the social scientist as historian may study utopian literature in order to learn

[17] See Richard Gerber, *Utopian Fantasy: A Study of English Utopian Fiction Since the End of the Nineteenth Century* (London: Routledge & Kegan Paul, 1955) and Northrop Frye, "Varieties of Literary Utopia," *Daedalus* 94 (Spring 1965): 323–47.

[18] See Manning Hawthorne, "Hawthorne and Utopian Socialism," *New England Quarterly* 12 (1939): 727–29.

more about the ideological conflicts and the ideal aspirations of a given culture as expressed by some of the most critical and advanced thinkers of the time. A careful study of Plato's *Republic* or of More's *Utopia* or of Zamiatin's *We* will increase, however slightly, one's overall understanding of Plato's fifth-century Athens, More's sixteenth-century England, or Zamiatin's postrevolutionary twentieth-century Russia. A study of certain phases or kinds of utopian experimentation during a certain period (such as communitarian socialism from the late seventeenth to the early nineteenth century) in a certain country or state (in the United States, or, specifically, in California) can expand and enrich one's knowledge of the history of the time, while furnishing perspectives from which other and larger historical developments can be viewed and often clarified.[19]

The Sociologist's Viewpoint

Another kind of social scientist, the sociologist, may read utopian literature in order to understand better certain social ideals which have influenced the behavior of a group or a community.[20] It would be impossible, for example, to understand fully the behavior of the Icarians, a nineteenth century group of French utopian colonists who started several communities in the United States, without understanding the utopian ideals and schemes of their leader, the utopian artist and organizer Étienne Cabet, who presented his proposals in elaborate detail in *A Voyage to Icaria*. Sociological studies of actual utopian experiments have often shed new light on social processes, such as cohesion, acculturation, and change, and suggested new approaches to the interpretation of social phenomena.[21]

The Psychologist's Viewpoint

Still another kind of social scientist, the psychologist, may analyze utopian literature in order to get insight into the psychological problems of an individual (e.g. a utopian organizer) or of a group. He may, if he is a Freudian, look for evidence of unconscious conflicts over sexuality, or, if he is a Jungian, he may seek evidence of racial memory or of archetypal

[19] See, for example, Arthur E. Bestor, *Backwoods Utopias: The Sectarian and Owenite Phases of Communitarian Socialism in America: 1663–1829* (Philadelphia: University of Pennsylvania Press, 1950); Robert V. Hine, *California's Utopian Colonies* (New Haven: Yale University Press, 1966); William H. Pease and Jane Pease, *Black Utopias: Negro Communal Experiments in America* (Madison, Wisconsin: The State Historical Society of Wisconsin, 1963).

[20] See, for example, Karl Mannheim, *Ideology and Utopia* (New York: Harcourt, Brace & World, 1936) and David Riesman, "Some Observations on Community Plans and Utopias" in *Selected Essays from Individualism Reconsidered* (New York: Doubleday, 1955).

[21] For example, Lee Emerson Deets, *The Hutterites: A Study in Social Cohesion* (Gettysburg, Pa., 1939); also, Joseph W. Eaton, "Controlled Acculturation: A Survival Technique of the Hutterites," *American Sociological Review* 17 (June 1952): 331–40.

images. Utopian experimentation can also furnish him with much new material for analysis and interpretation. He may study utopian communities in terms of their effects on human development and mental health; he may evaluate their success with reference to the extent to which they succeed in meeting the overall psychic needs of human beings; or he may be interested in planned communities as means for conditioning and controlling human behavior.[22]

The Political Theorist's Viewpoint

If the social scientist is a political theorist, he may try to discover in utopian literature plans for political reorganization and social reform which may have influenced political thought and action.[23] Utopian communities may be studied as exemplifications of political doctrines or of governmental arrangements the effects of which may be more apparent than in more highly developed, complex societies. Sometimes a political theorist will undertake a wide-ranging study of the concept of utopia as it relates to a whole complex of social problems or institutions.[24]

The Anthropologist's Viewpoint

If the social scientist is an anthropologist, works of utopian literature will be of interest as expressions of various cultures. Utopian experiments can be analyzed and interpreted as examples of planned cultures.[25]

The Economist's Viewpoint

And, finally, if the social scientist is an economist, he may find in utopian literature plans for economic systems or evidence of the influence of economic ideas which may throw light on the development of economic theory in other contexts.[26] Problems of production and distribution, for instance, can be studied in the context of the planned community and in relationship to society at large.

[22] See, for example, Joseph W. Eaton and Robert J. Weil, *Culture and Mental Disorders: A Comparative Study of the Hutterites and Other Populations* (Glencoe, Ill.: The Free Press, 1955); also Frank E. Manuel, "Toward a Psychological History of Utopias," *Daedalus* 94 (Spring 1965): 293–322.

[23] For example, Hugh F. Russell-Smith, *Harrington and his Oceana: A Study of a Seventeenth Century Utopia and its Influence in America* (Cambridge, Mass.: Harvard University Press, 1914).

[24] See George Kateb, *Utopia and Its Enemies* (New York: The Free Press of Glencoe, 1963) as an example.

[25] See Margaret Mead, "Toward More Vivid Utopias," *Science* 126 (November 1957): 957–61; also Melford E. Spiro, *Kibbutz, Venture in Utopia* (New York: Schocken Books, 1963).

[26] For example, J. Fuz, *Welfare Economics in English Utopias from Francis Bacon to Adam Smith* (The Hague: M. Nijhoff, 1952); see also Robert Heilbroner, *The Worldly Philosophers* (New York: Simon & Schuster, 1953), Chap. V.

THE SOCIAL PHILOSOPHER AND UTOPIANISM

Social philosophy is a more encompassing discipline than any one or all of the social sciences. It is concerned with analyzing and relating concepts taken from the social sciences and from other areas of knowledge and with answering certain general questions which might provide a consistent and coherent explanation of the overall nature and meaning of man's social experience. The social philosopher is first of all a *philosopher*, which means, according to the word's Greek derivation, that he is a lover of wisdom (*philein*, to love; *sophia*, wisdom)—a man who is searching not just for knowledge as organized and systematized facts and principles, but for an understanding of the value of this knowledge. Like the scientist, he is critical and systematic, but he does not perform experiments, go on field trips, or deal in statistics. He reflects critically upon experience, in its interrelatedness, using the knowledge provided him by social scientists and others. Thus he can claim to be completely empirical in his basic approach. He attempts to understand the meaning of the totality of reality. At times he is analytical and at times speculative, depending upon the problem with which he is dealing. His perspective is wider and more synoptic than that of any social scientist. He is concerned not just with what *is*, but with what *ought* to be; with values and norms, as well as with facts and ideas.

The questions which the social philosopher raises and attempts to answer may seem to some to be too general to be of much practical value, but to him they are of crucial importance: What is the nature of the good society? Toward what goal ought social institutions be directed? What is the relation between human nature and the nature of society? What is the best form of social organization and government? What is meant by social freedom? Social justice? Social obligation? Social philosophers such as Plato and Aristotle in the ancient world, St. Thomas Aquinas in the Middle Ages, and Locke, Hegel, Rousseau, Mill, and Dewey in the modern world have tried to answer these and other questions related to man as a social being.

Since social philosophy represents the broadest approach to utopian speculation and creation, the following section will be concerned with suggesting relations between this branch of philosophy and utopian literature and experimentation.

IV. UTOPIAN THINKING AND SOCIAL GOALS

Utopian thinking, whether it be set forth in proposals, expressed in works of art, or embodied in actual communities, raises most of the questions which interest social philosophers and provides imaginative and thought-provoking answers. What should be the goals of an ideal social order?

THE GOALS OF AN IDEAL SOCIAL ORDER

Plato and More, Bacon and Campanella, Wells and Morris, Skinner and Huxley, and countless other utopian artists have chosen to answer this question through the presentation of a vision of an ideal society which achieved the goals each believed to be supreme.

Plato in the *Republic*, for example, had Socrates apply his dialectical method to formulate the structure of an ideal social order in which all institutions worked together to promote justice and harmony. We are given a conception of the ideal city-state which has an imaginative, intellectual, and aesthetic unity. Its ideational appeal is far greater than any which might have been propounded systematically and defended critically in a carefully reasoned philosophical treatise.

Edward Bellamy and H. G. Wells both answered the question as to the goal of the ideal society in essays and articles, but their most persuasive and influential answers were presented in literary utopias. Bellamy's idea of a "commonwealth of the golden rule" which could come about through social regimentation and economic equality, and Wells' vision of a socialistic "modern utopia" ruled by idealistic experts ("samurai") retain vividness and credibility today primarily because they were given literary reality in works of art, *Looking Backward* and *A Modern Utopia*.

More recently B. F. Skinner has presented and defended his neo-behavioristic conception of man and culture in a number of books and articles. The implications of his approach to present and future community design were not widely recognized and popularized, however, until he presented his viewpoints imaginatively in his utopian novel *Walden Two*. Then his vision of a community set up by means of the techniques of behavioral engineering to reinforce and perpetuate the kind of behavior which an individual or group deemed desirable aroused strong and continual controversy.[27]

THE UTOPIAN COMMUNITY AS THE EXPRESSION OF A GOAL

When we turn from utopian literature to actual utopian communities, we find that here, too, the question of the goal of a social order is of paramount concern. Each of these communities represents an implicit or explicit attempt to put into practice a social ideal which usually had already been set forth by a utopian designer or utopian artist. Each is based on certain goals or values—security, equality, freedom, love—which are assumed to be the highest social ends and are promoted by the institutions of the community. Thus these utopian communities are invaluable pilot experiments which the social scientist and social philosopher can study in order to understand better the ways in which a community meets its needs, how it maintains its identity through development and change, and, most important, how it promotes the goals which make up the inhabitants' idea of the good life.

The Christian Commonwealth

Just as one picture is worth a thousand words, so is one community worth a thousand commentaries. A small community which called itself "The Christian Commonwealth" was established near Columbus, Georgia, in 1899

---

[27] See part 3.

for the express purpose "of demonstrating to the world the practicality and desirability of Christian cooperation as the best method of earning a livelihood, of developing nobility of character and promoting all the ends of a pure Christian civilization."[28] The members of this little utopia did not claim to be a perfected brotherhood (as some utopians elsewhere had claimed), but to be "a school of brotherhood" in which they were learning to practice "the patience of love." Their belief in God, whom they conceived to be their "common father with whom is all power and love," consoled them for the human shortcomings which became increasingly apparent as the members of the community got better acquainted with one another, especially as new members joined. Although they persevered in practicing the maxim "Bear ye the burdens of one another" and attempted to "overcome evil with good," their communal experiment in good will, common sharing, and loving fellowship failed after four years of hard effort. Poor land, typhoid fever, poverty, and inner dissension contributed to the end of the Christian Commonwealth, but while it lasted, it gave valuable evidence of what a whole community coherently organized on Christian principles could be like. Compared with the more successful ventures of the Shakers, Rappites, Perfectionists, Hutterites, and several other groups which were able to establish utopias based on Christian doctrines, the Georgia experiment may be minor, but it does illustrate how a utopian social ideal can guide practice and determine policy. The experiment did succeed, at least temporarily, in improving the quality of life by the conscientious application of an idealistic philosophy.

V. UTOPIAS AND DIFFERENT FORMS OF SOCIAL ORDER

CONTRASTING SOCIAL IDEALS

Another question with which utopian thinkers as well as social philosophers have been concerned is, What advantages does one form of social and political organization have over another? Or, to formulate it another way, Why should one be committed to one form of social order rather than another? To be sure, this question can and has been answered in works on social and political philosophy and on comparative government, but it has also been answered directly or indirectly by utopian designers, artists, and organizers.

Plato, for example, devoted a part of his *Republic* to the delineation and critique of what he considered to be imperfect or deteriorated forms of government—timocracy, oligarchy, democracy, and despotism—which he contrasted with the ideal he proposed, government by philosopher-rulers. In book one of his *Utopia* Thomas More has his characters describe the defects of several different kinds of government; in book two the narrator describes the Utopian form of government, a democratic, representative

[28] Hinds, *American Communities*, p. 522.

government which seems to avoid these defects. In *Looking Backward*, Edward Bellamy contrasts sharply the advantages of life under a socialistic order with the disadvantages of life under capitalism. In Ayn Rand's *Atlas Shrugged* the opposite is the case: capitalism and individualism are defended vehemently against the supposed defects of planned socialistic economies and welfare states. One of the most devastating and influential critiques of totalitarianism delivered in the twentieth century, and indirectly also one of the most powerful arguments for social freedom, social justice, and social honesty, is to be found in George Orwell's anti-utopian novel *1984*. A superb and prophetic attack on the hedonistic planned state with its tendencies toward overorganization, standardization, and stabilization was presented by Aldous Huxley in his satirical *Brave New World*. Later, in his constructive utopia *Island*, Huxley contrasted the advantages of the decentralized, free social order prevailing on his imaginary island Pala with the inhumane, profit-oriented outside society which threatens and eventually overwhelms it.

COMPARISONS OF UTOPIAN COMMUNITIES

One can also get insight into the advantages and disadvantages of different forms of political and social organization by comparing actual utopian communities—their goals, their success in achieving them, the obstacles which they were able to overcome, and the causes of their success or failure. The criteria according to which the various communities are compared will depend upon the philosophical orientation of the observer or appraiser.

Unless the student of utopias is able to discover and visit a number of existing intentional communities, he must base his evaluation upon historical records, reports, and other such data. The precedent for this sort of approach goes back to Aristotle, who was one of the first systematic students of comparative government. Aristotle collected and made a study of the constitutions of a large number of Greek city-states, and drew upon his research in writing his famous *Politics*. In criticizing Plato's conception of an ideal city-state, he attacked Plato's plan by comparing it with others, both actual and ideal. Following Aristotle's example, later political theorists have devoted a good deal of attention to the analysis and comparison of different forms of government, sometimes looking beyond the immediate differences to differences in ultimate moral and social ideals.

Less attention has been paid to the comparison of utopian communities partly because they were often considered too transitory, too inconsequential, and sometimes too absurd to merit the serious attention of scholars. Fortunately, several surveys of utopian communities have been made, however, the most important of which were accomplished in the last century in this country while intentional communities were widely flourishing.

Noyes and Nordhoff

The pioneering and best efforts to survey the nineteenth-century utopian scene were made by John Humphrey Noyes, the utopian organizer of the

Oneida Community in upstate New York, and Charles Nordhoff, a newspaperman who visited most of the communities he wrote about.[29] Noyes's work, based on material gathered by a predecessor, J. A. MacDonald, is more a work of exposition than comparison, but in his conclusion he did evaluate different forms of social order. (This chapter is reprinted in Part 2 under the title, "Why Utopias Fail.") Nordhoff's book concluded with an important "Comparative View and Review" giving his opinion of the merits and liabilities of the various communities he had studied. "The fundamental principle of communal life," he wrote, "is the subordination of the individual will to the general interest or the general will."[30] In practice, he pointed out, "this takes the shape of unquestioning obedience by the members towards the leaders, elders, or chiefs of their society."[31] Nordhoff does not think that this compliancy causes much hardship on members since utopian leaders (at least the ones he observed) "take no important step without the unanimous consent of the membership" and see to it that each person is usually assigned to do what he can do best and does not have to work as hard as he would have to do outside the community.[32] Comparing the political systems of the various communities, Nordhoff judges the pure democracy of Icaria to be the worst in that it constrains excessively the freedom of its leaders. "The president," Nordhoff is informed, "could not sell a bushel of corn without instructions from the meeting of the people."[33] Among the best and most successful governments in his opinion are the theocratic regimes of the Shakers and the Inspirationists. The authorities in these societies "have, almost, but not quite, unlimited power and authority."[34] However, Nordhoff thinks that the absolute equality which prevails in such communes, the security everybody has against want, misfortune, disability, and old age, and the order and system usually characteristic of communal life compensate members for the lack of freedom, variety, and amusement.[35]

VI. UTOPIAN VIEWS OF HUMAN NATURE

HUMAN NATURE IN UTOPIAN LITERATURE

Utopian literature has also dealt with another question which has been of considerable importance to social philosophy: What is the relationship

[29] John Humphrey Noyes, *History of American Socialisms* (Philadelphia: J. B. Lippincott, 1870); Charles Nordhoff, *The Communistic Societies of the United States* (New York: Harper & Brothers, 1875).

[30] Nordhoff, op. cit., p. 392.

[31] Ibid., p. 392.

[32] Ibid.

[33] Ibid., p. 393.

[34] Ibid.

[35] Ibid., pp. 394–95.

between the nature of man—his drives, needs, potentialities, and aspirations —and the nature of society? Generally utopian authors from Plato to B. F. Skinner have been optimistic about the possibility of establishing harmonious accord between the characteristics of an ideal social order and the characteristics of human beings. Not that there has been agreement among utopian authors as to the nature of man or the nature of the society appropriate to man. Like social philosophers, they have differed among themselves as to how human nature should be defined: whether man is basically rational or irrational, sociable or selfish, peace-loving or pugnacious, benevolent or malevolent, malleable or fixed in characteristics. They have usually shared the conviction, however, that ultimately man can achieve enough rationality, sociability, and benevolence to make a utopia feasible and workable.

Some authors of utopias, believing that institutions can never improve so long as the individuals composing them are corrupt, have held that reform must begin by bringing about moral changes in individual men. These utopians, however, have been in the minority; most have argued that institutions, the molders and directors of human activities, must be reconstructed and restructured according to moral principle in order to produce a mass of improved individuals. If a social order can be established which provides the kind of environment in which the more admirable endowments of human nature are nurtured and protected, then, and only then, will men reach their highest fulfillment individually. Envisaging such an order in *Looking Backward*, Edward Bellamy expresses the optimistic faith of many utopians when he writes:

> As in the old society the generous, the just, the tender-hearted had been placed at a disadvantage by the possession of those qualities, so in the new society the cold-hearted, the greedy, and self-seeking found themselves out of joint with the world. Now that the conditions of life for the first time ceased to operate as a forcing process to develop the brutal qualities of human nature, and the premium which had heretofore encouraged selfishness was not only removed but placed upon unselfishness, it was for the first time possible to see what unperverted human nature really was like. The depraved tendencies, which had previously overgrown and obscured the better to so large an extent, now withered like cellar fungi in the open air, and the nobler qualities showed a sudden luxuriance which turned cynics into panegyrists and for the first time in human history tempted mankind to fall in love with itself. Soon was fully revealed what the divines and philosophers of the old world never would have believed—that human nature in its essential qualities is good, not bad; that men by their natural intention and structure are generous, not selfish; pitiful, not cruel; sympathetic, not arrogant; godlike in aspirations, instinct with divinest impulses of tenderness and self-sacrifice; images of God indeed, not the travesties upon Him they had seemed. The constant pressure, through numberless generations, of conditions of life which might have perverted angels had not been able to essentially alter the natural nobility of the stock, and these conditions once removed, like a bent tree it had sprung back to its normal uprightness.[36]

---

[36] Edward Bellamy, *Looking Backward: 2000–1887,* 2nd ed. (Boston: Houghton Mifflin Co., 1888), chap. 26, p. 282.

CONCEPTS OF HUMAN NATURE AND UTOPIAN COMMUNITIES

Human nature and its relation to social goals was also a topic about which founders and members of utopian communities had every reason to be concerned. While social philosophers, utopian designers, and utopian artists could speculate about the nature of man usually without repercussions, utopian organizers and their followers could lose their possessions, common or individual, and even their lives because of misconceptions about the nature of their fellowmen.

John Humphrey Noyes, the founder of Oneida, held that the chief cause of the failure of most utopian experiments was "human depravity." (See Part 2.) As a Christian Perfectionist, however, he believed that it was possible, at least for some fortunate people, to overcome this depravity and to live a life untainted by what he considered to be sin. At Oneida he attempted, through the teaching and practice of "Bible Communism" and "Free Love" to show how a heaven on earth could be achieved. As we shall see, this community eventually failed due to outside pressure and internal dissension.

While the Shakers also had a low opinion of man's natural inclinations, his "worldly nature" or his "fleshly connections", they believed that by practicing the Shaker way of life with its emphasis on love, communal discipline, and "virgin purity" or celibacy one could eventually attain perfection. As a Shaker song put it quite simply:

> Away with the sluggard, the glutton, and beast,
>> For none but the bee and the dove
> Can truly partake of this heavenly feast
>> Which springs from the fountains of love.[37]

EFFECTS OF EXPERIMENTAL COMMUNITIES ON HUMAN NATURE

The effects which these communal experiments and others had upon human beings were, according to Charles Nordhoff who observed most of the important nineteenth-century experimental communities, on the whole good. To be sure, he found that they produced few "highly educated, refined, cultivated, or elegant men or women" while they produced many utilitarians. "They profess no exalted view of humanity or destiny," he noticed, and "they are not enthusiasts; they do not speak much of the Beautiful with a big B."[38] Nordhoff also was struck by the fact that their conception of the good life usually did not include either art or recreation. Although members of the communities were industrious, they did not overwork. They were clean; they were honest and temperate; they were humane and charitable. Creature comforts they usually secured and enjoyed. Their health seemed better than average to Nordhoff, and their life-span seemed longer than that of outsiders. If one compared the communal life, then, not with the highest kind of life achieved by some fortunate people "in pleasant circumstances in our great cities," but rather with ordinary urban mechanics and laborers,

---

[37] Nordhoff, *Communistic Societies,* p. 221.
[38] Ibid., p. 399.

Nordhoff was convinced that communitarianism provided a far better way of life.[39]

THE UTOPIAN SOCIALIST'S VIEW OF HUMAN NATURE

Although most of the communities visited by Nordhoff were based on a Christian view that man is a sinful depraved creature standing in need of salvation, his observations could also be seen as lending support to Bellamy's view that human nature can be molded for good or bad by the social environment. The nineteenth-century American social reformer Albert Brisbane expressed succinctly the "orthodox" utopian socialist view of human nature when, after rejecting the view that social evils were rooted "in the imperfection of human nature, or in the depravity of the passions," he remarked that "the root of the evil is in the social organization itself; and, until we attack it there, no permanent or beneficial reforms can be expected."[40]

Robert Owen, the "father of English socialism" and the founder of an American utopian community, New Harmony, had expressed the same doctrine even earlier in his *New View of Society*:

> . . . any general character, from the best to the worse, may be given to any community even to the world at large, by the application of proper means; which means are to a great extent at the command and under the control of those who have influence in the affairs of men.[41]

EDUCATION AS MOLDER OF HUMAN NATURE

In light of this environmentalist approach, it is not surprising that utopian socialists stressed the importance of education, which would provide the means for molding human nature according to the community design worked out by "those who have influence in the affairs of men." Unlike the Christian autocrats who usually looked with suspicion on education which included more than training in practical skills and indoctrination in religious attitudes, practices, and beliefs, Saint-Simon, Fourier, Owen, and their followers stressed education in its fuller sense, which went beyond training and indoctrination to free and creative use of intelligence. It is no accident that in the Owenite community of New Harmony and in the Fourierist community of Brook Farm the most vital and influential institution was the school.

VII. UTOPIAS AND THE PROBLEM OF FREEDOM

A number of questions concerning freedom have arisen to challenge both social philosophers and utopian thinkers. In an ideal society, how free ought

[39] Ibid., p. 406.

[40] Quoted in Bestor, *Backwoods Utopias*, p. 8.

[41] Quoted in Harry W. Laidler, *Social-Economic Movements* (New York: Thomas Y. Crowell, 1944), p. 89.

an individual to be? What aspects of his existence ought to be controlled by public authority? What rights does a citizen of an ideal society have? What duties? Under what circumstances ought a citizen be willing to sacrifice his own personal interests for the public interest?

RESTRICTIONS UPON INDIVIDUAL FREEDOM: PLATO AND BELLAMY

In answer to such questions, many utopian designers and artists have thought it necessary to establish a rigorous and wide-ranging control of the lives and conduct of individual members of their utopias in order to secure and protect the ends of the ideal state which they have envisaged. Plato, for example, in proposing that the philosopher-rulers of his ideal city-state should control the education, property, wealth, art, and even reproduction of citizens, justified his action by expressing his concern for the happiness of all, not only a minority of citizens. A condition of justice in which the harmonious interaction between and among classes of the state for the promotion of the common welfare could only be brought about and kept in existence, he believed, by men guided by love of divine wisdom, aided by a loyal military force and supported by a cooperative working force which accept strong leadership and discipline patriotically.

In Edward Bellamy's ideal socialistic "Commonwealth of the Golden Rule," more attention was paid than in Plato's *Republic* to the preservation of some domain of personal freedom for individual men, but Bellamy did not hesitate to restrict the individual's range of choice and action when it interfered with his ideals of social regimentation and economic equality. Everyone had to do his duty to the state and his fellowmen by serving in the industrial army for an appointed time. If he tried to escape from this obligation, he would quickly find that he had "excluded himself from the world, cut himself off from his kind, in a word, committed suicide."[42]

CONTROL REPLACES FREEDOM IN SKINNER'S UTOPIA

Despite the restrictions which Plato and Bellamy imposed for idealistic reasons upon individuals in their ideal societies, their schemes proposed far less complete control than that proposed in B. F. Skinner's utopia, *Walden Two*. Although an individual may feel free in Walden Two and want to do all the things he does, in reality every aspect of his behavior has been carefully studied and controlled through the latest techniques of behavioral engineering. As a complete determinist, Skinner rules out freedom as a useless concept and concentrates on the design, the purposeful control of a community. He has Frazier, the creator of the Walden Two community, put it:

> I deny that freedom exists at all. I must deny it—or my program would be absurd. You don't have a science about a subject matter which hops capriciously around. Perhaps we can never *prove* that man isn't free; it's an assump-

---

[42] Bellamy, *Looking Backward*, chap. 6, p. 132.

tion. But the increasing success of a science of behavior makes it more and more plausible.[43]

DEFENDERS OF INDIVIDUAL RESPONSIBILITY

Skinner's deterministic approach aroused strong objection among contemporary anti-utopian thinkers such as Joseph Wood Krutch, who argued against using science to restrict the range of human choice and to rob man of his sense of moral and social responsibility. (See Part 3.) Long before Krutch expressed concern over Skinner's "ignoble utopia," critics of utopias and authors of dystopias had vehemently opposed any kind of all-embracing control of human behavior, whether based on force or on psychological conditioning. Feodor Dostoyevsky in Russia, John Stuart Mill in England, and Henry David Thoreau in the United States wrote brilliantly and persuasively in defense of freedom of thought, action, and speech. In the twentieth century, three of the most important anti-utopian literary works—Zamiatin's *We*, Huxley's *Brave New World*, and Orwell's *1984*—focus on the heroic but hopeless rebellion of a lone individual against a state which cooly, calculatingly, and with the public interest in view, curtails freedom of choice and destroys individuality.[44]

TRADITION OF INDIVIDUAL FREEDOM IN UTOPIAN LITERATURE

In addition to the recent anti-utopian attacks on excessive state control and restriction of individual liberty, a tradition in constructive utopian literature itself has opposed authoritarianism in utopian thinking and has supported individual initiative, spontaneity, and freedom of choice against dictatorship by public or private authority in accord with total planning. In the Renaissance, the French humanist and humorist François Rabelais described an imaginary Abbey of Thélème in which the only rule for its inhabitants was "do what thou wilt." A seventeenth-century French preacher, Gabriel de Foigny, who was, according to one authority on utopian thought, the first utopian to conceive of a utopia without government,[45] had one of his characters in his *New Discovery of Terra Australis Incognita* (1676) defend a philosophy of anarchism based on the view that the essence of man is liberty. One of the great figures of the eighteenth-century French enlightenment, Denis Diderot, believing that "Nature gave no man the right to rule over others," dreamed of utopians as carefree, free-loving South Sea islanders far removed from the restrictions and tyranny of modern life.[46] During the

[43] B. F. Skinner, *Walden Two* (New York: The Macmillan Co., 1948), p. 214. Reprinted with permission of The Macmillan Company from *Walden Two* by B. F. Skinner. Copyright 1948 by B. F. Skinner.

[44] See Martin Kessler, "Power and the Perfect State, a Study in Disillusionment as Reflected in Orwell's *1984* and Huxley's *Brave New World*," *Political Science Quarterly* 72 (1957): 565–77.

[45] See Marie Louise Berneri, *Journey Through Utopia* (London: Routledge & Kegan Paul, 1950), pp. 184–201.

[46] See Berneri, op. cit., pp. 201–6.

same period, the Marquis de Sade in his bizarre utopian visions called upon Frenchmen to reject religion in order to have equality, and to assert their love of freedom not only in the legislature, in the marketplace, and on the battlefield, but also in the bedroom.[47]

Along with these French defenders of freedom in utopia, two great English writers of utopias were later to speak out in favor of greater personal autonomy and individuality. The first of these, William Morris, presented in *News from Nowhere* (1890) a vision of a postrevolutionary society in which the state has withered away, allowing each individual to satisfy without hindrance his longing for freedom, equality, and creative labor. The second, H. G. Wells, in his two major utopian works *A Modern Utopia* (1905) and *Men Like Gods* (1923), struggled to reconcile individualism and socialism, freedom and organization. In the latter work he outlines a utopian scheme in which unnecessary bureaucracy, legislation, and control have been eliminated, where education *is* government, and the activities of the world "are all coordinated to secure the general freedom."

FREEDOM LIMITED IN EXPERIMENTAL COMMUNITIES

Turning now from the fictional to the factual realm of utopianism, critics of actual utopian communities have pointed out that the security, prosperity, and stability have only been achieved at the sacrifice of man's individuality and freedom. If to achieve a stable and happy society men must become either sheep or robots, they ask, then is utopia not purchased at too high a price? As we shall see in Part 3, this question has been given a strong affirmative answer by the anti-utopians.

If one looks at the history of utopian communities in the United States, it is apparent that the most successful ones in the sense of long-lasting have been the authoritarian religious utopias—the Shakers, the Harmonists, the Inspirationists, and the Hutterites. In these communities, almost every aspect of an individual's life was under the strict and continuous control of one person or of a group. The authority governing the lives of the individual members may have been, and in most cases actually was, benevolent; it may have been a collective rather than a personal leadership, but it was nonetheless dictatorial. The government of the Shakers resembled that of the military, Nordhoff noted, not only in that all looked "for counsel and guidance to those immediately before them," but also in the rigorous discipline and conformity imposed upon all members of the organization by their superiors.[48] For example:

> Not a single action of life, whether spiritual or temporal, from the initiative of confession, or cleansing the habitation of Christ, to that of dressing the right side first, stepping first with the right foot as you ascend a flight of stairs, folding the hands with the right-hand thumb and fingers above those of the left, kneeling and rising again with the right leg first, and harnessing

---

[47] Ibid., pp. 178–81.
[48] Nordhoff, *Communistic Societies*, pp. 171–72.

first the right-hand beast, but that has a rule for its perfect and strict performance.[49]

Conformity and Belief in Divine Sanction

The Shakers were willing to accept this discipline from their spiritual leaders only because they regarded them as "mediators between God and their souls" or as "links of divine communication."[50] The Amana Community of True Inspiration, in Iowa, also believed that their elders and leaders in ruling the community were carrying out divine ordinances for which purpose they had "chosen and nominated to this purpose by God."[51] This belief in a divine sanction for rulers was also common in most if not all of the other religious utopias in the United States in the nineteenth century. As long as members of communities accepted this belief unquestionably, they were little troubled by their lack of freedom of choice and action. Perhaps they even felt freer in that they were at least free *from* insecurity, need, and fear, even while they were not free *to* question or reject authority, to rule themselves, or to do what they pleased. They were willing to live without freedom so long as their leaders ruled them with the "authority, mystery, and miracle" which Dostoyevsky's Grand Inquisitor claimed made the mass of men content to live as sheep under the care of an all-powerful shepherd.

Anarchist Utopias

But one can find a number of examples of utopias which stressed freedom as much as others stressed conformity. Except for their communitarian spirit, these offered quite a different model of the good life from that of religious autocracies. Before the end of the last century, several American utopian communities had tried to bring about a unity of interest without sacrificing individualism and freedom but today, except for their appealing names (Prairie Home, The Progressive Community, The Social Freedom Community), their idealistic constitutions, and their fragmentary autobiographies, little remains to commemorate their brief and bold existence.[52]

In the present century, the best examples of communities preoccupied with the value of freedom were founded in Europe on the basis of anarchism. As a philosophical and utopian doctrine developed by such thinkers as William Godwin, P. J. Proudhon, and Pëtr Kropotkin, anarchism rejected the authority of all secular and sacred institutions, accepted the intrinsic goodness and sociability of man, and exalted as the highest human values equality, community, and freedom. The founders of anarchist utopias were not usually too concerned with the consistent philosophical justification of these values so long as they could be put into practice.

[49] Ibid., pp. 177–78.
[50] Ibid., p. 172.
[51] Ibid., p. 46.
[52] These and other such communities are discussed in Nordhoff, op. cit.

Colony of the Free Environment

A typical example of an anarchist utopian community was the Colony of the Free Environment which was established at Vaux, France, in 1902.[53] The members of this colony, about twenty persons, occupied a house and plot of land donated by a peasant. Before joining, they had to sign a statement that they were acting on their own initiative as supporters of the principle of absolute freedom; that they would never commit acts of violence against fellow members; that they believed that work could be freely performed without being forced; and that if they decided to leave the colony, their travel expenses back to their native countries would be paid. For a while the experiment was fairly successful. Each member contributed according to his abilities and received what he needed from the common goods. But eventually dissension broke out among members. The peasant sued for the return of his house, and the colonists were forced to move to a new location. The founder of the colony, a Frenchman by the name of Butaud, was accused of "a tendency to disruption, of moral authoritarianism, of excess of logic"—in other words, of being a dictator, and he and his Russian mistress were asked to leave the colony. They left, followed by other "deserters," and soon afterwards the Colony of the Free Environment was no more. Other anarchist colonies sprang up elsewhere but they, too, were usually short-lived.

ART IN RELIGIOUS UTOPIAS

Since artistic creation is considered to be one of the freest of human activities, the discussion of freedom in utopian communities raises the question of the place of art in communitarian experiments. In the authoritarian religious utopias, usually the only arts permitted were those which were strictly functional and utilitarian, either in relation to essential human activities (e.g. building and crafts) or in relation to spiritual goals (e.g. music and dancing). "Art for art's sake" was virtually unknown, and purely aesthetic pleasures were usually considered to be sinful or at least useless.

The Shakers

The Shakers, in whose villages even flowers were once forbidden, expressed their attitude toward beauty in no uncertain terms. When one of their leaders, Elder Frederick Evans, was once asked by an outsider whether if they were building their villages anew the Shakers would aim at architectural effects and beautiful designs, he said, "No, the beautiful, as you call it, is absurd and abnormal. It has no business with us. The divine man has no right to waste money upon what you would call beauty, in his house or his daily life, while there are people living in misery."[54] Often, however, despite

[53] The following account is based on that in Charles Gide, *Communist and Co-operative Colonies*, translated by E. R. Row (New York: Thomas Y. Crowell, n.d.).

[54] Quoted by Nordhoff, *Communistic Societies*, p. 164.

this attitude and without intending to, Shaker builders and craftsmen achieved beautiful effects through their austere functionalism.

The Oneida Community

The founder of the Oneida Community, John Humphrey Noyes, was also opposed to art which served no communal purpose or involved no community participation. "It seems to me," he stated, "that the great condemnation of mere literary art, and indeed of art of any kind insubordinate to religion and science is that it is an enemy to earnestness."[55]

ART IN LIBERAL AND SECULAR UTOPIAS

The encouragement of free artistic creation, along with the utilization of the arts as means for creating and enriching man's ideal social and aesthetic environment, were characteristic of the most important of the liberal and secular utopian experiments in America. The men by whom these experiments were directly inspired—Robert Owen, Charles Fourier, and Étienne Cabet—had an appreciation of art and discussed it in their works. Orchestral music and dancing were popular at Owen's New Harmony. Theatrical performances were popular at Cabet's Icarian communities. A variety of different kinds of artists found a hearty welcome at Brook Farm. Later, some utopian communities were founded specifically for the purpose of creating an environment in which art and aesthetic appreciation would be stimulated and improved. One of the most interesting of these—an inspired idea but a crashing failure—was founded in 1876 in Anaheim, California, by a group of Polish artists and intellectuals, including the actress Helena Modjeska and the writer Henryk Sienkiewicz, later author of Quo Vadis.[56]

VIII. UTOPIA: A SUBJECT FOR CONTROVERSY

DIFFERING VIEWS OF THE NATURE OF A UTOPIA

One man's utopia is another man's dystopia. The Brook Farmers with their love of art and learning would have considered the Iowa Inspirationists culturally deprived. The staunchly religious Inspirationists would have been deeply offended by the atheistic freedom-loving anarchist colonies of early twentieth-century Europe. And the anarchists, in turn, would have found even the amount of regimentation acceptable at Brook Farm quite intolerable. Today, while many people can quickly see that the society depicted in

[55] Quoted in Donald D. Egbert and Stow Persons, eds., *Socialism and American Life* (Princeton: Princeton University Press, 1952), vol. I, p. 458. This volume and the second bibliographical volume (compiled by T. D. S. Bassett) provide invaluable help to the student of art in utopia.

[56] See the account of this colony in Hine, *California's Utopian Colonies*, pp. 137–40.

George Orwell's *1984* with its crushing dictatorship and its ruthless thought-control is a horrendous anti-utopia, they may be unable to see that Aldous Huxley's superhedonistic *Brave New World* is equally revolting, even though this work is meant to depict satirically the torments of a free and potentially creative individual in a pleasure-obsessed society. Huxley believed that because powerful forces in our present society are pushing us closer and closer to the ideals of Brave New World, "Community, Identity, and Stability," we are unable to see that the achievement of these ideals would mean the destruction of genuine individual self-realization as surely as would the imposition of a completely totalitarian regime.

Unpopularity of Some Previous Utopian Ideals

Confrontations with totalitarian regimes, whether Nazi, Fascist, or Communist, have made twentieth century readers more critical of literary utopias which previously were received with enthusiasm. Plato's *Republic* with its dictatorship of philosophers, Edward Bellamy's *Looking Backward* with its regimented industrial army, and H. G. Wells' *Modern Utopia* with its ruling intelligentsia seem less appealing to those who have fought to preserve democratic freedoms, who have seen the results of forced labor, and who have followed with disgust the sorry history of party-dictated purges under totalitarianism. A recent critic's comment on H. G. Wells' *Modern Utopia* (1905) suggests how with time one generation's utopia can become another generation's dystopia.

> Time has been cruel to *A Modern Utopia*. It would be difficult to arouse any enthusiasm for this vision of the good life today. Most of the things against which the current wave of youthful protest is directed in the Western world are to be found hopefully foreshadowed in Wells' Utopia: an examination-selected-meritocracy, a mixed economy, paternalistic state welfare, bureaucratic control over personal freedom, privilege based on productivity but controlled by fiscal means, minority participation in government, academic monopoly over culture, and a generally low-keyed, rather conformist contentment regarded as the desirable norm in behavior. Wells' Utopia is a class society in which the classes are distinguished not by breeding or by cash, but by intelligence and vocational aptitude, with a decent middle-class standard of living available to all. In a sense it was a generous attempt on Wells' part to imagine a social structure which would make available to everyone the kind of success and happiness he had personally achieved in the teeth of great disadvantages. Or, more cynically, you could call it the paradise of little fat men.[57]

Value of Utopian Speculation Questioned

If the major utopian thinker such as Wells seems so irrelevant today, does this suggest something about the relevance and value of utopian speculation? The enemies of utopia would answer with a resounding yes!

"Utopian speculation is a waste of time," one might point out. "The task of

[57] David Lodge, "Utopia and Criticism," *Encounter* XXXII (April 1969): 68–69.

the practical man is to solve social problems, not to spend time constructing imaginary perfect societies in which all problems can be solved mentally."

"Besides," another might remark, "utopian speculation is unrealistic, not only because it oversimplifies complex economic, political, and social problems, but also because it fails to take into account the unalterable facts of the imperfections of human nature. Man is basically a selfish, irrational, aggressive, depraved animal who will foul up any utopian scheme, no matter how carefully designed, how foolproof it is."

"Furthermore," a third might chime in, "no utopia could work without a strict and complete control of the conditions under which its inhabitants were to live, and if that is the case, how is freedom, the most important of all human values, to be preserved?"

"A real live utopia," another critic might interject, "would turn me off for good. With all the grief and pain taken out of life, how could I appreciate the joy and pleasure I would be experiencing all the time? A voyage to Icaria would be a bad trip since you'd never come down to go up again. Believe me, man, news from Nowhere is no news at all."

These imaginary comments suggest the wide range of criticism which can and has been leveled against utopian speculation. Some of these criticisms, and others, are developed in full in Part 3 (Contra Utopia). Possible answers to them are given in Part 4 (Utopian Rejoinders).

Idea of Utopia Continues to Attract Interest

Yet despite its perennial critics and the fact that many people view it with open hostility, bored scepticism, or ironic ridicule, the idea of utopia refuses to die. A utopian ideal still has vital significance as an incentive for personal involvement and as an aim for social action, especially in undeveloped countries, not because it has been so well defended against its enemies, but for other reasons. One of these is that many who accept it do so uncritically, enthusiastically, and wholeheartedly as they accept the associated beliefs that life has a meaning, that happiness is possible, and that the conditions under which they live can and must be improved. An American authority on Cuba, Joseph A. Kahl, writing in *Transaction* about the new generation of Cubans, remarks that they seem to lack genuine curiosity about the outside world but are satisfied with the caricatures of it presented to them. Continuing, he states:

> This dogmatism is perhaps the automatic result of militant belief in the vision of utopia. True believers of any creed lose objectivity and curiosity. They know the answers in advance. American youthful militants (at least the white ones) have too often lost all belief and become nihilists and destroyers; Cuban youthful militants have the security of conviction and the narrowness that goes with it. They are building utopia, and it completely absorbs their energies. The independent intellectual, the critic of all societies and all beliefs, is a luxury they cannot afford.[58]

---

[58] Joseph A. Kahl, "The Moral Economy of a Revolutionary Society," *Transaction* 6 (April 1969): p. 37.

WHY EXAMINATION OF UTOPIAN IDEALS IS IMPORTANT

To the philosopher who considers self-scrutiny a necessity rather than a luxury and who insists with Socrates that the unexamined life is not worth living, no belief, no matter how tenaciously it is held or how sacred it be considered, should be exempt from rational scrutiny. To be sure, critical examination of beliefs, like dogmatic assertion of them, has its risks; misdirected or short-circuited it can lead to nihilism as dogmatism can lead to fanaticism. But the uncritical acceptance of belief—whether the belief be in God, freedom, or immortality, or in progress, patriotism, or utopia—is far more dangerous to the life and vitality of democratic institutions in a free society than the critical appraisal of it. In his basic intuition Plato was right: if there is to be a utopia, it must be a society in which philosophers not fanatics are honored and heeded.

If the vision of utopia turns out to be only a beautiful mirage, a dangerous delusion, or a pernicious fantasy, then the sooner it is dispelled so that we can concern ourselves with other matters the better. But if it can be shown that utopia is a live option, a genuine possibility, even a necessity, then the sooner we dedicate ourselves to achieving it the better off we, and the world, will be. In order to decide rationally we must reflect. Let us begin with the first question, Why utopia?

I

Why Utopia?

These things shall be! a loftier race
Than e'er the world has known shall rise
With flame of freedom in their souls
And light of science in their eyes.
New arts shall bloom of loftier mould,
And mightier music thrill the skies,
And every life shall be a song,
When all the earth is paradise.

John Addington Symonds

1

Two Kinds of Utopia

LEWIS MUMFORD'S DISCUSSION OF UTOPIAS OF ESCAPE
AND UTOPIAS OF RECONSTRUCTION

One of the clearest and most convincing answers to the question, Why utopia? was given in a little book entitled *The Story of Utopias* by the American social philosopher Lewis Mumford (b. 1895). When this book was first published in 1922, Mumford was a promising young intellectual at the very beginning of his distinguished career, which was to encompass a number of roles—critic, teacher, writer, philosopher, historian, sociologist, and consultant—all related integrally to an organic philosophy of life and culture. This philosophy was later given impressive and beautiful expression in Mumford's major works which included *Technics and Civilization* (1934), *The Culture of Cities* (1938), *The Condition of Man* (1944), and *The Conduct of Life* (1951).

Mumford had a wide and deep acquaintance with several specialized fields of knowledge as well as the orientation of a generalist and humanist. Throughout his works he directed his readers along a path which he believed could lead toward personal and social renewal. In an age of complexity he urged his fellowmen, as had Thoreau before him, to simplify. In an age of uncertainty, he called upon men to commit themselves to worthy tasks and to transform themselves and their world according to ideals having permanence and universal significance. In an age in which nihilism seemed triumphant, he reaffirmed and defended certain basic "values for survival." And in a time when humanity had finally achieved the means by which it could easily succeed in destroying itself, he spoke powerfully and persuasively "in the name of sanity" against any such prospect as atomic warfare as a solution to international and human problems. Harmony and balance, love and integration, reaffirmation and reunion, sacrifice and self-discipline —until these were given more important roles in the conduct of life Mumford thought there could be little hope for modern man.

In *The Story of Utopias*, Mumford pointed out that utopias, as implicit criticisms of the civilizations which nurtured them and as affirmations of human potentialities which have been ignored by existing institutions, can offer fresh prospects and ideals for critical consideration. He recognized, of course, that utopians, in their enthusiasm for ideals, often neglected concrete realities and tended to overestimate the malleability of society and to underestimate the importance and strength of the past in producing present conditions. But these defects were compensated for to some extent, Mumford believed, by the utopian thinkers' refusal to consider institutions separately but instead to view them as dynamically interrelated parts of an entire social order. This aspect of utopian thinking especially appealed to young Mumford's blossoming organicism, just as the utopian habit of synoptic thinking appealed strongly to his already apparent generalist perspective.

Even though some critics and commentators have seen in Mumford's later works a broadly conceived utopian scheme for the reorganization and renewal of society, Mumford himself disclaims the title of utopian thinker and would not care to accept a place in the tradition of utopian thinking, which he believes has serious shortcomings. Nor does he admit to having his own private utopia. "My utopia," he states in his new (1962) preface to *The Story of Utopias*, "is actual life, here or anywhere, pushed to the limits of its ideal possibilities." Thus Mumford's interest in utopian thinking and his appreciation of it does not necessarily imply a conversion to it. Reading his *Story of Utopias* is worthwhile, if only to see how his serious and appreciative treatment of utopian literature ends up as "an anti-utopian tract."

From Lewis Mumford, The Story of Utopias *(New York: The Viking Press, 1962), pp. 11–26. Reprinted by permission of Lewis Mumford.*

1

Utopia has long been another name for the unreal and the impossible. We have set utopia over against the world. As a matter of fact, it is our utopias that make the world tolerable to us: the cities and mansions that people dream of are those in which they finally live. The more that men react upon their environment and make it over after a human pattern, the more continuously do they live in utopia; but when there is a breach between the world of affairs and the overworld of utopia, we become conscious of the part that the will-to-utopia has played in our lives, and we see our utopia as a separate reality.

It is the separate reality of utopia that we are going to explore in the course of this book—Utopia as a world by itself, divided into ideal commonwealths, with all its communities clustered into proud cities, aiming bravely at the good life.

This discussion of ideal commonwealths gets its form and its color from the time in which it is written. Plato's Republic dates from the period of social disintegration which followed the Peloponnesian War; and some of its mordant courage is probably derived from the hopelessness of conditions that came under Plato's eye. It was in the midst of a similar period of disorder and violence that Sir Thomas More laid the foundations for his imaginary commonwealth: Utopia was the bridge by which he sought to span the gap between the old order of the Middle Age, and the new interests and institutions of the Renascence.

In presenting this history and criticism of utopias we are perhaps pulled by the same interests that led Plato and More onwards, for it is only after the storm that we dare to look for the rainbow. Our fall into a chasm of disillusion has stimulated us to discuss in a more thorough way the ultimate goods, the basic aims, the whole conception of the "good life" by which, in modern times, we have been guided. In the midst of the tepid and half-hearted discussions that continue to arise out of prohibition laws and strikes and "peace" conferences let us

31

break in with the injunction to talk about fundamentals—consider Utopia!

2

Man walks with his feet on the ground and his head in the air; and the history of what has happened on earth—the history of cities and armies and of all the things that have had body and form—is only one-half the Story of Mankind.

In every age, the external scenery in which the human drama has been framed has remained pretty much the same. There have been fluctuations in climate and changes in terrain; and at times a great civilization, like that of the Mayas in Central America, has arisen where now only a thick net of jungle remains; but the hills around Jerusalem are the hills that David saw; and during the historic period the drowning of a city in the Netherlands or the rise of a shifting bank of real estate along the coast of New Jersey is little more than the wearing off of the paint or a crack in the plaster. What we call the material world constantly changes, it goes without saying: mountains are stript of trees and become wastes, deserts are plowed with water and become gardens. The main outlines, however, hold their own remarkably well; and we could have travelled better in Roman days with a modern map than with the best chart Ptolemy could have offered us.

If the world in which men live were the world as it is known to the physical geographer, we should have a pretty simple time of it. We might follow Whitman's advice, and live as the animals, and stop whining for all time about our sins and imperfections.

What makes human history such an uncertain and fascinating story is that man lives in two worlds—the world within and the world without—and the world within men's heads has undergone transformations which have disintegrated material things with the power and rapidity of radium. I shall take the liberty of calling this inner world our idolum (ido'lum) or world of ideas. The word "ideas" is not used here precisely in the ordinary sense. I use it rather to stand for what the philosophers would call the subjective world, what the theologians would perhaps call the spiritual world; and I mean to include in it all the philosophies, fantasies, rationalizations, projections, images, and opinions in terms of which people pattern their behavior. This world of ideas, in the case of scientific truths, for example, sometimes has a rough correspondence with what people call the world; but it is important to note that it has contours of its own which are quite independent of the material environment.

Now the physical world is a definite, inescapable thing. Its limits are narrow and obvious. On occasion, if your impulse is sufficiently strong, you can leave the land for the sea, or go from a warm climate into a cool one; but you cannot cut yourself off from the physical environment without terminating your life. For good or ill, you must breathe air, eat food, drink water; and the penalties for refusing to meet these conditions are inexorable. Only a lunatic would refuse to recognize this physical environment; it is the substratum of our daily lives.

But if the physical environment is the earth, the world of ideas corresponds to the heavens. We sleep under the light of stars that have long since ceased to exist, and we pattern our behavior by ideas which have no reality as soon as we cease to credit them. Whilst it holds together this world of ideas—this idolum—is almost as sound, almost as real, almost as inescapable as the bricks of our houses or the asphalt beneath our feet. The "belief" that the world was flat was once upon a time more important than the "fact" that it was round; and that belief kept the sailors of the medieval world from wandering out of sight of land as effectively as would a string of gunboats or floating mines. An idea is a solid fact, a theory is a solid fact, a superstition is a solid fact as long as people continue to regulate their actions in terms of the idea, theory, or superstition; and it is none the less solid because it is conveyed as an image or a breath of sound.

3

This world of ideas serves many purposes. Two of them bear heavily upon our investigation of utopia. On one hand the pseudo-environment or idolum is a substitute for the external world; it is a sort of house of refuge to which we flee when our contacts with "hard facts" becomes too complicated to carry through or too rough to face. On the other hand, it is by means of the idolum that the facts of the everyday world are brought together and assorted and sifted, and a new sort of reality is projected back again upon the external world. One of these functions is escape or compensation; it seeks an immediate release from the difficulties or frustrations of our lot. The other attempts to provide a condition for our release in the future. The utopias that correspond to these two functions I shall call the utopias of escape and the utopias of reconstruction. The first leaves the external world the way it is; the second seeks to change it so that one may have intercourse with it on one's own terms. In one we build impossible castles in the air; in the other we consult a surveyor and an architect and a mason and proceed to build a house which meets our essential needs;

as well as houses made of stone and mortar are capable of meeting them.

4

Why, however, should we find it necessary to talk about utopia and the world of ideas at all? Why should we not rest secure in the bosom of the material environment, without flying off into a region apparently beyond space and time? Well, the alternative before us is not whether we shall live in the real world or dream away our time in utopia; for men are so constituted that only by a deliberate discipline—such as that followed by a Hindu ascetic or an American business man—can one or the other world be abolished from consciousness. The genuine alternative for most of us is that between an aimless utopia of escape and a purposive utopia of reconstruction. One way or the other, it seems, in a world so full of frustrations as the "real" one, we must spend a good part of our mental lives in utopia.

Nevertheless this needs a qualification. It is plain that certain types of people have no need for private utopias and that certain communities seem to be without them. The savages of the Marquesas whom Herman Melville described seem to have had such a jolly and complete adjustment to their environment that, except for the raids of hostile tribes—and this turned out to be chiefly sport which only whetted their appetites for the feast that followed—everything needed for a good life at the South Sea level could be obtained by direct attack. The Marquesans had no need to dream of a happier existence; they had only to grab it.

At times, during childhood perhaps, life has the same sort of completeness; and without doubt there are many mature people who have manufactured out of their limitations a pretty adequate response to a narrow environment; and have let it go at that. Such people feel no need for utopia. As long as they can keep their contacts restricted, only a deliberate raid from the outside world would create such a need. They are like the sick man in the parable of the Persian poet, whose only desire was that he might desire something; and there is no particular reason to envy them. People who will not venture out into the open sea pay the penalty of never having looked into the bright eyes of danger; and at best they know but half of life. What such folk might call the good life is simply not good enough. We cannot be satisfied with a segment of existence, no matter how safely we may be adjusted to it, when with a little effort we can trace the complete circle.

But there have been few regions, few social orders, and few people in which the adjustment has not been incomplete. In the face of perpetual difficulties and obstructions—the wind and the weather and the impulses of other men and customs that have long outlived their use—there are three ways, roughly, in which a man may react. He may run away. He may try to hold his own. He may attack. Looking around at our contemporaries who have survived the war, it is fairly evident that most of them are in the first stage of panic and despair. In an interesting article on The Dénouement of Nihilism, Mr. Edward Townsend Booth characterized the generation born in the late eighties as suffering a complete paralysis of will, or else, "if any initiative remains to them, they emigrate to Europe or the South Sea Islands, or crawl off into some quiet corner of the United States—but most of them continue where they were stricken in a state of living death."

Speaking more generally, running away does not always mean a physical escape, nor does an "attack" necessarily mean doing something practical "on the spot." Let us use Dr. John Dewey's illustration and suppose that a man is denied intercourse with his friends at a distance. One kind of reaction is for him to "imagine" meeting his friends, and going through, in fantasy, a whole ritual of meeting, repartee, and discussion. The other kind of reaction, as Dr. Dewey says, is to see what conditions must be met in order to cement distant friends, and then invent the telephone. The so-called extrovert, the type of man who has no need for utopias, will satisfy his desire by talking to the nearest human being. ("He may try to hold his own.") But it is fairly plain that the extrovert, from the very weakness and inconstancy of his aims, is incapable of contributing anything but "good nature" to the good life of the community; and in his hands both art and invention would probably come to an end.

Now putting aside the extrovert, we find that the two remaining types of reaction have expressed themselves in all the historic utopias. It is perhaps well that we should see them first in their normal, everyday setting, before we set out to explore the ideal commonwealths of the past.

More or less, we have all had glimpses of the utopia of escape: it is raised and it collapses and it is built up again almost daily. In the midst of the clanking machinery of a paper factory I have come across a moving picture actress's portrait, stuck upon an inoperative part of the machine; and it was not hard to reconstruct the private utopia of the wretch who minded the levers, or to picture the world into which he had fled from the roar and throb and muck of the machinery about him. What man has not had this utopia from the dawn of adolescence onwards—the desire to possess and be possessed by a beautiful woman?

Perhaps for the great majority of men and women that small, private Utopia is the only one for which they feel a perpetual, warm interest; and ultimately every other utopia must be translatable to them in some such intimate terms. Their conduct would tell us as much if their words did not confess it. They leave their bleak office buildings and their grimy factories, and night after night they pour into the cinema theater in order that they may live for a while in a land populated by beautiful, flirtatious women and tender, lusty men. Small wonder that the great and powerful religion founded by Mahomet puts that utopia in the very foreground of the hereafter! In a sense, this is the most elementary of utopias; for, on the interpretation of the analytical psychologist, it carries with it the deep longing to return to and remain at rest in the mother's womb—the one perfect environment which all the machinery and legislation of an eager world has never been able to reproduce.

In its most elemental state, this utopia of escape calls for a complete breach with the butcher, the baker, the grocer, and the real, limited, imperfect people that flutter around us. In order to make it more perfect, we eliminate the butcher and baker and transport ourselves to a self-sufficient island in the South Seas. For the most part, of course, this is an idle dream, and if we do not grow out of it, we must at any rate thrust other conditions into it; but for a good many of us, idleness without a dream is the only alternative. Out of such fantasies of bliss and perfection, which do not endure in real life even when they occasionally bloom into existence, our art and literature have very largely grown. It is hard to conceive of a social order so complete and satisfactory that it would rob us of the necessity of having recourse, from time to time, to an imaginary world in which our sufferings could be purged or our delights heightened. Even in the great idyll painted by William Morris, women are fickle and lovers are disappointed; and when the "real" world becomes a little too hard and too sullen to face, we must take refuge, if we are to recover our balance, into another world which responds more perfectly to our deeper interests and desires—the world of literature.

Once we have weathered the storm, it is dangerous to remain in the utopia of escape; for it is an enchanted island, and to remain there is to lose one's capacity for dealing with things as they are. The girl who has felt Prince Charming's caresses too long will be repulsed by the clumsy embraces of the young man who takes her to the theater and wonders how the deuce he is going to pay the rent if they spend more than a week on their honeymoon. Moreover, life is too easy in the utopia of escape, and too blankly perfect—there is nothing to sharpen your teeth upon. It is not for this that men have gone into the jungle to hunt beasts and have cajoled the grasses and roots to be prolific, and have defied, in little open boats, the terror of the wind and sea. Our daily diet must have more roughage in it than these daydreams will give us if we are not to become debilitated.

In the course of our journey into utopia we shall remain a little while in these utopias of escape; but we shall not bide there long. There are plenty of them, and they dot the waters of our imaginary world as the islands that Ulysses visited dotted the Aegean Sea. These utopias however belong to the department of pure literature, and in that department they occupy but a minor place. We could dispense with the whole lot of them, bag and baggage, in exchange for another Anna Karenin or The Brothers Karamazov.

5

The second kind of utopia which we shall encounter is the utopia of reconstruction.

The first species represents, the analytical psychologist would tell us, a very primitive kind of thinking, in which we follow the direction of our desires without taking into account any of the limiting conditions which we should have to confront if we came back to earth and tried to realize our wishes in practical affairs. It is a vague and messy and logically inconsequent series of images which color up and fade, which excite us and leave us cold, and which—for the sake of the respect our neighbors have for our ability to add a ledger or plane a piece of wood—we had better confine to the strange box of records we call our brain.

The second type of utopia may likewise be colored by primitive desires and wishes; but these desires and wishes have come to reckon with the world in which they seek realization. The utopia of reconstruction is what its name implies: a vision of a reconstituted environment which is better adapted to the nature and aims of the human beings who dwell within it than the actual one; and not merely better adapted to their actual nature, but better fitted to their possible developments. If the first utopia leads backward into the utopian's ego, the second leads outward—outward into the world.

By a reconstructed environment I do not mean merely a physical thing. I mean, in addition, a new set of habits, a fresh scale of values, a different net of relationships and institutions, and possibly—for almost all utopias emphasize the factor of breeding—an alteration of the physical and mental characteristics of the people chosen, through education, biological selection, and so forth. The reconstructed environ-

ment which all the genuine utopians seek to contrive is a reconstruction of both the physical world and the idolum. It is in this that the
utopian distinguishes himself from the practical inventor and the
industrialist. Every attempt that has been made to domesticate animals, cultivate plants, dredge rivers, dig ditches, and in modern times,
apply the energy of the sun to mechanical instruments, has been an
effort to reconstruct the environment; and in many cases the human
advantage has been plain. It is not for the utopian to despise Prome-
theus who brought the fire or Franklin who captured the lightning. As
Anatole France says: "Without the Utopians of other times, men
would still live in caves, miserable and naked. It was Utopians who
traced the lines of the first city. . . . Out of generous dreams come
beneficial realities. Utopia is the principle of all progress, and the
essay into a better future."

Our physical reconstructions however have been limited; they have
touched chiefly the surfaces of things. The result is that people live in
a modern physical environment and carry in their minds an odd
assortment of spiritual relics from almost every other age, from that of
the primitive, taboo-ridden savage, to the energetic Victorian disciples
of Gradgrind and Bounderby. As Mr. Hendrik van Loon pithily says:
"A human being with the mind of a sixteenth century tradesman driving a 1921 Rolls-Royce is still a human being with the mind of a sixteenth century tradesman." The problem is fundamentally a human
problem. The more completely man is in control of physical nature,
the more urgently we must ask ourselves what under the heavens is to
move and guide and keep in hand the controller. This problem of an
ideal, a goal, an end—even if the aim persist in shifting as much as
the magnetic north pole—is a fundamental one to the utopian.

Except in the writings of the utopians, and this is an important
point to notice in our travels through utopia, the reconstruction of the
material environment and the reconstitution of the mental framework
of the creatures who inhabit it, have been kept in two different com-
partments. One compartment is supposed to belong to the practical
man; the other to the idealist. The first was something whose aims
could be realized in the Here and Now; the other was postponed very
largely to the sweet by-and-bye. Neither the practical man nor the
idealist has been willing to admit that he has been dealing with a
single problem; that each has been treating the faces of a single thing
as if they were separate.

Here is where the utopia of reconstruction wins hands down. It
not merely pictures a whole world, but it faces every part of it at the
same time. We shall not examine the classic utopias without becoming
conscious of their weaknesses, their sometimes disturbing idiosyncra-

sies. It is important at present that we should realize their virtues; and should start on our journey without the feeling of disparagement which the word utopian usually calls up in minds that have been seduced by Macaulay's sneer that he would rather have an acre in Middlesex than a principality in utopia.

6

Finally, be convinced about the reality of utopia. All that has happened in what we call human history—unless it has left a building or a book or some other record of itself—is just as remote and in a sense just as mythical as the mysterious island which Raphael Hythloday, scholar and sailor, described to Sir Thomas More. A good part of human history is even more insubstantial: the Icarians who lived only in the mind of Étienne Cabet, or the Freelanders who dwelt within the imagination of a dry little Austrian economist, have had more influence upon the lives of our contemporaries than the Etruscan people who once dwelt in Italy, although the Etruscans belong to what we call the real world, and the Freelanders and Icarians inhabited— Nowhere.

Nowhere may be an imaginary country, but News from Nowhere is real news. The world of ideas, beliefs, fantasies, projections, is (I must emphasize again) just as real whilst it is acted upon as the post which Dr. Johnson kicked in order to demonstrate that it was solid. The man who wholly respects the rights of property is kept out of his neighbor's field perhaps even more effectively than the man who is merely forbidden entrance by a no-trespass sign. In sum, we cannot ignore our utopias. They exist in the same way that north and south exist; if we are not familiar with their classical statements we at least know them as they spring to life each day in our own minds. We can never reach the points of the compass; and so no doubt we shall never live in utopia; but without the magnetic needle we should not be able to travel intelligently at all. It is absurd to dispose of utopia by saying that it exists only on paper. The answer to this is: precisely the same thing may be said of the architect's plans for a house, and houses are none the worse for it.

We must lose our sense of remoteness and severity in setting out on this exploration of ideal commonwealths, as some of the fine minds of the past have pictured them. Our ideals are not something that we can set apart from the main facts of our existence, as our grandmothers sometimes set the cold, bleak, and usually moldy parlor apart from the living rooms of the house: on the contrary, the things we dream of tend consciously or unconsciously to work themselves out in the pattern of our daily lives. Our utopias are just as human and warm and jolly as the world out of which they are born. Looking out from the top of a high tenement, over the housetops of Manhattan, I can see a pale tower with its golden pinnacle gleaming through the soft morning haze; and for a moment all the harsh and ugly lines in the landscape have disappeared. So in looking at our utopias. We need not abandon the real world in order to enter these realizable worlds; for it is out of the first that the second are always coming.

Finally, an anticipation and a warning. In our journey through the utopias of the past we shall not rest content when we have traversed the whole territory between Plato and the latest modern writer. If the story of utopia throws any light upon the story of mankind it is this: our utopias have been pitifully weak and inadequate; and if they have not exercised enough practical influence upon the course of affairs, it is because, as Viola Paget says in Gospels of Anarchy, they were simply not good enough. We travel through utopia only in order to get beyond utopia: if we leave the domains of history when we enter the gates of Plato's Republic, we do so in order to re-enter more effectively the dusty midday traffic of the contemporary world. So our study of the classic utopias will be followed by an examination of certain social myths and partial utopias that have played an important part in the affairs of the Western World during the last few centuries. In the end, I promise, I shall make no attempt to present another utopia; it will be enough to survey the foundations upon which others may build.

In the meanwhile, our ship is about to set sail; and we shall not heave anchor again until we reach the coasts of Utopia.

2

The Uses of Utopia

ARTHUR E. MORGAN'S JUSTIFICATION OF THE
STUDY OF UTOPIAN LITERATURE

Arthur E. Morgan (b. 1878) is an engineer, educator, and philosopher with a wide and deep knowledge of utopists and utopian literature. Research for a biography of Edward Bellamy led Morgan to attempt to trace the previously unexplored sources which had probably influenced Bellamy in writing the famous utopian novel *Looking Backward*. Morgan became convinced that Bellamy, in his proposed scheme for the reorganization of society, had been inspired by the example of the Incas of Peru. He also found striking similarities between the supposedly imaginary social order described by Sir Thomas More in his *Utopia* and the organization of the Inca empire. In Bellamy's ideal new society, in More's Utopia, and in the Peru of the Incas, private ownership of land had been eliminated; public work and rotation of labor were practiced; periodical censuses and inventories were taken; a system of storehouses had been instituted; money was not used generally; supervision of labor was skillfully managed; and an economy of abundance had been achieved. These and numerous other parallels among the three societies were discussed by Morgan in his informative and delightful book *Nowhere Was Somewhere: How History Makes Utopias and How Utopias Make History* (1946). This work is of importance not only because of the light it throws on specific works of utopian literature and how they sometimes imitate or reflect actual human experience and historical fact, but also because it contains one of the most lucid and thought-provoking answers to the question, Of what use are utopias?

Morgan holds that utopias have been "among the most powerful formative forces" in the history of civilization. By presenting "designs of a good society," they have provided a wide range of alternative possibilities to serve as inspiration and guidance, either directly or indirectly, for creators of new governments. As Morgan points out, Napoleon was influenced by the utopian constitution of Abbe Sieyès; the American Constitution was an offspring of utopias; and the American Democratic party was the inheritor

41

of utopian doctrines popularized by Bellamy's *Looking Backward.* The knowledge of utopian philosophy and literature, then, is not merely a pleasurable diversion or a cultural embellishment to legislators and social reformers; it is essential to them and to everyone interested in reconstructing political and social institutions. Morgan suggests that if the study of utopian literature and philosophy were more widespread, the mass of men would be less credulous of social panaceas and more critical of ideologies. For, as he puts it, utopias constitute "one of the greatest reservoirs of human experience and aspiration."[1]

Morgan's interest in utopias extends back to the origin of utopian images in dim racial memories of a Golden Age and forward to the problem of what man would do if utopia were achieved in the future. The problem of achieving utopia will not be, according to Morgan, as difficult for man to solve as the problem of living in it. The boredom which might come from his getting what he wanted might present as many problems as did the frustration previously experienced from not having what he desired. In speculating about "what lies beyond utopia," Morgan hopes that the realization of utopia, of economic security and social stability, will not mean the end of human striving and a disappointment of human hopes, but rather will provide new opportunities for individual self-realization and "achievements of imperishable worth."

[1] Arthur E. Morgan, *Nowhere Was Somewhere: How History Makes Utopias and How Utopias Make History* (Chapel Hill, N.C.: The University of North Carolina Press, 1946), p. 14.

From Arthur E. Morgan, Nowhere Was Somewhere: How History Makes Utopias and How Utopias Make History *(Chapel Hill, N.C.: The University of North Carolina Press, 1946), pp. 152–64. Reprinted by permission of The University of North Carolina Press.*

We have drawn no narrow boundaries for the utopian theme. Any picture or pattern which has gone beyond current achievement in presenting the possibilities of a good society has been considered within the range of interest. Some such writings are in the twilight zone between utopia and philosophy, as for instance, Plato's *Republic.*

In the marginal zone between utopia and government are numerous treatises which fall into one class or the other depending on circumstances or outlook. The biblical book of Deuteronomy is looked upon by some as a utopian picture of a good society, by others as a code of laws that to a considerable degree was actually lived by. The idealized code drafted in the cabin of the *Mayflower* during the long slow months of the passage overseas, which breathed the spirit of Watt Tyler, has come to be considered utopian.

Joseph Smith, a Vermont boy, in all probability a *Mayflower* descendant, and with some of the *Mayflower* spirit in him, outlined a political and social code which seemed strongly utopian. Yet the brotherhood which the boy had planned did come into existence; and, under the forceful leadership of his successors, three quarters of a million Mormons maintain a highly significant pattern of social and economic organization, and have made the desert bloom as the rose. Our federal Constitution, if it had not worked out successfully, would have been called utopian. Having succeeded in large degree it is practical government with us, whereas in certain Latin American countries, where it was copied but did not work, it is utopian.

An interesting case of a social pattern which was at one time a program of actual government, and later a utopia, is "The Memorial of a Myriad Words," which was produced by the Chinese statesman Wang An Shih in A.D. 1058, and which under the emperor Jin Tsung was the actual program of a "new deal" government for twenty years. Thereafter it was repudiated by a reactionary regime, its adherents were eliminated, and almost every copy of the document was destroyed. Long afterward two copies were found, one of them sealed up in the brick wall of a house. Through the centuries it has existed as a utopian dream.

In the region between ethics and religion, on the one hand, and utopia, on the other, we find similar indefiniteness of boundary. The Hebrew prophets, followed by the bearer of a message of world brotherhood, and St. Augustine and his *City of God*, all have been classified in both fields.

So we might continue our list of those writings that are in the no-man's-land between utopia and other fields. We might inquire whether Rousseau and his *Social Contract*, and Harrington and his *Oceana*, were utopians or authors of treatises on political philosophy. We might wonder whether the utopian spirit or the spirit of satire for its own sake is dominant in Aristophanes' *Ecclesiazusae*, Swift and his *Gulliver*, Butler and his *Erewhon*, and Voltaire and his *Zadig*. The same question might be asked about the Chinese travel tales, "Flowers in the Mirror."

Even in works of fiction utopian elements appear. We find them in Defoe's *Robinson Crusoe* and in the large number of imitators known as "Robinsons," the best known among them being *The Swiss Family Robinson* and, in German, *Insel Felsenburg*. We may even trace utopian features in such "pure" fantasies as Jules Verne's *Twenty Thousand Leagues Under the Sea* and E. Rider Haggard's *King Solomon's Mines*. The great Shakespeare could not resist playing about the margins of utopia, as in *The Tempest* and *As You Like It*. Occasionally a man like H. G. Wells ranges all around the borders of utopia, through religion, philosophy, government, and economics, to adventures and pure fantasy.

Should a commission of the wisest men be set up to define exactly the boundaries of utopia, they must fail; for no sooner would they turn their backs than some intrepid people would put some utopian scheme to work and bring it into the domain of practical life. Why, then, should the author trouble himself about whether he has ignored the proper boundaries of his subject? The author has not so troubled himself. Wherever the utopian theme appears, in whatever form of literature, he has considered it to be within his domain. . . .

When a man makes a garden or builds a house or a city, he begins to express a design of orderly arrangement—to make his work conform to a preconceived pattern. Almost every single item in our vast and complex American civilization was first a design in some man's mind before it was worked out into reality. The quality of our civilization is the quality of those designs. Occasionally there are men in whom this sense of design extends its range of action until it achieves an inclusive view of life as a whole in all its relationships. A description of such an inclusive view, especially if it is in the form of a picture of an ideal society as though it actually existed, may properly be called utopia.

Every intelligent and active-minded person is to some degree a utopian. In our leisure moments we try to picture to ourselves the political, social and technical conditions under which we should like to live, and, at least in some small degree, we try to realize those conditions. The process of uncritical trying of this and that to see whether it will work is better than completely inert conservatism, at least as regards simple circumstances. However, in complex situations the wrong ways may so vastly outnumber the right ones that the prospect of success by unsystematic, impulsive experiment may be very, very remote. The results of that type of experiment are chiefly waste of resources, disillusionment, and the discrediting of creative effort.

Up to the present, much of political and social experiment has been of that uncritical, impulsive character. Where the total resources and energies of great nations are involved in such experiments, the process is exceedingly wasteful and dangerous. Repeatedly the people have had high hopes, only to have them dashed to the ground; and such will continue to be common experience except to the extent that a new method of social pioneering becomes general. The new social process, of critical analysis and of orderly, creative design disciplined by the results of such analysis, makes possible a great reduction of risk and waste in making social changes, and promises greater and more rapid achievement.

The process of critical inquiry and analysis, with orderly design controlled by established principles and pertinent facts, is called engineering. Only as a similar process comes to prevail in the field of human relations will the conditions of society greatly improve. The social engineer is imperative.

The engineer does not dispense with the use of imagination or intuition. He is as much artist as he is analyst. He does not build from nothing. He begins with suggestions from his experience, or from the designs of others, or from imagination. He must have mental pictures of possible solutions before he can analyze and test and compare. The more nearly he is equipped with mental pictures of all possible solutions to his problem, the greater is the probability that he will reach the best possible result.

So it is with the social engineer. His is not an abstract mathematical process. He should have mental pictures of all possible solutions of his problem, so that in the process of analysis, test, and comparison, no significant prospect may be overlooked. Utopias are among the chief sources of suggestion for the social engineer. At their best they represent the essence of the world's thought regarding the possibilities of human society.

Most suggestions of design which are helpful to an engineer come from men who are disciplined and experienced in their field. Similarly, most utopias of any value are the work of intelligent and imagi-native men who have been active participants or disciplined observers of affairs. They are by no means the work of idle dreamers.

The two general reasons why human societies do not reach per-fection have already been suggested. One is that, like the trees in the forest, different societies crowd each other, trying to win "a place in the sun," and also are thwarted, injured, and blighted by flood, famine, pestilence, and other adverse natural circumstances. The other reason for social imperfection is no less important. Unlike a tree of the forest, human society is without a single common, definite pattern of growth, or idea or ideal. In an anthill there apparently is no rebellion or internal discord. The prevailing type of social organization is completely recog-nized and accepted. In human society no such fixed social pattern exists. Fortunately men are still free to explore the vast ranges of possible social organization and to work out new designs as human experience and insight increase, or as conditions of living change.

Much of the discord, grief, and conflict in the world today is the result, not of men's inability to achieve social aims, but of the absence of agreement concerning social aims on which to unite their efforts. When we observe how far from agreement on a social program those men are who are ablest in the field of government and social organi-zation, we realize that it is not yet time for any single type of govern-ment to be fixed on society. The existence of disagreement and con-flict, and the lack of unity of inner impulse toward achieving an ideal design, are not necessarily a hopeless or even an undesirable condi-tion. Such discord indicates that society is in active evolution and is feeling its way toward larger and better patterns. We are as yet in the dim morning twilight of social science. Premature unity might result in fixing on society an unnecessarily imperfect type.

For a design for society to find expression in the actual structure of society and of government there is necessary a vast expenditure of life and resources, no small part of which expenditure at present is made in efforts to eliminate competing designs. The world today is in the throes of conflict between competitive utopias that are struggling for realization. Each of the social philosophies now fighting for self-preservation or for dominance is presented to the peoples who live under it as ideal and as suitable for universal application. Each one is a product of tradition and experience, combined with partly un-tested theory. Each one is in some respects so crude and imperfect as to raise doubts about whether it should become dominant, at least until further evolution and development have taken place. However, there is scarcely one of these social philosophies which does not in-clude wholesome and desirable elements which might be universally adopted with profit.

If each of these social philosophies were being held by a people tentatively, with open minds, and with the aim of correcting and refining it, but not with the purpose of imposing it on others, then the resulting variety would be enlightening and stimulating. In the process of critical examination, comparison, and refinement the excellences of each system of social organization would emerge, and weaknesses would become evident and could be removed.

When a people is taught to hold its social philosophy, not tentatively and open-mindedly, but as the finally best form of society which all the world must sometime accept, then destructive competition and conflict follow, of which the recent world war is an example. While Americans are passionately, emotionally loyal to the name of democracy, its actual operation in our own political life is seen to be very imperfect, and relatively few people are wholly committed to it in practice. The best outcome of the recent world war would not be the imposition upon the world of what we call democracy, but the emergence of an attitude of mutual tolerance for different types of social organization. Our utopias should have only tentative adoption and use on a limited scale until they can be thoroughly examined, tested, and criticized. In the end it is by practical results and not only by theory that they must be judged.

Therefore the great social need today is not that men shall agree on a single type of social organization, but that they shall come to recognize principles of integrity, mutual respect, tolerance, and local autonomy combined with interdependence, which will make possible a continuing process of social experiment and exploration without destructive conflict. The colossal waste of life and resources which takes place in the competitive struggle for a pattern of government, both by class and party struggles within nations and by war between nations, might be largely eliminated if men but realized that they are blindly feeling their way toward a good organization of society. With tolerance, patience, and good will; with free inquiry and aggressive exploration; with absence of dogmatism and without reliance on revelation or panacea, unprecedented progress might be made. Instead of a spirit of desperation and hatred—of fighting for life—there might be the zest and interest of exploration and adventure. Should such a change of social feeling once take place, any thought of reverting to present methods of violent competition would be looked upon as insanity. No change of human nature is needed, but only a change in the "conditioning" of the human spirit.

Pictures of a good life that have come to us range all the way from the daydreams of unrestrained wishful thinking to appeals for rigorous discipline and reconstruction of life as essential preparation for a better day. At one extreme, only the rubbing of Aladdin's magic lamp is necessary to turn a shiftless ne'er-do-well into an opulent prince. In contrast is the prophet Amos, calling for a radical reformation of life and character as essential to any real hope for his people. Some of the Arabian Nights stories seem to have come down from a remote past. It may be that in the light of the same moon, while Amos was rehearsing his stern theme to the herdsmen on the mountain, a pampered son of luxury or a parasitic plebeian in Egypt or Babylon was getting a vicarious sense of validity from stories of the magic lamp or the magic carpet.

The expression "creative vision" may seem a contradiction of terms; yet it is the quality of some men to see that which never has been but which can be within the framework of reality and would add to the quality of living. Such creative vision may become an active cause of events, without which they would not occur. At their best utopians have that gift.

Whatever stirs men deeply tends to result in pictures of a good society. When, a short time before the discovery of America, the Turks overran Greece and drove Greek scholars to Italy, there was a burst of utopian thinking and undertaking in Italian cities. Columbus inspired utopias by opening the doors of what had seemed like a closed world. When the Tudors broke up the ancient land system of England, other pictures of a good society appeared. The Industrial Revolution, one of the great disturbances of history, stimulated the appearance of utopias at an unprecedented rate. Whenever circumstances press especially hard upon men, unless their spirits are completely broken they persist in picturing a good world that for the present is denied them. When men cease to produce utopias it will be because they are all dead, in spirit, if not in body—or else because life is so good that they cannot imagine it to be better.

A sense of human brotherhood, a craving to find some way in which all men, and not just the favored few, could escape from drudgery, has been one of the dominant incentives to the writing of utopias. As Bellamy said, the crux of the problem in his boyhood discussions was "Who would do the dirty work?" To imagine labor-saving technology may have seemed like a psychology of escape; yet that term may sometimes be too easily applied. What seems like wishful thinking may be a refusal to surrender the hope of better things.

This craving to be relieved from the deadening burden of physical drudgery is constantly in evidence in utopian writing and leads to the prophesying of many inventions. Thomas More cautiously felt his way to modern technology, as in forecasting artificial incubation of eggs.

First, perhaps, among the moderns to see the freeing of men from drudgery as an important element of the good life was Robert Owen, who spoke and wrote from his knowledge as a successful manufacturer. J. H. Etzler, in one of the first American utopias, *The Paradise Within the Reach of All Men*, published in Pennsylvania in 1833, forecast plastics, synthetic fabrics, and air conditioning. Henry Thoreau read this thin little volume and, repulsed by the crude picture it presented of a mechanized civilization, was confirmed in his preference for simple living. About three years later, in 1836, another Pennsylvanian, Mrs. Mary Griffith, in her little utopia, *Three Hundred Years Hence*, forecast many of the technical inventions which have since taken place. In 1840 came Cabet's *Icarie* in which technical inventions were among the most prominent features of a somewhat mechanically organized society.

Then, at about the time of *Looking Backward*, came another burst of utopian writing in which inventions and technical developments were to relieve men of drudgery. Bellamy generally is looked upon as the first to anticipate broadcasting of the human voice, but at least two utopians had preceded him in this: Macnie in *The Diothas*, and Cridge in *Utopia: The History of an Extinct Planet*. Both were published in 1884, the first in New York and the second in California. Macnie also forecast internal combustion engines, wheat "combine harvesters," artificial milk, microphotographs, television, a universal language, and numerous other useful developments. Yet, for all the imaginative daring of utopian writers, the developments of technology in general have already outrun their predictions.

In contrast with most utopians, William Morris was very skeptical of modern technology. In his *News from Nowhere* we have a record of his disgust at the dirty, ugly England of the Industrial Revolution, and his love of his quiet, old-time rural English home where he was reared in simple luxury. Thus typical utopian writings criticize the shortcomings of the prevailing social order as they see them and contrast them to the finest the creator of the utopia has seen or heard about. The sheer creative element generally is small, though the best that the utopian has seen becomes refined and perfected in his own mind, and that process of itself is creative.

As already suggested, there is, in the more responsible utopian literature, a great and largely untapped reservoir of creative ideas and shrewd practical devices, with records of experience, insight, and wisdom. In these writings thoughtful and experienced men have considered what are the principal handicaps to the achievement of personal and social well-being. Sometimes with creative minds, and often with daring originality, they have devised a great variety of ways of meeting social issues. A collection of utopian literature is like a convention of philosophers and statesmen, determined to find ways in which their hard-won philosophies can be put into effect in the actual lives of men.

It would be an important service to mankind, a service which has never yet been rendered, to assemble all such material which is not simply ephemeral or trivial, to organize it into conveniently usable form, and to make it available. One part of such a work would be an analysis and codification of all principles, methods, and devices used in utopias and in near utopias. Under any subject, such as education or money or economic equality or freedom of thought and expression, would be presented the best-thought-out and best-expressed observations, opinions, and policies of utopian writers, with indication of the extent to which different viewpoints prevailed among utopians. From some utopians, such as Plato, More, Rousseau, or Bellamy, a considerable number of significant ideas would be extracted and codified. From the writings of many a minor utopian but a single idea or proposal would be worth recording; yet in the aggregate these scattered contributions would constitute an important part of the whole. Such a "classified compendium of utopian principles and usages," gathered from the entire range of utopian literature, would be an invaluable handbook for lawmakers and all those who formulate public policy.

Not only does utopian literature supply such background material for social design, but the unconventional creative approach of utopians helps us to break through the rigid and formidable barriers of conventional thinking and see things fresh, from unusual standpoints. To some extent utopians provide choice of method, which is the very essence of freedom.

"To write properly the history of utopias from the time of Sir Thomas More to the present is to write the history of the progress of human thought in the past five centuries." Such was the opinion of Charles M. Andrews in his introduction to *Ideal Empires and Republics*. There is reason to believe that the British Royal Society was a direct outgrowth of two or three utopias—Andreae's *Christianopolis,* Bacon's *New Atlantis,* and *Nova Solyma.* Perhaps the most obviously productive of all utopias was Harrington's *Oceana,* which has been discussed. Practical-minded congressmen seldom realize, when they argue for the separation of the legislative, executive, and judicial functions of government, that they are going over the arguments of *Oceana.* Neither are the people of Massachusetts, Pennsylvania, and other states generally aware that their constitutions contain substantial elements borrowed from that source; nor are the French aware of the extent to which the Napoleonic organization of France was, through Sieyès, probably indebted to *Oceana*.

Robert Owen, through his utopian writing and his personal work, gave rise to the great co-operative movement, had a profound effect on education, gave its name and much of its content to socialism, greatly influenced the trade union movement, and was forerunner of the ethical culture movement. The influence of Rousseau's *Social Contract* on government in Europe and America is common knowledge. His influence on education through Pestalozzi, Froebel, Elizabeth Peabody, and Horace Mann is less well known.

The efforts of statesmen to put their plans into practical effect often are blocked by lack of a great pattern which they can follow. In the aggregate men have a vast amount of energy, but possess small capacity for creative design. They spend their energies in wars, in building economic empire, in ostentation of wealth, because no finer design for living possesses their spirits. Whenever an apparently hopeful design is powerfully presented so as to capture men's attention and loyalty, they will pour vast energies into its realization, even though the design is extremely faulty. Witness the energies which have been poured into efforts to realize the designs presented by Buddha, Mohammed, Rousseau, Karl Marx, Mary Baker Eddy, Joseph Smith of the Mormons, and Adolph Hitler.

No greater service can be done to men than to contribute to the correction, refinement, and enlargement of the designs of life they live by. Efforts to do this by means of pictures of ideal societies, called utopias, rank high among effective means to that end. It is not the immediate application of such a picture to a particular society that is the measure of their greatest usefulness, but the fact that they exist as bases for measuring what has been done and as suggestions of what might be.

3

Invitation to Utopia

GEORGE RIPLEY'S PLAN FOR AN IDEAL ASSOCIATION

The following letter written by the New England Transcendentalist George Ripley (1802–1880) to Ralph Waldo Emerson is not just a letter of invitation but also a statement of utopian faith. A more typical example of utopian thinking could scarcely be imagined. Most if not all of the characteristics of utopianism are here: the plan which works out so well on paper; the glowing vision of an ideal community in which economic security, personal happiness, and social harmony have become realities; the conviction that the quality of life can and must be improved; the desire to escape from or to solve the problems of everyday life; and the conviction that human nature can be radically remolded by social institutions, especially by education. As is usually the case, the utopian reformer Ripley claims to be a practical man, and like all reformers, he claims there is an urgency to his cause: the times are ripe for his proposed social changes, and if they are not put into effect shortly a better opportunity may not arise again in the future. Typical utopian that he is, Ripley further expresses the belief that if (or rather, when) his experiment succeeds, it will provide a valuable example to the world by proving that a heaven can indeed be achieved here on earth.

Although Ripley's letter could almost be taken for a parody of utopian faith, from its idealization of labor to its invocation of the divine, there is no doubt that his faith was genuine and his application of it unique. Because of this faith, he manifested clearly what David Riesman admired in utopians, "the nerve of failure." Even though his beloved association Brook Farm failed after a few years, while it lasted Ripley and his associates gave powerful witness to the utopian conviction, which they expressed so beautifully in the revised constitution of Brook Farm in 1844, "that human life shall yet be developed, not in discord and misery, but in harmony and joy, and the perfected earth shall at last bear on her bosom a race of men worthy of the name."[1]

Finally, the reader may wonder whether Emerson accepted Ripley's invitation to become a charter member of Brook Farm. He did not. The reasons for Emerson's refusal—and it was a polite refusal of course—will be brought out later in Part 3. For the present the letter is presented here as a testament of utopianism and as an answer to the question of why men seek to create utopias.

---

[1] The entire introductory statement to Brook Farm's revised constitution is given in part 3.

A letter from George Ripley to Ralph Waldo Emerson. Reprinted from Octavius B. Frothingham, George Ripley *(Boston: Houghton Mifflin & Company, 1882), pp. 307–12.*

Boston, November 9, 1840

My dear Sir:

Our conversation in Concord was of such a general nature that I do not feel as if you were in complete possession of the idea of the association which I wish to see established. As we have now a prospect of carrying it into effect, at an early period, I wish to submit the plan more distinctly to your judgment, that you may decide whether it is one that can have the benefit of your aid and cooperation.

Our objects, as you know, are to insure a more natural union between intellectual and manual labor than now exists; to combine the thinker and the worker, as far as possible, in the same individual; to guarantee the highest mental freedom by providing all with labor adapted to their tastes and talents, and securing to them the fruits of their industry; to do away with the necessity of menial services by opening the benefits of education and the profits of labor to all; and thus to prepare a society of liberal, intelligent, and cultivated persons whose relations with each other would permit a more simple and wholesome life than can be led amidst the pressure of our competitive institutions.

To accomplish these objects, we propose to take a small tract of land, which, under skillful husbandry, uniting the garden and the farm, will be adequate to the subsistence of the families; and to connect with this a school or college in which the most complete instruction shall be given, from the first rudiments to the highest culture. Our farm would be a place for improving the race of men that lived on it; thought would preside over the operations of labor, and labor would contribute to the expansion of thought; we should have industry without drudgery, and true equality without its vulgarity.

An offer has been made to us of a beautiful estate, on very reasonable terms, on the borders of Newton, West Roxbury, and Dedham.

I am very familiar with the premises, having resided on them a part of last summer, and we might search the country in vain for anything more eligible. Our proposal now is for three or four families to take possession on the first of April next, to attend to the cultivation of the farm and the erection of buildings, to prepare for the coming of as many more in the autumn, and thus to commence the institution in the simplest manner, and with the smallest number with which it can go into operation at all. It would thus be not less than two or three years before we should be joined by all who mean to be with us; we should not fall to pieces by our own weight; we should grow up slowly and strong; and the attractiveness of our experiment would win to us all whose society we should want.

The step now to be taken at once is the procuring of funds for the necessary capital. According to the present modification of our plan, a much less sum will be required than that spoken of in our discussions at Concord. We thought then $50,000 would be needed; I find now, after a careful estimate, that $30,000 will purchase the estate and buildings for ten families, and give the required surplus for carrying on the operations for one year.

We propose to raise this sum by a subscription to a joint stock company among the friends of the institution, the payment of a fixed interest being guaranteed to the subscribers, and the subscription itself secured by the real estate. No man then will be in danger of losing; he will receive as fair an interest as he would from any investment, while at the same time he is contributing toward an institution in which, while the true use of money is retained, its abuses are done away. The sum required cannot come from rich capitalists; their instinct would protest against such an application of their coins; it must be obtained from those who sympathize with our ideas, and who are willing to aid their realization with their money, if not by their personal cooperation. There are some of this description on whom I think I can rely; among ourselves we can produce perhaps $10,000; the remainder must be subscribed for by those who wish us well, whether they mean to unite with us or not.

I can imagine no plan which is suited to carry into effect so many divine ideas as this. If wisely executed, it will be a light over this country and this age. If not the sunrise, it will be the morning star. As a practical man, I see clearly that we must have some such arrangement, or all changes less radical will be nugatory. I believe in the divinity of labor; I wish to "harvest my flesh and blood from the land"; but to do this, I must either be insulated and work to disadvantage, or avail myself of the services of hirelings who are not of my order and whom I can scarce make friends, for I must have another to drive the plow which I hold. I cannot empty a cask of lime upon my grass alone. I wish to see a society of educated friends, working, thinking, and living together, with no strife except that of each to contribute the most to the benefit of all.

Personally, my tastes and habits would lead me in another direction. I have a passion for being independent of the world and of every man in it. This I could do easily on the estate which is now offered, and which I could rent at a rate that, with my other resources, would place me in a very agreeable condition as far as my personal interests were involved. I should have a city of God on a small scale of my own; and please God, I should hope one day to drive my own cart to market and sell greens. But I feel bound to sacrifice this private feeling in the hope of a great social good. I shall be anxious to hear from you. Your decision will do much toward settling the question with me, whether the time has come for the fulfillment of a high hope, or whether the work belongs to a future generation. All omens now are favorable; a singular union of diverse talents is ready for the enterprise; everything indicates that we ought to arise and build; and if we let slip this occasion, the unsleeping Nemesis will deprive us of the boon we seek. For myself, I am sure that I can never give so much thought to it again; my mind must act on other objects, and I shall acquiesce in the course of fate, with grief that so fair a light is put out. A small pittance of the wealth which has been thrown away on ignoble objects during this wild contest for political supremacy would lay the cornerstone of a house which would ere long become the desire of nations.

I almost forgot to say that our friends, the "Practical Christians," insist on making their "Standard,"—a vritten document,—a prescribed test. This cuts them off. Perhaps we are better without them. They are good men; they have salt, which we needed with our spice; but we might have proved too liberal, too comprehensive, too much attached to the graces of culture, to suit their ideas. Instead of them, we have the offer of ten or twelve "Practical Men," from Mr. S. G. May, who himself is deeply interested in the proposal, and would like one day to share in its concerns. Pray write me with as much frankness as I have used towards you, and believe me ever your friend and faithful servant,

George Ripley

P.S. I ought to add, that in the present stage of the enterprise no proposal is considered as binding. We wish only to know what can probably be relied on, provided always, that no pledge will be accepted until the articles of association are agreed on by all parties.

I recollect you said that if you were sure of compeers of the right stamp you might embark yourself in the adventure: as to this, let me suggest the inquiry, whether our Association should not be composed of various classes of men? If we have friends whom we love and who love us, I think we should be content to join with others, with whom our personal sympathy is not strong, but whose general ideas coincide with ours, and whose gifts and abilities would make their services important. For instance, I should like to have a good washerwoman in my parish admitted into the plot. She is certainly not a Minerva or a Venus; but we might educate her two children to wisdom and varied accomplishments, who otherwise will be doomed to drudge through life. The same is true of some farmers and mechanics, whom we should like with us.

4

Intentional Living

Henry David Thoreau's Experiment
in Simplifying Existence

"Sage of Concord" and citizen of the universe, Henry David Thoreau (1817–1862) is important to utopianism for two reasons. First, he challenged the traditional communitarian conception of utopia with its quest for collective security and happiness by withdrawing from society to cultivate his inner resources in hope of discovering the essential wisdom of life. Unencumbered by useless possessions and contemptuous of all luxuries, Thoreau, like an ancient Cynic, sought and found meaning just in being a philosopher. And, in his words, "to be a philosopher, is not merely to have subtle thoughts, nor even to found a school, but so to love wisdom as to live according to its dictates, a life of simplicity, independence, magnanimity, and trust."[1] Further, to be a philosopher a man must find practical as well as theoretical solutions to some of the problems of life.

Fiercely independent in his beliefs and actions, highly critical of all authority except that of reason and "higher laws," Thoreau had no confidence in social panaceas, communal visions of salvations, or government-sponsored reforms. The best kind of government was, in his view, that government which governs least or, better still, not at all. In his masterpiece *Walden* (1854) and in his briefer but more influential essay "On the Duty of Civil Disobedience" (1849), Thoreau spoke as "a majority of one" who frankly admitted that he had come into this world "not chiefly to make it a good place to live in, but to live in it, be it good or bad."[2]

In light of his critical stance and extreme individualism, it is easy to view Thoreau as an enemy of the establishment, as an anti-utopian, even as a precursor of the hippies. But Thoreau can also be viewed from a different perspective, which leads to the second reason why he is so important to utopianism. He was one of the most influential utopian thinkers ever pro-

[1] *Writings of Thoreau*, vol. 2 (*Walden*), p. 16.
[2] Ibid., vol. 4 (*Civil Disobedience*), p. 368.

58

duced by America, a designer of a kind of minimum utopia, a do-it-yourself utopist. No hermit, no misanthrope, no cynic, no hater of actual or ideal society could have written works which in our century have inspired utopian planners as different as Mahatma Gandhi, who derived his powerful policy of passive resistance from Thoreau, and B. F. Skinner, who envisioned in his novel *Walden Two* a utopia in which a whole community enjoyed the values of Thoreau's way of life—a Walden not for one, but for two (or more). A reading of Thoreau's works has also awakened in innumerable young people a longing to remold the world nearer to their hearts' desire, a determination to begin to live intentionally, either in solitude or communally, and a willingness to put foundations under their castles in the air.

A conservative revolutionist who usually preferred to hoe beans than to defy authorities, Thoreau never hesitated to act upon his radical beliefs when he was convinced it was necessary. "Under a government which imprisons any unjustly, the true place for a just man is also in prison."[3] Believing this, Thoreau went without hesitation to jail rather than pay a tax to support a government whose policies (during the Mexican War) he condemned. Despite his low opinion of most worldly governments, Thoreau apparently had his own vision of a utopian government under which everyone from bean hoers to philosophers would be free to "do their own thing." This free and enlightened state would only come about, Thoreau suggested, when the state recognized the individual "as a higher and independent power, from which all its own power and authority are derived, and treats him accordingly."[4]

[3] Ibid., p. 370.
[4] Ibid., p. 387.

From The Writings of Henry David Thoreau, *vol. 2*
(Walden) *(Boston: Houghton Mifflin & Co., 1893),*
chap. 2, 100–109; chap. 18, 355–56.

I went to the woods because I wished to live deliberately, to front
only the essential facts of life, and see if I could not learn what it had
to teach, and not, when I came to die, discover that I had not lived. I
did not wish to live what was not life, living is so dear; nor did I wish
to practise resignation, unless it was quite necessary. I wanted to live
deep and suck out all the marrow of life, to live so sturdily and
Spartan-like as to put to rout all that was not life, to cut a broad swath
and shave close, to drive life into a corner, and reduce it to its lowest
terms, and, if it proved to be mean, why then to get the whole and
genuine meanness of it, and publish its meanness to the world; or if it
were sublime, to know it by experience, and be able to give a true
account of it in my next excursion. For most men, it appears to me,
are in a strange uncertainty about it, whether it is of the devil or of
God, and have *somewhat hastily* concluded that it is the chief end of
man here to "glorify God and enjoy him forever."

Still we live meanly, like ants; though the fable tells us that we
were long ago changed into men; like pygmies we fight with cranes; it
is error upon error, and clout upon clout, and our best virtue has for
its occasion a superfluous and evitable wretchedness. Our life is frit-
tered away by detail. An honest man has hardly need to count more
than his ten fingers, or in extreme cases he may add his ten toes, and
lump the rest. Simplicity, simplicity, simplicity! I say, let your affairs
be as two or three, and not a hundred or a thousand; instead of a
million count half a dozen, and keep your accounts on your thumb-
nail. In the midst of this chopping sea of civilized life, such are the
clouds and storms and quicksands and thousand-and-one items to be
allowed for, that a man has to live, if he would not founder and go to
the bottom and not make his port at all, by dead reckoning, and he
must be a great calculator indeed who succeeds. Simplify, simplify.
Instead of three meals a day, if it be necessary eat but one; instead of
a hundred dishes, five; and reduce other things in proportion. Our life
is like a German Confederacy, made up of petty states, with its
boundary forever fluctuating, so that even a German cannot tell you

how it is bounded at any moment. The nation itself, with all its so-called internal improvements, which, by the way are all external and superficial, is just such an unwieldy and overgrown establishment, cluttered with furniture and tripped up by its own traps, ruined by luxury and heedless expense, by want of calculation and a worthy aim, as the million households in the land; and the only cure for it, as for them, is in a rigid economy, a stern and more than Spartan simplicity of life and elevation of purpose. It lives too fast. Men think that it is essential that the *Nation* have commerce, and export ice, and talk through a telegraph, and ride thirty miles an hour, without a doubt, whether *they* do or not; but whether we should live like baboons or like men, is a little uncertain. If we do not get out sleepers, and forge rails, and devote days and nights to the work, but go to tinkering upon our *lives* to improve *them*, who will build railroads? And if railroads are not built, how shall we get to heaven in season? But if we stay at home and mind our business, who will want railroads? We do not ride on the railroad; it rides upon us. Did you ever think what those sleepers are that underlie the railroad? Each one is a man, an Irish-man, or a Yankee man. The rails are laid on them, and they are covered with sand, and the cars run smoothly over them. They are sound sleepers, I assure you. And every few years a new lot is laid down and run over; so that, if some have the pleasure of riding on a rail, others have the misfortune to be ridden upon. And when they run over a man that is walking in his sleep, a supernumerary sleeper in the wrong position, and wake him up, they suddenly stop the cars, and make a hue and cry about it, as if this were an exception. I am glad to know that it takes a gang of men for every five miles to keep the sleepers down and level in their beds as it is, for this is a sign that they may sometime get up again.

Why should we live with such hurry and waste of life? We are determined to be starved before we are hungry. Men say that a stitch in time saves nine, and so they take a thousand stitches to-day to save nine to-morrow. As for *work*, we haven't any of any consequence. We have the Saint Vitus' dance, and cannot possibly keep our heads still. If I should only give a few pulls at the parish bell-rope, as for a fire, that is, without setting the bell, there is hardly a man on his farm in the outskirts of Concord, notwithstanding that press of engagements which was his excuse so many times this morning, nor a boy, nor a woman, I might almost say, but would forsake all and follow that sound, not mainly to save property from the flames, but, if we will confess the truth, much more to see it burn, since burn it must, and we, be it known, did not set it on fire,—or to see it put out, and have a hand in it, if that is done as handsomely; yes, even if it were the parish church itself. Hardly a man takes a half-hour's nap after dinner, but when he wakes he holds up his head and asks, "What's the news?" as if the rest of mankind had stood his sentinels. Some give directions to be waked every half-hour, doubtless for no other purpose; and then, to pay for it, they tell what they have dreamed. After a night's sleep the news is as indispensable as the breakfast. "Pray tell me anything new that has happened to a man anywhere on this globe,"—and he reads it over his coffee and rolls, that a man has had his eyes gouged out this morning on the Wachito River; never dreaming the while that he lives in the dark unfathomed mammoth cave of this world, and has but the rudiment of an eye himself.

For my part, I could easily do without the post office. I think that there are very few important communications made through it. To speak critically, I never received more than one or two letters in my life—I wrote this some years ago—that were worth the postage. The penny-post is, commonly, an institution through which you seriously offer a man that penny for his thoughts which is so often safely offered in jest. And I am sure that I never read any memorable news in a newspaper. If we read of one man robbed, or murdered, or killed by accident, or one house burned, or one vessel wrecked, or one steamboat blown up, or one cow run over on the Western Railroad, or one mad dog killed, or one lot of grasshoppers in the winter,—we never need read of another. One is enough. If you are acquainted with the principle, what do you care for a myriad instances and applications? To a philosopher all *news*, as it is called, is gossip, and they who edit and read it are old women over their tea. Yet not a few are greedy after this gossip. There was such a rush, as I hear, the other day at one of the offices to learn the foreign news by the last arrival, that several large squares of plate glass belonging to the establishment were broken by the pressure,—news which I seriously think a ready wit might write a twelvemonth or twelve years beforehand with sufficient accuracy. As for Spain, for instance, if you know how to throw in Don Carlos and the Infanta, and Don Pedro and Seville and Granada, from time to time in the right proportions,—they may have changed the names a little since I saw the papers,—and serve up a bullfight when other entertainments fail, it will be true to the letter, and give us as good an idea of the exact state or ruin of things in Spain as the most succinct and lucid reports under this head in the newspapers: and as for England, almost the last significant scrap of news from that quarter was the revolution of 1649; and if you have learned the history of her crops for an average year, you never need attend to that thing again, unless your speculations are of a merely pecuniary character. If one may judge who rarely looks into the newspapers, nothing new does ever happen in foreign parts, a French revolution not excepted.

What news! how much more important to know what that is which was never old! "Kieou-he-yu (great dignitary of the state of Wei) sent a man to Khoung-tseu to know his news. Khoung-tseu caused the messenger to be seated near him, and questioned him in these terms: What is your master doing? The messenger answered with respect: My master desires to diminish the number of his faults, but he cannot come to the end of them. The messenger being gone, the philosopher remarked: "What a worthy messenger! What a worthy messenger!" The preacher, instead of vexing the ears of drowsy farmers on their day of rest at the end of the week,—for Sunday is the fit conclusion of an ill-spent week, and not the fresh and brave beginning of a new one,—with this one other draggle-tail of a sermon, should shout with thundering voice, "Pause! Avast! Why so seeming fast, but deadly slow?"

Shams and delusions are esteemed for soundest truths, while reality is fabulous. If men would steadily observe realities only, and not allow themselves to be deluded, life, to compare it with such things as we know, would be like a fairy tale and the Arabian Nights' Entertainments. If we respected only what is inevitable and has a right to be, music and poetry would resound along the streets. When we are unhurried and wise, we perceive that only great and worthy things have any permanent and absolute existence—that petty fears and petty pleasures are but the shadow of the reality. This is always exhilarating and sublime. By closing the eyes and slumbering, and consenting to be deceived by shows, men establish and confirm their daily life of routine and habit everywhere, which still is built on purely illusory foundations. Children, who play life, discern its true law and relations more clearly than men, who fail to live it worthily, but who think that they are wiser by experience, that is, by failure. I have read in a Hindoo book, that "there was a king's son, who, being expelled in infancy from his native city was brought up by a forester, and, growing up to maturity in that state, imagined himself to belong to the barbarous race with which he lived. One of his father's ministers having discovered him, revealed to him what he was, and the misconception of his character was removed, and he knew himself to be a prince. So soul," continues the Hindoo philosopher, "from the circumstances in which it is placed, mistakes its own character, until the truth is revealed to it by some holy teacher, and then it knows itself to be *Brahme*." I perceive that we inhabitants of New England live this mean life that we do because our vision does not penetrate the surface of things. We think that that *is* which *appears* to be. If a man should walk through this town and see only the reality, where, think you, would the "Mill-dam" go to? If he should give us an account of the realities he beheld there, we should not recognize the place in his description. Look at a meeting-house, or a court-house, or a jail, or a shop, or a dwelling-house, and say what that thing really is before a true gaze, and they would all go to pieces in your account of them. Men esteem truth remote, in the outskirts of the system, behind the farthest star, before Adam and after the last man. In eternity there is indeed something true and sublime. But all these times and places and occasions are now and here. God himself culminates in the present moment, and will never be more divine in the lapse of all the ages. And we are enabled to apprehend at all what is sublime and noble only by the perpetual instilling and drenching of the reality that surrounds us. The universe constantly and obediently answers to our conceptions; whether we travel fast or slow, the track is laid for us. Let us spend our lives in conceiving then. The poet or the artist never yet had so fair and noble a design but some of his posterity at least could accomplish it.

Let us spend one day as deliberately as Nature, and not be thrown off the track by every nutshell and mosquito's wing that falls on the rails. Let us rise early and fast, or break fast, gently and without perturbation; let company come and let company go, let the bells ring and the children cry,—determined to make a day of it. Why should we knock under and go with the stream? Let us not be upset and overwhelmed in that terrible rapid and whirlpool called a dinner, situated in the meridian shallows. Weather this danger and you are safe, for the rest of the way is down hill. With unrelaxed nerves, with morning vigor, sail by it, looking another way, tied to the mast like Ulysses. If the engine whistles, let it whistle till it is hoarse for its pains. If the bell rings, why should we run? We will consider what kind of music they are like. Let us settle ourselves, and work and wedge our feet downward through the mud and slush of opinion, and prejudice, and tradition, and delusion, and appearance, that alluvion which covers the globe, through Paris and London, through New York and Boston and Concord, through church and state, through poetry and philosophy and religion, till we come to a hard bottom and rocks in place, which we can call *reality*, and say, This is, and no mistake; and then begin, having a *point d'appui*, below freshet and frost and fire, a place where you might found a wall or a state, or set a lamp-post safely, or perhaps a gauge, not a Nilometer, but a Realometer, that future ages might know how deep a freshet of shams and appearances had gathered from time to time. If you stand right fronting and face to face to a fact, you will see the sun glimmer on both its surfaces, as if it were a cimeter, and feel its sweet edge dividing you through the heart and marrow, and so you will happily conclude your mortal career. Be it life or death, we crave only reality. If we are really dying, let us hear the rattle in our throats and feel cold in the extremities; if we are alive, let us go about our business. . . .

I left the woods for as good a reason as I went there. Perhaps it seemed to me that I had several more lives to live, and could not spare any more time for that one. It is remarkable how easily and insensibly we fall into a particular route, and make a beaten track for ourselves. I had not lived there a week before my feet wore a path from my door to the pond-side; and though it is five or six years since I trod it, it is still quite distinct. It is true, I fear, that others may have fallen into it, and so helped to keep it open. The surface of the earth is soft and impressible by the feet of men; and so with the paths which the mind travels. How worn and dusty, then, must be the highways of the world, how deep the ruts of tradition and conformity! I did not wish to take a cabin passage, but rather to go before the mast and on the deck of the world, for there I could best see the moonlight amid the mountains. I do not wish to go below now.

I learned this, at least, by my experiment: that if one advances confidently in the direction of his dreams, and endeavors to live the life which he has imagined, he will meet with a success unexpected in common hours. He will put some things behind, will pass an invisible boundary; new, universal, and more liberal laws will begin to establish themselves around and within him; or the old laws be expanded, and interpreted in his favor in a more liberal sense, and he will live with the license of a higher order of beings. In proportion as he simplifies his life, the laws of the universe will appear less complex, and solitude will not be solitude, nor poverty poverty, nor weakness weakness. If you have built castles in the air, your work need not be lost; that is where they should be. Now put the foundations under them.

5

Utopian Socialism

FRIEDRICH ENGELS' CRITIQUE OF
PRE-MARXIAN COMMUNITARIANS

Utopianism—or one variety of it, "Critical-Utopian Socialism"—was considered important enough by Karl Marx and Friedrich Engels to be given some attention in the third section of their *Communist Manifesto* (1848). Their appraisal was not very favorable.

Since the Critical-Utopian Socialists—Saint-Simon, Fourier, Owen and others—had lived at a time when the struggle between the proletariat and the bourgeoisie had not yet reached a high point, they could not comprehend the historical significance or predict the inevitable outcome of the all-important class conflict. While the utopians had recognized the injustices and class antagonisms and sympathized with the working class, they had not formulated a realistic plan which could lead to the emancipation of the workers from capitalistic exploitation. Instead they made grandiose and often fantastic plans for social salvation which they believed would bring harmony and happiness to all classes—rulers and ruled—once they were carried out. They rejected political and revolutionary action and planned to achieve their altruistic goals peacefully and compassionately through making universal and continual appeals. Believers in the power of example, the utopians sought to prove the validity and relevance of their social blueprints by using them to construct actual utopian communities. Thus went Marx's and Engels' interpretation of the Critical-Utopian Socialists.

But the authors of the *Communist Manifesto* recognized that the Critical-Utopian Socialists were more than tender-minded speculators. They were also keen and sometimes stringent critics of the society in which they lived. Because the Utopians attacked "every principle of existing society," Marx and Engels found in their writings "the most valuable materials for the enlightenment of the working class." For this reason the authors of the *Manifesto* showed considerable respect for the chief utopian socialists, Saint-Simon, Fourier and Owen, but only contempt for their disciples, the men who were attempting to carry on the tradition of utopian socialism.

Marx and Engels claimed that the latter-day utopian socialists had become more reactionary rather than more progressive; they were trying to play down class conflicts and to discourage political action by workers. Worse still (to the authors of the *Manifesto*), they were even attempting to bring about a reconciliation between workers and capitalists! Marx and Engels felt completely justified in dismissing them as uncritical and pedantic, as well as fanatical and superstitious, utopians.

> They still dream of experimental realization of their social Utopias, of founding isolated "Phalansteres," of establishing "Home Colonies," of setting up a "Little Icaria"—duodecimo editions of the New Jerusalem, and to realize all these castles in the air they are compelled to appeal to the feelings and purses of the bourgeois.[1]

Utopian socialism was given further attention by Friedrich Engels (1820–1895) later in an extensive work in which he attempted to answer Eugen Dühring, one of Marx's critics. The following selection is taken from a part of his larger polemic entitled *Socialism: Utopian and Scientific*. Engels gave a brief survey of utopian socialism as well as sketches of three of its chief representatives: Claude Henri de Saint-Simon (1760–1825), Charles Fourier (1772–1837), and Robert Owen (1771–1858). His paramount concern was, of course, critical rather than appreciative; he had not come to praise utopian socialism but to bury it.

Marx's "Scientific Socialism" had already provided him with a viable alternative to Critical-Utopian Socialism. If he now discussed the earlier form of socialism, it was only to reveal its shortcomings to others. Critical-Utopian Socialism had been able to criticize capitalism but had not been able to explain its essential nature. Utopians could denounce the exploitation of the working class by capitalists, but they were unable to analyze the mechanisms by which this exploitation arose and thus were helpless to do anything about it. Only after Marx had formulated his materialist interpretation of history, Engels believed, was a sound basis for a scientific socialism established. "From that time forward," Engels wrote, "socialism was no longer an accidental discovery of this or that ingenious brain." It could now "present the capitalistic method of production in its historical connection and its inevitableness during a particular historical period, and therefore, also, to present its inevitable downfall."[2] Thus the task of socialism was, in Engels' view, "no longer to manufacture a system of society as perfect as possible," but rather to explain actual society and to change it.

Having discredited utopian socialism (at least in his eyes), Engels was now ready to present the Marxian version of socialism. This alone, he claimed, deserves to be called "scientific." As he proceeded to expound and defend Marx's dialectical materialism, he allowed himself to make statements and predictions, the scientific basis of which seems doubtful to say

[1] *The Communist Manifesto*, sec. 3.

[2] Friedrich Engels, *Socialism, Utopian and Scientific*, trans. Edward Aveling (London: Swan Sonnenschein & Co., 1892), pp. 42–43.

the least. Looking ahead to the ultimate consummation of a socialistic social order, he envisaged a time at which "the government of persons is replaced by the administration of things, and by the conduct of processes of production."[3] Then and only then, Engels pontificates, "the political authority of the State dies out" and "Man, at last the master of his own form of social organization, becomes at the same time the lord over Nature, his own master—free."[4] Engels' critique of utopian socialism thus concludes with his own socialist utopian vision.

[3] Ibid., pp. 76–77.
[4] Ibid., p. 86.

From Friedrich Engels, Socialism, Utopian and Scientific, *translated by Edward Aveling (London: Swan Sonnenschein & Co., 1892), pt. 1, pp. 1–27.*

Modern Socialism is, in its essence, the direct product of the recognition, on the one hand, of the class antagonisms, existing in the society of to-day, between proprietors and non-proprietors, between capitalists and wage-workers; on the other hand, of the anarchy existing in production. But, in its theoretical form, modern Socialism originally appears ostensibly as a more logical extension of the principles laid down by the great French philosophers of the eighteenth century. Like every new theory, modern Socialism had, at first, to connect itself with the intellectual stock-in-trade ready to its hand, however deeply its roots lay in material economic facts.

The great men, who in France prepared men's minds for the coming revolution, were themselves extreme revolutionists. They recognised no external authority of any kind whatever. Religion, natural science, society, political institutions, everything, was subjected to the most unsparing criticism: everything must justify its existence before the judgment-seat of reason, or give up existence. Reason became the sole measure of everything. It was the time when, as Hegel says, the world stood upon its head; first, in the sense that the human head, and the principles arrived at by its thought, claimed to be the basis of all human action and association; but by and by, also, in the wider sense that the reality which was in contradiction to these principles had, in fact, to be turned upside down. Every form of society and government then existing, every old traditional notion was flung into the lumber-room as irrational; the world had hitherto allowed itself to be led solely by prejudices; everything in the past deserved only pity and contempt. Now, for the first time, appeared the light of day, the kingdom of reason; henceforth superstition, injustice, privilege, oppression, were to be superseded by eternal truth, eternal Right, equality based on Nature and the inalienable rights of man.

We know to-day that his kingdom of reason was nothing more that the idealised kingdom of the bourgeoisie; that this eternal Right found its realisation in bourgeois justice; that this equality reduced itself to bourgeois equality before the law; that bourgeois property was proclaimed as one of the essential rights of man; and that the government of reason, the Contrat Social of Rousseau, came into being, and only could come into being, as a democratic bourgeois republic. The great thinkers of the eighteenth century could, no more than their predecessors, go beyond the limits imposed upon them by their epoch.

But, side by side with the antagonism of the feudal nobility and the burghers, who claimed to represent all the rest of society, was the general antagonism of exploiters and exploited, of rich idlers and poor workers. It was this very circumstance that made it possible for the representatives of the bourgeoisie to put themselves forward as representing, not one special class, but the whole of suffering humanity. Still further. From its origin, the bourgeoisie was saddled with its antithesis: capitalists cannot exist without wage-workers, and, in the same proportion as the mediaeval burgher of the guild developed into the modern bourgeois, the guild journeyman and the day-labourer, outside the guilds, developed into the proletarian. And although, upon the whole, the bourgeoisie, in their struggle with the nobility, could claim to represent at the same time the interests of the different working-classes of that period, yet in every great bourgeois movement there were independent outbursts of that class which was the forerunner, more or less developed, of the modern proletariat. For example, at the time of the German reformation and the peasants' war, the Anabaptists and Thomas Münzer; in the great English revolution, the Levellers; in the great French revolution, Baboeuf.

There were theoretical enunciations corresponding with these revolutionary uprisings of a class not yet developed; in the sixteenth and seventeenth centuries, Utopian pictures of ideal social conditions; in the eighteenth, actual communistic theories (Morelly and Mably). The demand for equality was no longer limited to political rights; it was extended also to the social conditions of individuals. It was not simply class privileges that were to be abolished, but class distinctions themselves. A Communism, ascetic, denouncing all the pleasures of life, Spartan, was the first form of the new teaching. Then came the three great Utopians: Saint-Simon, to whom the middle-class movement, side by side with the proletarian, still had a certain significance; Fourier; and Owen, who in the country where capitalist production was most developed, and under the influence of the antagonisms begotten of this, worked out his proposals for the removal of class distinction systematically and in direct relation to French materialism.

One thing is common to all three. Not one of them appears as a representative of the interests of that proletariat, which historical development had, in the meantime, produced. Like the French philosophers, they do not claim to emancipate a particular class to begin with, but all humanity at once. Like them, they wish to bring in the kingdom of reason and eternal justice, but this kingdom, as they see it, is as far as heaven from earth, from that of the French philosophers.

For, to our three social reformers, the bourgeois world, based upon the principles of these philosophers, is quite as irrational and unjust, and, therefore, finds its way to the dust-hole quite as readily as feudalism and all the earlier stages of society. If pure reason and justice have not, hitherto, ruled the world, this has been the case only because men have not rightly understood them. What was wanted was the individual man of genius, who has now arisen and who understands the truth. That he has now arisen, that the truth has now been clearly understood, is not an inevitable event, following of necessity in the chain of historical development, but a mere happy accident. He might just as well have been born 500 years earlier, and might then have spared humanity 500 years of error, strife, and suffering.

We saw how the French philosophers of the eighteenth century, the forerunners of the Revolution, appealed to reason as the sole judge of all that is. A rational government, rational society, were to be founded; everything that ran counter to eternal reason was to be remorselessly done away with. We saw also that this eternal reason was in reality nothing but the idealised understanding of the eighteenth century citizen, just then evolving into the bourgeois. The French Revolution had realised this rational society and government.

But the new order of things, rational enough as compared with earlier conditions, turned out to be by no means absolutely rational. The State based upon reason completely collapsed. Rousseau's Contrat Social had found its realisation in the Reign of Terror, from which the bourgeoisie, who had lost confidence in their own political capacity, had taken refuge first in the corruption of the Directorate, and, finally, under the wing of the Napoleonic despotism. The promised eternal peace was turned into an endless war of conquest. The society based upon reason had fared no better. The antagonism between rich and poor, instead of dissolving into general prosperity, had become intensified by the removal of the guild and other privileges, which had to some extent bridged it over, and by the removal of the charitable institutions of the Church. The "freedom of property" from feudal fetters, now veritably accomplished, turned out to be, for the small capitalists and small proprietors, the freedom to sell their small property, crushed under the overmastering competition of the large capitalists and landlords, to these great lords, and thus, as far as the small capitalists and peasant proprietors were concerned, became "freedom *from* property." The development of industry upon a capitalistic basis made poverty and misery of the working masses conditions of existence of society. Cash payment became more and more, in Carlyle's phrase, the sole nexus between man and man. The number of crimes increased from year to year. Formerly, the feudal vices had openly stalked about in broad daylight; though not eradicated, they were now at any rate thrust into the background. In their stead, the bourgeois vices, hitherto practised in secret, began to blossom all the more luxuriantly. Trade became to a greater and greater extent cheating. The "fraternity" of the revolutionary motto was realised in the chicanery and rivalries of the battle of competition. Oppression by force was replaced by corruption; the sword, as the first social lever, by gold. The right of the first night was transferred from the feudal lords to the bourgeois manufacturers. Prostitution increased to an extent never heard of. Marriage itself remained, as before, the legally recognised form, the official cloak of prostitution, and, moreover, was supplemented by rich crops of adultery.

In a word, compared with the splendid promises of the philosophers, the social and political institutions born of the "triumph of reason" were bitterly disappointing caricatures. All that was wanting was the men to formulate this disappointment, and they came with the turn of the century. In 1802 Saint-Simon's Geneva letters appeared; in 1808 appeared Fourier's first work, although the groundwork of his theory dated from 1799; on January 1, 1800, Robert Owen undertook the direction of New Lanark.

At this time, however, the capitalist mode of production, and with it the antagonism between the bourgeoisie and the proletariat, was still very incompletely developed. Modern Industry, which had just arisen in England, was still unknown in France. But Modern Industry develops, on the one hand, the conflicts which make absolutely necessary a revolution in the mode of production, and the doing away with its capitalistic character—conflicts not only between the classes begotten of it, but also between the very productive forces and the forms of exchange created by it. And, on the other hand, it develops, in these very gigantic productive forces, the means of ending these conflicts. If, therefore, about the year 1800, the conflicts arising from the new social order were only just beginning to take shape, this holds still more fully as to the means of ending them. The "have-nothing" masses of Paris, during the Reign of Terror, were able for a moment to gain the mastery, and thus to lead the bourgeois revolution to victory in spite of the bourgeoisie themselves. But, in doing so, they only proved how impossible it was for their domination to last under the conditions then obtaining. The proletariat, which then for the first time evolved itself from these "have-nothing" masses as the nucleus of a new class, as yet quite incapable of independent political action, appeared as an oppressed, suffering order, to whom, in its incapacity to help itself, help could, at best, be brought in from without, or down from above.

This historical situation also dominated the founders of Socialism. To the crude conditions of capitalistic production and the crude class conditions corresponded crude theories. The solution of the social problems, which as yet lay hidden in undeveloped economic conditions, the Utopians attempted to evolve out of the human brain. Society presented nothing but wrongs; to remove these was the task of reason. It was necessary, then, to discover a new and more perfect system of social order and to impose this upon society from without by propaganda, and, wherever it was possible, by the example of model experiments. These new social systems were foredoomed as Utopian; the more completely they were worked out in detail, the more they could not avoid drifting off into pure phantasies.

These facts once established, we need not dwell a moment longer upon this side of the question, now wholly belonging to the past. We can leave it to the literary small fry to solemnly quibble over these phantasies, which to-day only make us smile, and to crow over the superiority of their own bald reasoning, as compared with such "insanity." For ourselves, we delight in the stupendously grand thoughts and germs of thought that everywhere break out through their phantastic covering, and to which these Philistines are blind.

Saint-Simon was a son of the great French Revolution, at the outbreak of which he was not yet thirty. The Revolution was the victory of the third estate, i.e., of the great masses of the nation, *working* in production and in trade, over the privileged *idle* classes, the nobles and the priests. But the victory of the third estate soon revealed itself as exclusively the victory of a small part of this "estate," as the conquest of political power by the socially privileged section of it, i.e., the propertied bourgeoisie. And the bourgeoisie had certainly developed rapidly during the Revolution, partly by speculation in the lands of the nobility and of the Church, confiscated and afterwards put up for sale, and partly by frauds upon the nation by means of army contracts. It was the domination of these swindlers that, under the Directorate, brought France to the verge of ruin, and thus gave Napoleon the pretext for his *coup-d'état*.

Hence, to Saint-Simon the antagonism between the third estate and the privileged classes took the form of an antagonism between "workers" and "idlers." The idlers were not merely the old privileged classes, but also all who, without taking any part in the production or distribution, lived on their incomes. And the workers were not only the wage-workers, but also the manufacturers, the merchants, the bankers. That the idlers had lost the capacity for intellectual leadership and political supremacy had been proved, and was by the Revolution finally settled. That the non-possessing classes had not this capacity seemed to Saint-Simon proved by the experiences of the Reign of Terror. Then, who was to lead and command? According to Saint-Simon, science and industry, both united by a new religious bond, destined to restore that unity of religious ideas which had been lost since the time of the Reformation—a necessarily mystic and rigidly hierarchic "new Christianity." But science, that was the scholars; and industry, that was, in the first place, the working bourgeois, manufacturers, merchants, bankers. These bourgeoisie were, certainly, intended by Saint-Simon to transform themselves into a kind of public officials, of social trustees; but they were still to hold, *vis-à-vis* of the workers, a commanding and economically privileged position. The bankers especially were to be called upon to direct the whole of social production by the regulation of credit. This conception was in exact keeping with a time in which Modern Industry in France and, with it, the chasm between bourgeoisie and proletariat was only just coming into existence. But what Saint-Simon especially lays stress upon is this: what interests him first, and above all other things, is the lot of the class that is the most numerous and the most poor (*"la classe la plus nombreuse et la plus pauvre"*).

Already, in his Geneva letters, Saint-Simon lays down the proposition that "all men ought to work." In the same work he recognises also that the Reign of Terror was the reign of the non-possessing masses. "See," says he to them, "what happened in France at the time when your comrades held sway there; they brought about a famine." But to recognise the French Revolution as a class war, and not simply one between nobility and bourgeoisie, but between nobility, bourgeoisie, and the non-possessors, was, in the year 1802, a most pregnant discovery. In 1816, he declares that politics is the science of production, and foretells the complete absorption of politics by economics. The knowledge that economic conditions are the basis of political institutions appears here only in embryo. Yet what is here already very plainly expressed is the idea of the future conversion of political rule over men into an administration of things and a direction of processes of production—that is to say, the "abolition of the State," about which recently there has been so much noise.

Saint-Simon shows the same superiority over his contemporaries, when in 1814, immediately after the entry of the allies into Paris, and again in 1815, during the Hundred Days' War, he proclaims the alliance of France with England, and then of both these countries with Germany, as the only guarantee for the prosperous development and peace of Europe. To preach to the French in 1815 an alliance with the victors of Waterloo required as much courage as historical foresight.

If in Saint-Simon we find a comprehensive breadth of view, by virtue of which almost all the ideas of later Socialists, that are not strictly economic, are found in him in embryo, we find in Fourier a criticism of the existing conditions of society, genuinely French and witty, but not upon that account any the less thorough. Fourier takes the bourgeoisie, their inspired prophets before the Revolution, and their interested eulogists after it, at their own word. He lays bare remorselessly the material and moral misery of the bourgeois world. He confronts it with the earlier philosophers' dazzling promises of a society in which reason alone should reign, of a civilisation in which happiness should be universal, of an illimitable human perfectibility, and with the rose-coloured phraseology of the bourgeois ideologists of his time. He points out how everywhere the most pitiful reality corresponds with the most high-sounding phrases, and he overwhelms this hopeless fiasco of phrases with his mordant sarcasm.

Fourier is not only a critic; his imperturbably serene nature makes him a satirist, and assuredly one of the greatest satirists of all time. He depicts, with equal power and charm, the swindling speculations that blossomed out upon the downfall of the Revolution, and the shop-keeping spirit prevalent in, and characteristic of, French commerce at that time. Still more masterly is his criticism of the bourgeois form of the relations between the sexes, and the position of women in bourgeois society. He was the first to declare that in any given society the degree of woman's emancipation is the natural measure of the general emancipation.

But Fourier is at his greatest in his conception of the history of society. He divides its whole course, thus far, into four stages of evolution—savagery, barbarism, the patriarchate, civilisation. This last is identical with the so-called civil, or bourgeois, society of to-day—i.e., with the social order that came in with the sixteenth century. He proves "that the civilised stage raises every vice practised by barbarism in a simple fashion, into a form of existence, complex, ambiguous, equivocal, hypocritical"—that civilisation moves in "a vicious circle," in contradictions which it constantly reproduces without being able to solve them; hence it constantly arrives at the very opposite to that which it wants to attain, or pretends to want to attain, so that, e.g. "under civilization poverty is born of superabundance itself."

Fourier, as we see, uses the dialectic method in the same masterly way as his contemporary, Hegel. Using these same dialectics, he argues against the talk about illimitable human perfectibility, that every historical phase has its period of ascent and also its period of descent, and he applies this observation to the future of the whole human race. As Kant introduced into natural science the idea of the ultimate destruction of the earth, Fourier introduced into historical science that of the ultimate destruction of the human race.

Whilst in France the hurricane of the Revolution swept over the land, in England a quieter, but not on that account less tremendous, revolution was going on. Steam and the new tool-making machinery were transforming manufacture into modern industry, and thus revolutionising the whole foundation of bourgeois society. The sluggish march of development of the manufacturing period changed into a veritable storm and stress period of production. With constantly increasing swiftness the splitting-up of society into large capitalists and non-possessing proletarians went on. Between these, instead of the former stable middle-class, an unstable mass of artisans and small shopkeepers, the most fluctuating portion of the population, now led a precarious existence.

The new mode of production was, as yet, only at the beginning of its period of ascent; as yet it was the normal, regular method of production—the only one possible under existing conditions. Nevertheless, even then it was producing crying social abuses—the herding together of a homeless population in the worst quarters of the large towns; the loosening of all traditional moral bonds, of patriarchal subordination, of family relations; overwork, especially of women and children, to a frightful extent; complete demoralisation of the working-class, suddenly flung into altogether new conditions, from the country into the town, from agriculture into modern industry, from stable conditions of existence into insecure ones that changed from day to day.

At this juncture there came forward as a reformer a manufacturer 29 years old—a man of almost sublime, childlike simplicity of character, and at the same time one of the few born leaders of men. Robert Owen had adopted the teaching of the materialistic philosophers: that man's character is the product, on the one hand, of heredity, on the other, of the environment of the individual during his lifetime, and especially during his period of development. In the industrial revolution most of his class saw only chaos and confusion, and the opportunity of fishing in these troubled waters and making large fortunes quickly. He saw in it the opportunity of putting into practice his favourite theory, and so of bringing order out of chaos. He had already tried it with success, as superintendent of more than five hundred men in a Manchester factory. From 1800 to 1829, he directed the great cotton mill at New Lanark, in Scotland, as managing partner, along the same lines, but with greater freedom of action and with a success that made him a European reputation. A population, originally consisting of the most diverse and, for the most part, very demoralised elements, a population that gradually grew to 2,500, he turned into a model colony, in which drunkenness, police, magistrates, lawsuits, poor laws, charity, were unknown. And all this simply by placing the people in conditions worthy of human beings, and especially by carefully bringing up the rising generation. He was the founder of infant schools, and introduced them first at New Lanark. At the age of two the children came to school, where they enjoyed themselves so much that they could scarcely be got home again. Whilst his competitors worked their people thirteen or fourteen hours a day, in New Lanark the working-day was only ten and a half hours. When a crisis in cotton stopped work for four months, his workers received their full wages all the time. And with all this the business more than doubled in value, and to the last yielded large profits to its proprietors.

In spite of all this, Owen was not content. The existence which he secured for his workers was, in his eyes, still far from being worthy of human beings. "The people were slaves at my mercy." The relatively favourable conditions in which he had placed them were still far from allowing a rational development of the character and of the intellect in all directions, much less of the free exercise of all their faculties. "And yet [Owen wrote], the working part of this population of 2500 persons was daily producing as much real wealth for society as, less than half a century before, it would have required the working part of a population of 600,000 to create. I asked myself what became of the difference between the wealth consumed by 2500 persons and that which would have been consumed by 600,000?"[1]

The answer was clear. It had been used to pay the proprietors of the establishment 5 per cent on the capital they had laid out, in addition to over £300,000 clear profit. And that which held for New Lanark held to a still greater extent for all the factories in England. "If this new wealth had not been created by machinery, imperfectly as it has been applied, the wars of Europe, in opposition to Napoleon, and to support the aristocratic principles of society, could not have been maintained. And yet this new power was the creation of the working classes."[2] To them, therefore, the fruits of this new power belonged. The newly-created gigantic productive forces, hitherto used only to

---

[1] From "The Revolution in Mind and Practice," p. 21, a memorial addressed to all the "red Republicans, Communists and Socialists of Europe," and sent to the provisional government of France, 1848, and also "to Queen Victoria and her responsible advisers."

[2] Note, l.c., p. 22.

enrich individuals and to enslave the masses, offered to Owen the foundations for a reconstruction of society; they were destined, as the common property of all, to be worked for the common good of all.

Owen's Communism was based upon this purely business foundation, the outcome, so to say, of commercial calculation. Throughout, it maintained this practical character. Thus, in 1823, Owen proposed the relief of the distress in Ireland by Communist colonies, and drew up complete estimates of costs of founding them, yearly expenditure, and probable revenue. And in his definite plan for the future, the technical working out of details is managed with such practical knowledge—ground plan, front and side and bird's-eye views all included—that the Owen method of social reform once accepted, there is from the practical point of view little to be said against the actual arrangement of details.

His advance in the direction of Communism was the turning-point in Owen's life. As long as he was simply a philanthropist, he was rewarded with nothing but wealth, applause, honour, and glory. He was the most popular man in Europe. Not only men of his own class, but statesmen and princes listened to him approvingly. But when he came out with his Communist theories, that was quite another thing. Three great obstacles seemed to him especially to block the path to social reform: private property, religion, the present form of marriage. He knew what confronted him if he attacked these—outlawry, excommunication from official society, the loss of his whole social position. But nothing of this prevented him from attacking them without fear of consequences, and what he had foreseen happened. Banished from official society, with a conspiracy of silence against him in the press, ruined by his unsuccessful Communist experiments in America, in which he sacrificed all his fortune, he turned directly to the working-class and continued working in their midst for thirty years. Every social movement, every real advance in England on behalf of the workers links itself on to the name of Robert Owen. He forced through in 1819, after five years' fighting, the first law limiting the hours of labour of women and children in factories. He was president of the first Congress at which all the Trade Unions of England united in a single great trade association. He introduced as transition measures to the complete communistic organisation of society, on the one hand, co-operative societies for retail trade and production. These have since that time, at least, given practical proof that the merchant and the manufacturer are socially quite unnecessary. On the other hand, he introduced labour bazaars for the exchange of the products of labour through the medium of labour-notes, whose unit was a single hour of work; institutions necessarily doomed to failure, but completely anticipating Proudhon's bank of exchange of a much later period, and differing entirely from this in that it did not claim to be the panacea for all social ills, but only a first step towards a much more radical revolution of society.

The Utopians' mode of thought has for a long time governed the socialist ideas of the nineteenth century, and still governs some of them. Until very recently all French and English Socialists did homage to it. The earlier German Communism, including that of Weitling was of the same school. To all these Socialism is the expression of absolute truth, reason, and justice, and has only to be discovered to conquer all the world by virtue of its own power. And as absolute truth is independent of time, space, and of the historical development of man, it is a mere accident when and where it is discovered. With all this, absolute truth, reason, and justice are different with the founder of each different school. And as each one's special kind of absolute truth, reason, and justice is again conditioned by his subjective understanding, his conditions of existence, the measure of his knowledge and his intellectual training, there is no other ending possible in this conflict of absolute truths than that they shall be mutually exclusive one of the other. Hence, from this nothing could come but a kind of eclectic, average Socialism, which, as a matter of fact, has up to the present time dominated the minds of most of the socialist workers in France and England. Hence, a mish-mash allowing of the most manifold shades of opinion; a mish-mash of such critical statements, economic theories, pictures of future society by the founders of different sects, as excite a minimum of opposition; a mish-mash which is the more easily brewed the more the definite sharp edges of the individual constituents are rubbed down in the stream of debate, like rounded pebbles in a brook.

To make a science of Socialism, it had first to be placed upon a real basis.

QUESTIONS ON PART I

Two Kinds of Utopia (Mumford)

1. Explain what Mumford means by "idolum" and why he considers this concept to be important.
2. How are the two types of utopia discussed by Mumford related to the "idolum"?
3. Why does Mumford consider each of the two types of utopia to be important to man's everyday life?
4. What evidence can be given to support the statement by Anatole France quoted by Mumford that "Utopia is the principle of all progress, and the essay into a better future"?

The Uses of Utopia (Morgan)

5. Why is Morgan hesitant to draw the boundaries of utopian literature more sharply?
6. Explain why Morgan believes that "every intelligent and active-minded person is to some degree a utopian."
7. What evidence does Morgan give which could be used to support the statement by Anatole France quoted by Mumford? (See question 4.)

Invitation to Utopia (Ripley)

8. Envisage a utopian community which would achieve in today's world the goals Ripley sets forth in the second paragraph of his letter to Emerson. Where would it be located? According to what criteria would you select its inhabitants? What institutions would you set up, and how would they be directed so as to achieve Ripley's (and your) goals?

Intentional Living (Thoreau)

9. What might be the characteristics of a utopia designed for today's world by a person adhering to Thoreau's views?

10. Thoreau is sometimes considered to be a critic of utopias rather than a utopian. What evidence do you find in the selections to support this view of Thoreau? What evidence is there that he is a utopian thinker?

11. Explain what Thoreau means by "living deliberately." What are the obstacles to this kind of living? How might they be removed or overcome?

UTOPIAN SOCIALISM (ENGELS)

12. How does Engels account for the development of utopian socialism? What are, in his opinion, its assets and limitations?

13. What, briefly, would the utopian societies envisaged by Saint-Simon, Fourier, and Owen have in common? How would they differ?

14. Compare Engels account of utopian socialism with that given by another author (e.g. Martin Buber or Robert Heilbroner).

SUPPLEMENTARY READINGS

(Works marked * are available in paperbound editions.)

Armytage, W. H. G. *Yesterday's Tomorrows: A Historical Survey of Future Societies.* London: Routledge & Kegan Paul, 1968.

Berneri, Marie Louise. *Journey Through Utopia.* London: Routledge & Kegan Paul, 1950.

Carew-Hunt, R. N. **The Theory and Practice of Communism: An Introduction.* Baltimore, Md.: Penguin Books, 1950.

Dubos, René. **The Dreams of Reason: Science and Utopia.* New York: Columbia University Press, 1961. Chap. 3.

Frothingham, Octavius B. *George Ripley.* Boston: Houghton Mifflin Co., 1884.

Goodman, Paul. **Utopian Essays and Practical Proposals.* New York: Random House, Vintage Books, 1964. Pp. 3–22.

Heilbroner, Robert L. **The Worldly Philosophers.* New York: Simon & Schuster, 1953. Chap. V.

Hertzler, Joyce O. *The History of Utopian Thought.* New York: Macmillan Co., 1923.

Johnson, J. W., ed. **Utopian Literature, a Selection.* New York: The Modern Library, 1968.

Kateb, George. *Utopia and Its Enemies.* New York: The Free Press of Glencoe, 1963. Chap. 1.

Krutch, Joseph Wood. *Henry David Thoreau.* New York: William Sloane, 1948.

Laidler, Harry W. *Social-Economic Movements.* New York: Thomas Y. Crowell Co., 1944. Part I.

Mannheim, Karl. **Ideology and Utopia: An Introduction to the Sociology of Knowledge,* translated by Louis Wirth and Edward Shils. New York: Harcourt, Brace & World, 1958. Chap. IV.

Manuel, Frank, ed. *Utopias and Utopian Thought.* Boston: Houghton Mifflin Co., 1966.

Marx, Karl. **Selected Writings in Sociology and Social Philosophy,* translated by T. B. Bottomore. New York: McGraw-Hill, 1956.

Morgan, Arthur E. *Nowhere Was Somewhere: How History Makes Utopias and Utopias Make History.* Chapel Hill, N. C.: University of North Carolina Press, 1946.

———. *The Small Community, Foundation of Democratic Life.* New York: Harper and Brothers, 1942.

———. *The Community of the Future.* Yellow Springs, Ohio: Community Service, 1957. Chap. XV.

Mumford, Lewis. *The Golden Age: A Study in American Experience and Culture.* Boston: Beacon Press, 1926.

———. *The Conduct of Life.* New York: Harcourt, Brace & World, 1951.

———. *The Story of Utopias.* New York: The Viking Press, 1962.

Murray, James G. *Henry David Thoreau.* New York: Washington Square Press, 1968.

Negley, Glenn R., and J. Max Patrick, eds. *The Quest for Utopia: An Anthology of Imaginary Societies.* Garden City, N. Y.: Doubleday and Company, 1962. Introduction.

Paul, Sherman. *Thoreau, a Collection of Critical Essays.* Englewood Cliffs, N. J.: Prentice-Hall, 1962.

Schonfield, Andrew. "Thinking About the Future," *Encounter* XXXII (February 1969): 15–26.

Thoreau, Henry David. "Paradise (To Be) Regained." In *The Writings of Henry David Thoreau,* vol. IV (Cape Cod and Miscellaneous), pp. 280–305. Boston: Houghton Mifflin & Co., 1893. (Thoreau's review of a work by the utopian designer J. A. Etzler.)

II

Utopias Revisited

The better life! Possibly it would hardly look so now; it is enough if it looked so then. The greatest obstacle to being heroic is the doubt whether one may not be going to prove one's self a fool; the truest heroism is to resist the doubt; and the profoundest wisdom to know when it ought to be resisted, and when to be obeyed.

Yet, after all, let us acknowledge it wiser, if not more sagacious, to follow out one's day-dream to its natural consummation, although if the vision have been worth the having, it is certain never to be consummated otherwise than by a failure. And what of that? Its airiest fragments, impalpable as they may be, will possess a value that lurks not in the most ponderous realities of any practicable scheme. They are not the rubbish of the mind. Whatever else I may repent of, therefore, let it be reckoned neither among my sins nor follies that I once had faith and force enough to form generous hopes of the world's destiny—yes! —and to do what in me lay for their accomplishment; even to the extent of quitting a warm fire-side, flinging away a freshly lighted cigar, and travelling far beyond the strike of city clocks, through a drifting snow-storm.

Nathaniel Hawthorne

6

Community of Celibates

THE SHAKERS

At the high point of their development, from about 1840 to 1850, the Shakers, as the members of the Millennial Church or United Society of Believers were popularly called, had about six thousand members. Today they have fewer than twenty. Only two of their eighteen formerly flourishing utopian villages have survived—at Canterbury, New Hampshire, and at Sabbathday Lake, Maine—and these are no longer active communities but homes for the aged remnant of the Shakers.

Students of the Shakers have had some difficulty in explaining why the movement, which has been called the most successful communitarian experiment in American history, began to deteriorate after 1860 and finally became defunct in the twentieth century. Among the factors mentioned as contributing to the decline and eventual end of Shakerism are the inability of Shaker industries to compete with modern assembly-line production; the cooling of the original religious ardor of the members; increased expenses of running the village communes; widespread improvements in the outside world which made the Shaker way of life less appealing to converts; the practice of celibacy which made it impossible to increase membership from within; and the lack of imagination and strong leadership in the latter stages of the movement.

In its heyday, however, communitarian Shakerism was an outstanding success. Presidents of the United States paid visits to Shaker villages and were impressed by their agricultural and horticultural industries. From Mexico, Spain, England, and Russia came observers interested in the day-to-day workings of a communal way of life. Writers such as Nathaniel Hawthorne and William Dean Howells used Shakers as subjects for their fiction. Other utopian experimenters such as Robert Owen of New Harmony, John Humphrey Noyes of Oneida, Bronson Alcott and Charles Lane of Fruitlands expressed their admiration for the wisdom and excellence of Shaker institutions. "Thus it is no more than bare justice to say that we are indebted to the Shakers," wrote Noyes, "more than to any or all other Social Architects of modern times."[1]

The Shakers considered themselves to be not primarily social but spiritual architects, designers of communities in which men and women could live together in Christian fellowship and love while awaiting ascent into the higher heavenly regions. Their founder was Ann Lee, or "Mother Ann," an English spiritualist who, her followers claimed, was the second embodiment (Jesus being the first) of the spirit of Christ. She gave the movement its original inspiration and impetus after she arrived in the United States with a group of disciples in 1774.

After Ann Lee's death in 1785, the Millennial Church was formally organized, and under a series of effective leaders its various church communities were established or "gathered." First in New York, then in Massachusetts, New Hampshire, Connecticut, and Maine, and finally in Kentucky, Ohio, and Indiana, land was bought and cleared, buildings were erected, crops were planted, and industries were established.

The members of the various societies were bound together by a common covenant, a common way of life, and a common source of authority. In accepting these common bonds, every Shaker had to give up all his or her private interests and property "to the service of God forever." This was not considered so much a sacrifice as essential for participating in the "Church of the Last Dispensation," the establishment of which by "Mother Ann" had already begun Christ's kingdom on earth.

Drawing their principles from what they conceived to be the practice of the original "Pentecostal Church" founded by Jesus, the Shakers preached and aspired to first, common possession of property; second, a life of strict celibacy; third, nonresistance to evil; fourth, separation from the world and reliance on their own distinct government; and fifth, power over physical disease. Except for the last, the Shakers were remarkably successful in embodying their principles, and even if they never attained power over disease, they often remained in excellent health and lived unusually long lives.

The long lives lived by the Shakers seem to have been quite happy lives, although the Shaker goal was not happiness but spiritual perfection. Typical of their attitude was the answer of a seventy-three year old Mt. Lebanon Shaker to a visitor's question whether on the whole, in reviewing his life, he thought it a success. "Certainly," the old man replied, "I have lived out the highest aspirations my mind was capable of. The best I knew has been realized for and around me here. With my ideas of society I should have been unfit for anything in the world, and unhappy because everything around me would have worked contrary to my belief in the right and the best. Here I found my place and my work, and have been happy and content, seeing the realization of the highest I had dreamed of."[2]

[1] Noyes, *American Socialisms*, p. 670.

[2] Nordhoff, *Communistic Societies*, p. 164.

Admirable as this answer and the attitude it reflects may seem to some, critics of Shakerism would point out that such contentment was achieved only by paying a heavy price: unquestioning reliance upon external authority for justifying individual decisions and actions; uncritical acceptance of revelation as a basis for fundamental religious beliefs; rejection of purely aesthetic and intellectual pursuits; and suppression of sexual drives.

The last of the Shakers, however, remain firm in their faith and convinced that the "Shaker adventure" was eminently worthwhile. They are optimists about the future. As one of them, Sister Marguerite Frost of the Canterbury Shakers, writes in her pamphlet *The Shaker Story*:

> We have called our church the Millennial Church and so it is. It will go on forever and ever for the Spirit of the Inner Christ is still in the hearts of men and women awaiting its discovery. As time goes on there will be a greater and greater fellowship of such souls though wide scatttered over the earth. Perhaps some will be gathered together at some future time.[3]

The following account of the Shakers was written by Charles Nordhoff after visiting most of the Shaker societies in the early 1870's.

[3] Sister Marquerite Frost, *The Shaker Story: Canterbury Shakers* (Canterbury, New Hampshire: n.d.), p. 21. Quoted by permission of the author.

From Charles Nordhoff, The Communistic Societies of the United States *(New York: Harper and Brothers, 1875), pp. 137–45; 147–51.*

A Shaker Society consists of two classes or orders: the Novitiate and the Church Order. There is a general similarity in the life of these two; but to the Novitiate families are sent all applicants for admission to the community or Church, and here they are trained; and the elders of these families also receive inquiring strangers, and stand in somewhat nearer relations with the outer world than the Church families.

To the Church family or commune belong those who have determined to seclude themselves more entirely from contact with the outer world; and who aspire to live the highest spiritual life. Except so far as necessary business obliges deacons and care-takers to deal with the world, the members of the Church Order aim to live apart; and they do not receive or entertain strangers or applicants for membership, but confine their intercourse to members of other societies.

Formerly there was a considerable membership living in the world, maintaining the family relation so far as to educate children and transact business, but conforming to the Shaker rule of celibacy. This was allowed because of the difficulty of disposing of property, closing up business affairs, and perhaps on account of the unwillingness of husband or wife to follow the other partner into the Shaker family. There are still such members, but they are fewer in number than formerly. The Novitiate elders and elderesses keep some oversight, by correspondence and by personal visits, over such outside members.

The Shaker family, or commune, usually consists of from thirty to eighty or ninety persons, men and women, with such children as may have been apprenticed to the society. These live together in one large house, divided as regards its upper stories into rooms capable of accommodating from four to eight persons. Each room contains as many simple cot-beds as it has occupants, the necessary washing utensils, a small looking-glass, a stove for the winter, a table for writing, and a considerable number of chairs, which, when not in use, are suspended from pegs along the wall. A wide hall separates the dormitories of the men from those of the women. Strips of home-made carpets, usually of very quiet colors, are laid upon the floors, but never tacked down.

On the first floor are the kitchen, pantry, storerooms, and the common dining-hall; and in a Novitiate family there is also a small separate room, where strangers—visitors—eat, apart from the family.

Ranged around the family house or dwelling are buildings for the various pursuits of the society: the sisters' shop, where tailoring, basket-making, and other female industries are carried on; the brothers' shop, where broom-making, carpentry, and other men's pursuits are followed; the laundry, the stables, the fruit-house, wood-house, and often machine shops, saw-mills, etc.

If you are permitted to examine these shops and the dwelling of the family, you will notice that the most scrupulous cleanliness is every where practiced; if there is a stove in the room, a small broom and dust-pan hang near it, and a wood-box stands by it; scrapers and mats at the door invite you to make clean your shoes; and if the roads are muddy or snowy, a broom hung up outside the outer door mutely requests you to brush off all the mud or snow. The strips of carpet are easily lifted, and the floor beneath is as clean as though it were a table to be eaten from. The walls are bare of pictures; not only because all ornament is wrong, but because frames are places where dust will lodge. The bedstead is a cot, covered with the bed-clothing, and easily moved away to allow of dusting and sweeping. Mats meet you at the outer door and at every inner door. The floors of the halls and dining-room are polished until they shine.

Moreover all the walls, in hall and rooms, are lined with rows of wooden pegs, on which spare chairs, hats, cloaks, bonnets, and shawls are hung; and you presently perceive that neatness, order and absolute cleanliness rule every where.

The government or administration of the Shaker societies is partly spiritual and partly temporal. "The visible Head of the Church of Christ on earth is vested in a Ministry, consisting of male and female, not less than three, and generally four in number, two of each sex. The first in the Ministry stands as the leading elder of the society. Those who compose the Ministry are selected from the Church, and appointed by the last preceding head or leading character; and their authority is confirmed and established by the spontaneous union of the whole body. Those of the United Society who are selected and called to the important work of the Ministry, to lead and direct the Church of Christ, must be blameless characters, faithful, honest, and upright, clothed with the spirit of meekness and humility, gifted with wisdom and understanding, and of great experience in the things of God. As faithful embassadors of Christ, they are invested with wisdom and authority, by the revelation of God, to guide, teach, and direct his Church on earth in its spiritual travel, and to counsel and advise in other matters of importance, whether spiritual or temporal.

"To the Ministry appertains, therefore, the power to appoint ministers, elders, and deacons, and with the elders to assign offices of care and trust to such brethren and sisters as they shall judge to be best qualified for the several offices to which they may be assigned. Such appointments, being communicated to the members of the Church concerned, and having received the mutual approbation of the Church, or the family concerned, are thereby confirmed and established until altered or repealed by the same authority."[1]

"Although the society at New Lebanon is the centre of union to all the other societies, yet the more immediate duties of the Ministry in this place extend only to the two societies of New Lebanon and Watervliet. [Groveland has since been added to this circle.] Other societies are under the direction of a ministry appointed to preside over them; and in most instances two or more societies constitute a bishopric, being united under the superintendence of the same ministry."

Each society has ministers, in the Novitiate family, to instruct and train neophytes, and to go out into the world to preach when it may be desirable. Each family has two elders, male and female, to teach, exhort, and lead the family in spiritual concerns. It has also deacons and deaconesses, who provide for the support and convenience of the family, and regulate the various branches of industry in which the members are employed, and transact business with those without Under the deacons are "caretakers," who are the foremen and forewomen in the different pursuits.

It will be seen that this is a complete and judicious system of administration. It has worked well for a long time. A notable feature of the system is that the members do not appoint their rulers, nor are they consulted openly or directly about such appointments. The Ministry are self-perpetuating; and they select and appoint all subordinates, being morally, but it seems not otherwise, responsible to the members.

Finally, "all the members are equally holden, according to their several abilities, to maintain one united interest, and therefore all labor *with their hands*, in some useful occupation, for the mutual comfort and benefit of themselves and each other, and for the general good of the society or family to which they belong. Ministers, elders, and deacons, all without exception, are industriously employed in some *manual* occupation, except in the time taken up in the neces-

[1] This quotation and the others below are apparently taken from *A Summary View of the Millennial Church, or United Society of Believers*, 2nd ed. revised. Albany, New York: C. Van Benthuysen, 1848. Nordhoff gives no page references.—Ed

sary duties of their respective callings." So carefully is this rule observed that even the supreme heads of the Shaker Church—the four who constitute the Ministry at Mount Lebanon, Daniel Boler, Giles B. Avery, Ann Taylor, and Polly Reed—labor at basket-making in the intervals of their travels and ministrations, and have a separate little "shop" for this purpose near the church. They live in a house built against the church, and eat in a separate room in the family of the first order; and, I believe, generally keep themselves somewhat apart from the people.

The property of each society, no matter of how many families it is composed, is for convenience held in the name of the trustees, who are usually members of the Church family, or first order; but each family or commune keeps its own accounts and transacts its business separately.

The Shaker family rises at half-past four in the summer, and five o'clock in the winter; breakfasts at six or half-past six; dines at twelve; sups at six; and by nine or half-past all are in bed and the lights are out.

They eat in a general hall. The tables have no cloth, or rather are covered with oil-cloth; the men eat at one table, women at another, and children at a third; and the meal is eaten in silence, no conversation being held at table. When all are assembled for a meal they kneel in silence for a moment; and this is repeated on rising from the table, and on rising in the morning and before going to bed.

When they get up in the morning, each person takes two chairs, and, setting them back to back, takes off the bedclothing, piece by piece, and folding each neatly once, lays it across the backs of the chairs, the pillows being first laid on the seats of the chairs. In the men's rooms the slops are also carried out of the house by one of them; and the room is then left to the women, who sweep, make the beds, and put every thing to rights. All this is done before breakfast; and by breakfast time what New Englanders call "chores" are all finished, and the day's work in the shops or in the fields may begin.

Each brother is assigned to a sister, who takes care of his clothing, mends when it is needed, looks after his washing, tells him when he requires a new garment, reproves him if he is not orderly, and keeps a general sisterly oversight over his habits and temporal needs.

In cooking, and the general labor of the dining-room and kitchen, the sisters take turns; a certain number, sufficient to make the work light, serving a month at a time. The younger sisters do the washing and ironing; and the clothes which are washed on Monday are not ironed till the following week.

Their diet is simple but sufficient. Pork is never eaten, and only a part of the Shaker people eat any meat at all. Many use no food produced by animals, denying themselves even milk, butter, and eggs. At Mount Lebanon, and in some of the other societies, two tables are set, one with, the other without meat. They consume much fruit, eating it at every meal; and the Shakers have always fine and extensive vegetable gardens and orchards.

After breakfast every body goes to work; and the "caretakers," who are subordinate to the deacons, and are foremen in fact, take their followers to their proper employments. When, as in harvest, an extra number of hands is needed at any labor, it is of course easy to divert at once a sufficient force to the place. The women do not labor in the fields, except in such light work as picking berries. Shakers do not toil severely. They are not in haste to be rich; and they have found that for their support, economically as they live, it is not necessary to make labor painful. Many hands make light work; and where all are interested alike, they hold that labor may be made and is made a pleasure.

Their evenings are well filled with such diversions as they regard wholesome. Instrumental music they do not generally allow themselves, but they sing well; and much time is spent in learning new hymns and tunes, which they profess to receive constantly from the spirit world. Some sort of meeting of the family is held every evening. At Mount Lebanon, for instance, on Monday evening there is a general meeting in the dining-hall, where selected articles from the newspapers are read, crimes and accidents being omitted as unprofitable; and the selections consisting largely of scientific news, speeches on public affairs, and the general news of the world. They prefer such matter as conveys information of the important political and social movements of the day; and the elder usually makes the extracts. At this meeting, too, letters from other societies are read. On Tuesday evening they meet in the assembly hall for singing, marching, etc. Wednesday night is devoted to a union meeting for conversation. Thursday night is a "laboring meeting," which means the regular religious service, where they "labor to get good." Friday is devoted to new songs and hymns; and Saturday evening to worship. On Sunday evening, finally, they visit at each other's rooms, three or four sisters visiting the brethren in each room, by appointment, and engaging in singing and in conversation upon general subjects.

In their religious services there is little or no audible prayer; they say that God does not need spoken words, and that the mental aspiration is sufficient. Their aim too, as they say, is to "walk with God," as with a friend; and mental prayer may be a large part of their lives without interruption to usual avocations. They do not regularly read the Bible.

The Sunday service is held either in the "meetinghouse," when two or three families, all composing the society, join together; or in the large assembly hall which is found in every family house. In the meeting-house there are generally benches, on which the people sit until all are assembled. In the assembly hall there are only seats ranged along the walls; and the members of the family, as they enter, take their accustomed places, standing, in the ranks which are formed for worship. The men face the women, the older men and women in the front, the elders standing at the head of the first rank. A somewhat broad space or gangway is left between the two front ranks. After the singing of a hymn, the elder usually makes a brief address upon holiness of living and consecration to God; he is followed by the eldress; and thereupon the ranks are broken, and a dozen of the brethren and sisters, forming a separate square on the floor, begin a lively hymn tune, in which all the rest join, marching around the room to a quick step, the women following the men, and all often clapping their hands.

The exercises are varied by reforming the ranks; by speaking from men and women; by singing; and by dancing as they march, "as David danced before the Lord"—the dance being a kind of shuffle. Occasionally one of the members, more deeply moved than the rest, or perhaps in some tribulation of soul, asks the prayers of the others; or one comes to the front, and, bowing before the elder and eldress, begins to whirl, a singular exercise which is sometimes continued for a considerable time, and is a remarkable performance. Then some brother or sister is impressed to deliver a message of comfort or warning from the spiritland; or some spirit asks the prayers of the assembly: on such occasions the elder asks all to kneel for a few moments in silent prayer.

In their marching and dancing they hold their hands before them, and make a motion as of gathering something to themselves: this is called gathering a blessing. In like manner, when any brother or sister asks for their prayers and sympathy, they, reversing their hands, push toward him that which he asks.

All the movements are performed with much precision and in exact order; their tunes are usually in quick time, and the singers keep time admirably. The words of the elder guide the meeting; and at his bidding all disperse in a somewhat summary manner. It is, I believe, an object with them to vary the order of their meetings, and thus give life to them.

New members are admitted with great caution. Usually a person who is moved to become a Shaker has made a visit to the Novitiate family of some society, remaining long enough to satisfy himself that membership would be agreeable to him. During this preliminary visit he lives separately from the family, but is admitted to their religious meetings, and is fully informed of the doctrines, practices, and requirements of the Shaker people. If then he still desires admission, he is expected to set his affairs in order, so that he shall not leave any unfulfilled obligations behind him in the world. If he has debts, they must be paid; if he has a wife, she must freely give her consent to the husband leaving her; or if it is a woman, her husband must consent. If there are children, they must be provided for, and placed so as not to suffer neglect, either within the society, or with other and proper persons.

It is not necessary that applicants for admission shall possess property. The only question the society asks and seeks to be satisfied upon is, "Are you sick of sin, and do you want salvation from it?" A candidate for admission is usually taken on trial for a year at least, in order that the society may be satisfied of his fitness; of course he may leave at any time.

The first and chief requirement, on admission, is that the neophyte shall make a complete and open confession of the sins of his whole past life to two elders of his or her own sex; and the completeness of this confession is rigidly demanded. . . .

Community of property is one of the leading principles of the Shakers. "It is an established principle of faith in the Church, that all who are received as members thereof do freely and voluntarily, of their own deliberate choice, dedicate, devote, and consecrate themselves, with all they possess, to the service of God forever." In accordance with this rule, the neophyte brings with him his property; but as he is still on trial, and may prove unfit, or find himself uncomfortable, he is not allowed to give up his property unreservedly to the society; but only its use, agreeing that so long as he remains he will require neither wages for his labor nor interest for that which he brought in. On these terms he may remain as long as he proves his fitness. But when at last he is moved to enter the higher or Church order, he formally makes over to the society, forever, and without power of taking it back, all that he owns. . . .

As under this agreement or convenant no accounts can be demanded, so the societies and families have no annual or business meetings, nor is any business report ever made to the members.

Agriculture and horticulture are the foundations of all the communes or families; but with these they have united some small manufactures. For instance, some of the families make brooms, others dry sweet corn, raise and put up garden seeds, make medicinal extracts; make mops, baskets, chairs; one society makes large casks, and so on.

A complete list of these industries in all the societies will be found further on. It will be seen that the range is not great.

Besides this, they aim, as far as possible, to supply their own needs. Thus they make all their own clothing, and formerly made also their own woolen cloths and flannels. They make shoes, do all their own carpentering, and, as far as is convenient, raise the food they consume. They have usually fine barns, and all the arrangements for working are of the best and most convenient. For instance, at Mount Lebanon the different families saw their firewood by a power-saw, and store it in huge wood-houses, that it may be seasoned before it is used. In their farming operations they spare no pains; but, working slowly year after year, redeem the soil, clear it of stones, and have clean tillage. They are fond of such minute and careful culture as is required in raising garden seeds. They keep fine stock, and their barns are usually admirably arranged to save labor.

Their buildings are always of the best, and kept in the best order and repair.

Their savings they invest chiefly in land; and many families own considerable estates outside of their own limits. In the cultivation of these outlying farms they employ hired laborers, and build for them comfortable houses. About Lebanon, I am told, a farmer who is in the employ of the Shakers is considered a fortunate man, as they are kind and liberal in their dealings. Every where they have the reputation of being strictly honest and fair in all their transactions with the world's people.

The dress of the men is remarkable for a very broad, stiff-brimmed, white or gray felt hat, and a long coat of light blue. The women wear gowns with many plaits in the skirt; and a singular head-dress or cap of light material, which so completely hides the hair, and so encroaches upon the face, that a stranger is at first unable to distinguish the old from the young. Out of doors they wear the deep sun-bonnet known in this country commonly as a Shaker bonnet. They do not profess to adhere to a uniform; but have adopted what they find to be a convenient style of dress, and will not change it until they find something better.

7

Owenites in Indiana

NEW HARMONY

The story of New Harmony is the story of a utopian socialist's brilliant vision, of those who rallied round him to try to make it a reality, and of the venture's early failure due primarily to its founder's bungling administration. It is also the story of the successes which sprang from the failure of a dream.

Having achieved fame and fortune as the manager of the industrial town of New Lanark in Scotland, Robert Owen (1771–1858) widened his ambition for social reform and preached that times were ripe for the establishment of "The New Moral World." This world, as he envisaged it, would provide opportunities for everyone to be educated and employed and would improve human existence by surrounding men with "superior circumstances only."

Owen was convinced "that the character of man is, without a single exception, always formed for him." Thus he called for an eventual reorganization of social institutions which would produce happy rather than unhappy human beings. By using what would today be called "behavioral engineering," Owen believed that a new world could be created, in which "to produce happiness will be the only religion of man" and "the worship of God will consist in the practice of useful industry, in the acquisition of knowledge, in uniformly speaking the language of truth, and in the expression of the joyful feeling which a life in accordance with nature and truth is sure to produce."[1]

Owen remained rather vague as to how this world could be brought about, but essential to its realization, he taught, was the gradual abolition of private property and the eventual establishment of communism. As a start, he proposed building carefully planned and well-organized villages of "unity and cooperation" in which the unemployed could be engaged in both

[1] Robert Owen, *The Book of the New Moral World*, pt. 2, p. 33. Quoted by Laidler, *Social Economic Movements*, p. 89.

manufacturing and agriculture. Each of these villages would be built in the form of a parallelogram and would be an independent and self-contained unit without being isolated, for "as the independent townships should increase in numbers, unions of them, federatively united, should be formed in circles of ten, hundreds, thousands, until they should embrace the entire world."[2]

Owen began the attempt to realize his grandiose scheme in 1825 when he bought a complete village in southwest Indiana. This village, originally called Harmonie, but renamed by the Owenites New Harmony, had been built ten years before by the Rappites, a community of German pietists who, after a decade of life in Indiana, had decided to resettle in Pennsylvania. Interest in Owen's plans for New Harmony at the time was widespread. He was invited to explain them to the House of Representatives and to the president of the United States.

Despite his enthusiasm and good intentions, the "father of English social-ism" was never able to nurture to maturity the utopian colony he had planted. He left its management to others during its crucial first year; he made little effort to select carefully its total population; he tried to solve problems by rewriting constitutions; and he failed hopelessly to put sound economic foundations under his dream castle. He was sometimes authori-tarian when he should have been permissive and (more often) permissive when he should have been authoritarian; he moved speedily when he should have "made haste slowly"; he encouraged diversity of approach while he should have insisted upon unity; and when all else failed, he took flight into clouds of rhetoric (sometimes inflammatory) instead of facing reality with tact and caution. By the time (1827) it became obvious to everyone, including belatedly its founder, that the utopian experiment at New Harmony was a complete failure, Owen had already disappointed a multitude, alienated his brilliant partner William MacLure, and lost a for-tune. But when he finally returned to England to pursue other schemes, his optimism was still unshaken. He remained throughout his long life a believer that a New Moral World could be brought about.

If New Harmony failed to be the "halfway house" to an ideal com-munitarianism, as Owen hoped it would be, this does not mean that the little town on the Wabash was a complete failure. Far from it. Some of the brilliant men and women whom Owen had gathered around him stayed on to teach, to write, to do scientific research, and to launch social reforms which affected not only New Harmony and Indiana, but also the Midwest and the nation. Especially for its educational innovations—its infant school, its kindergarten, its trade school, and its free public school system—New Harmony achieved wide renown.

The following account of New Harmony in its utopian period is taken from John Humphrey Noyes's *History of American Socialisms*. Noyes embodies material from an earlier unpublished work on utopian communi-ties compiled by A. J. Macdonald, an admirer of Owen who visited New Harmony in the early 1840's to gather information for his proposed book.

[2] Ibid., p. 92.

From John Humphrey Noyes, History of American
Socialisms *(Philadelphia: J. B. Lippincott, 1870),
pp. 30–43.*

American Socialisms, as we have defined them and grouped their
experiments, may be called *non-religious* Socialisms. Several religious
Communities flourished in this country before Owen's attempts, and
have continued to flourish here since the collapse of Fourierism. But
they were originally colonies of foreigners, and never were directly
connected with movements that could be called national. Owen was
the first Socialist that stirred the enthusiasm of the whole American
people; and he was the first, so far as we know, who tried the experiment of a non-religious Community. And the whole series of experiments belonging to the two great groups of the Owen and Fourier
epochs, followed in his footsteps. The exclusion of theology was their
distinction and their boast.

Our programme, limited as it is by its title to these national Socialisms, does not strictly include the religious Communities. Yet those
Communities have played indirectly a very important part in the
drama of American Socialisms, and will require considerable incidental
attention as we proceed.

In attempting to make out from Macdonald's collection an outline
of Owen's great experiment at New Harmony (which was the prototype of all the Owen and Fourier experiments), we find ourselves at
the outset quite unexpectedly dealing with a striking example of the
relation between the religious and non-religious Communities.

Owen did not build the village of New Harmony, nor create the
improvements which prepared his 30,000 acres for his family of nine
hundred. He bought them outright from a previous religious Community; and it is doubtful whether he would have ever gathered his
nine hundred and made his experiment, if he had not found a place
prepared for him by a sect of Christian Communists.

Macdonald was an admirer, we might almost say a worshiper, of
Owen. He gloats over New Harmony as the very Mecca of his devotion. There he spent his first eighteen months in this country. The
finest picture in his collection is an elaborate India-ink drawing of the
village. But he scarcely mentions the Rappites who built it. No sepa-

rate account of them, such as he gives of the Shakers and Moravians, can be found in his manuscripts. This is an unaccountable neglect; for their pre-occupation of New Harmony and their transactions with Owen, must have thrust them upon his notice; and their history is intrinsically as interesting, to say the least, as that of any of the religious Communities.

A glance at the history of the Rappites is in many ways indispensable, as an introduction to an account of Owen's New Harmony. We must therefore address ourselves to the task which Macdonald neglected.

THE HARMONISTS

In the first years of the present century, old Würtemburg, a province always famous for its religious enthusiasms, was fermenting with excitement about the Millennium; and many of its enthusiasts were expecting the speedy personal advent of Christ. Among these George Rapp became a prominent preacher, and led forth a considerable sect into doctrines and ways that brought upon him and them severe persecutions. In 1803 he came to America to find a refuge for his flock. After due exploration he purchased 5000 acres of land in Butler Co., Pennsylvania, and commenced a settlement which he called Harmony. In the summer of 1804 two ship-loads of his disciples with their families—six hundred in all—came over the ocean and joined him. In 1805 the Society was formally organized as a Christian Community, on the model of the Pentecostal church. For a time their fare was poor and their work was hard. An evil eye from their neighbors was upon them. But they lived down calumny and suspicion by well-doing, and soon made the wilderness blossom around them like the rose. In 1807 they adopted the principle of celibacy; but in other respects they were far from being ascetics. Music, painting, sculpture, and other liberal arts flourished among them. Their museums and gardens were the wonder and delight of the region around them. In 1814, desiring warmer land and a better location for business, they sold all in Pennsylvania and removed to Indiana. On the banks of the Wabash they built a new village and again called it Harmony. Here they prospered more than ever, and their number increased to nearly a thousand. In 1824 they again became discontented with their location, on account of bad neighbors and malaria. Again they sold all, and returned to Pennsylvania; but not to their old home. They built their third and final village in Beaver Co., near Pittsburgh, and called it Economy. There they are to this day. They own railroads and oil wells and are reported to be millionaires of the unknown grade. In all their migrations from the old world to the new, from Pennsylvania to Indiana, and from Indiana back to Pennsylvania; in all their perils by persecutions, by false brethren, by pestilence, by poverty and wealth, their religion held them together, and their union gave them the strength that conquers prosperity. A notable example of what a hundred families can do when they have the wisdom of harmony, and fight the battle of life in a solid phalanx! A nobler "six hundred" than the famous dragoons of Balaklava!

Such were the people who gave Robert Owen his first lessons in Communism, and sold him their home in Indiana. Ten of their best years they spent in building a village on the Wabash, not for themselves (as it turned out), but for a theater of the great infidel experiment. Rev. Aaron Williams, D. D., the historian to whom we are indebted for the facts of the above sketch, thus describes the negotiations, and the transfer:

"The Harmonists, when they began to think of returning to Pennsylvania, employed a certain Richard Flower, an Englishman, and a prominent member of an English settlement in their vicinity, to negotiate for a sale of their real estate, offering him five thousand dollars to find a purchaser. Flower went to England for this purpose, and hearing of Robert Owen's Community at New Lanark, he sought him out and succeeded in selling to him the town of Harmony, with all its houses, mills, factories and thirty thousand acres of land, for one hundred and fifty thousand dollars. This was an immense sacrifice; but they were determined to leave the country, and they submitted to the loss. Having in the meantime made a purchase of their present lands in Pennsylvania, on the Ohio river, they built a steamboat and removed in detachments to their new and final place of settlement."

Thus Owen, the first experimenter in non-religious Association, had substantially the ready-made material conditions which Fourier and his followers considered indispensable to success.

We proceed now to give a sketch of the Owen experiment chiefly in Macdonald's words. When our own language occurs it is generally a condensation of his.

OWEN'S NEW HARMONY

"Robert Owen came to the United States in December 1824, to complete the purchase of the settlement at Harmony. Mr. Rapp had sent an agent to England to dispose of the property, and Mr. Owen fell in with him there. In the spring of 1825 Mr. Owen closed the bargain. The property consisted of about 30,000 acres of land; nearly 3,000 acres under cultivation by the society; 19 detached farms; 600 acres of improved land occupied by tenants; some fine orchards; eighteen acres of full-bearing vines; and the village, which was a regularly laid out town, with streets running at right angles to each other, and a public square, around which were large brick edifices, built by the Rappites for churches, schools, and other public purposes.

We can form some idea of the size of the village from the fact which we learn from Mr. Williams, that the Rappites, while at Harmony, numbered one thousand souls. It does not appear from Macdonald's account that Owen and his Community made any important additions to the village.

"On the departure of the Rappites, persons favorable to Mr. Owen's views came flocking to New Harmony (as it was thenceforth called) from all parts of the country. Tidings of the new social experiment spread far and wide; and, although it has been denied, yet it is undoubtedly true, that Mr. Owen in his public lectures invited the 'industrious and well disposed of all nations' to emigrate to new Harmony. The consequence was, that in the short space of six weeks from the commencement of the experiment, a population of eight hundred persons was drawn together, and in October 1825, the number had increased to nine hundred."

As to the character of this population, Macdonald insists that it was "as good as it could be under the circumstances," and he gives the names of "many intelligent and benevolent individuals who were at various times residents at New Harmony." But he admits that there were some "black sheep" in the flock. "It is certain," he says, "that there was a proportion of needy and idle persons, who crowded in to avail themselves of Mr. Owen's liberal offer; and that they did their share of work more in the line of *destruction* than *construction.*"

CONSTITUTION NO. 1

On the 27th of April 1825, Mr. Owen instituted a sort of provisional government. In an address to the people in New Harmony Hall, he informed them, "that he had bought that property, and had come there to introduce the practice of the new views; but he showed them the impossibility that persons educated as they were, should change at once from an irrational to a rational system of society, and the necessity for a 'half-way house,' in which to be prepared for the new system." Whereupon he tendered them a *Constitution,* of which we find no definite account, except that it was not fully Communistic, and was to hold the people in probationary training three years, under the title of the *Preliminary Society of New Harmony.* "After these proceedings Mr. Owen left New Harmony for Europe, and the Society was managed by the *Preliminary Committee.* (!)" We may imagine, each one for himself, what the nine hundred did while Mr. Owen was away. Macdonald compiled from the *New Harmony Gazette* a very rapid but evidently defective account of the state of things in this important interval. He says nothing about the work on the 30,000 acres, but speaks of various minor businesses as "doing well." The only manufacturers that appear to have "exceeded consumption" were those of soap and glue. A respectable apothecary "dispensed medicines without charge," and "the store supplied the inhabitants with all necessaries"—probably at Mr. Owen's expense. Education was considered "public property," and one hundred and thirty children were schooled, boarded and clothed from the public funds—probably at Mr. Owen's expense. Amusements flourished. The Society had a band of music; Tuesday evenings were appropriated to balls; Friday evenings to concerts—both in the old Rappite church. There was no provision for religious worship. Five military companies, "consisting of infantry, artillery, riflemen, veterans and fusileers," did duty from time to time on the public square.

CONSTITUTION NO. 2

"Mr. Owen returned to New Harmony on the 12th of January, 1826, and soon after the members of the Preliminary Society held a convention, and adopted a constitution of a Community, entitled *The New Harmony Community of Equality*. Thus in less than a year, instead of three years as Mr. Owen had proposed, the 'half-way house' came to an end, and actual Communism commenced. A few of the members, who, on account of a difference of opinions, did not sign the new constitution, formed a second Community on the New Harmony estate about two miles from the town, in friendly connection with the first."

The new government instituted by Mr. Owen, was to be in the hands of an *Executive Council*, subject at all times to the direction of the Community; and six gentlemen were appointed to this function. But Macdonald says: "Difficulties ensued in organizing the new Community. It appears that the plan of government by executive council would not work, and that the members were unanimous in calling upon Mr. Owen to take the sole management, judging from his experience that he was the only man who could do so. This call Mr. Owen accepted, and we learn that soon after general satisfaction and individual contentment took the place of suspense and uncertainty."

This was in fact the inauguration of

CONSTITUTION NO. 3

"In March the *Gazette* says that under the indefatigable attention of Mr. Owen, order had been introduced into every department of business, and the farm presented a scene of active and steady industry. The Society was rapidly becoming a Community of Equality. The streets no longer exhibited groups of idle talkers, but each one was busily engaged in the occupation he had chosen. The public meetings, instead of being the arenas for contending orators, were changed into meetings of business, where consultations were held and measures adopted for the comfort of all the members of the Community.

"In April there was a disturbance in the village on account of negotiations that were going on for securing the estate as private property. Some persons attempted to divide the town into several societies. Mr. Owen would not agree to this, and as he had the power, he made a selection, and by solemn examination constituted a *nucleus* of twenty-five men, which *nucleus* was to admit members, Mr. Owen reserving the power to *veto* every one admitted. There were to be three grades of members, viz., conditional members, probationary members, and persons on trial. (?) The Community was to be under the direction of Mr. Owen, until two-thirds of the members should think fit to govern themselves, provided the time was not less than twelve months."

This may be called,

CONSTITUTION NO. 4

In May a third Community had been formed; and the population was divided between No. 1, which was Mr. Owen's Community, No. 2, which was called Macluria, and No. 3, which was called *Feiba Peven* —a name designating in some mysterious way the latitude and longitude of New Harmony.

"May 27. The immigration continued so steadily, that it became necessary for the Community to inform the friends of the new views that the accommodations were inadequate, and call upon them by advertisement not to come until further notice."

CONSTITUTION NO. 5

"May 30. In consequence of a variety of troubles and disagreements, chiefly relating to the disposal of the property, a great meeting of the whole population was held, and it was decided to form four separate societies, each signing its own contract for such part of the property as it should purchase, and each managing its own affairs; but to trade with each other by paper money."

Mr. Owen was now beginning to make sharp bargains with the independent Communities. Macdonald says, "He had lost money, and no doubt he tried to regain some of it, and used such means as he thought would prevent further loss."

On the 4th of July Mr. Owen delivered his celebrated *Declaration of Mental Independence*, from which we give the following specimen: "I now declare to you and to the world, that Man, up to this hour, has been in all parts of the earth a slave to a Trinity of the most monstrous evils that could be combined to inflict mental and physical evil upon his whole race. I refer to Private or Individual Property, Absurd and Irrational systems of Religion, and Marriage founded on Individual Property, combined with some of these Irrational systems of Religion."

"August 20. After Mr. Owen had given his usual address, it was unanimously agreed by the meeting that the entire population of New Harmony should meet three times a week in the Hall, for the purpose of being educated together. This practice was continued about six weeks, when Mr. Owen became sick and it was discontinued."

CONSTITUTION NO. 6

"August 25. The people held a meeting at which they *abolished all officers* then existing, and appointed three men as *dictators*."

CONSTITUTION NO. 7

"Sept. 17. A large meeting of all the Societies and the whole population of the town took place at the Hall, for the purpose of considering a plan for the '*amelioration of the Society*, to improve the condition of the people, and make them more contented.' A message was received from Mr. Owen proposing to form a Community with as many as would join him, and put in all their property, save what might be thought necessary to reserve to help their friends; the government to consist of Robert Owen and four others of his choice, to be appointed by him every year; and not to be altered for five years. This movement of course nullified all previous organizations. Disagreements and jealousies ensued, and, as was the case on a former change being made, many persons left New Harmony.

"Nov. 1. The *Gazette* says: 'Eighteen months' experience has proved to us, that the requisite qualifications for a permanent member of the Community of Common Property are, 1, Honesty of purpose; 2, Temperance; 3, Industry; 4, Carefulness; 5, Cleanliness; 6, Desire for knowledge; 7, A conviction of that fact that the character of man is formed for, and not by, himself.'

"Nov. 8. Many persons leaving. The *Gazette* shows how impossible it is for a Community of common property to exist, unless the members comprising it have acquired the genuine Community character.

"Nov. 11. Mr. Owen reviewed the last six months' progress of the Community in a favorable light.

"In December the use of ardent spirits was abolished.

"Jan. 1827. Although there was an appearance of increased order and happiness, yet matters were drawing to a close. Owen was selling property to individuals; the greater part of the town was now resolved into individual lots; a grocery was established opposite the tavern; painted sign-boards began to be stuck up on the buildings, pointing out places of manufacture and trade; a sort of wax-figure-and-puppet-show was opened at one end of the boarding-house; and every thing was getting into the old style."

It is useless to follow this wreck further. Everybody sees it must go down, and *why* it must go down. It is like a great ship, wallowing helpless in the trough of a tempestuous sea, with nine hundred *passengers*, and no captain or organized crew! We skip to Macdonald's picture of the end.

"June 18, 1827. The *Gazette* advertised that Mr. Owen would meet the inhabitants of New Harmony and the neighborhood on the following Sunday, to bid them farewell. I find no account of this meeting, nor indeed of any further movements of Mr. Owen in the *Gazette*. After his departure the majority of the population also removed and scattered about the country. Those who remained returned to individualism, and settled as farmers and mechanics in the ordinary way. One portion of the estate was owned by Mr. Owen, and the other by Mr. Maclure. They sold, rented, or gave away the houses and lands, and their heirs and assigns have continued to do so to the present day."

Fifteen years after the catastrophe Macdonald was at New Harmony, among the remains of the old Community population, and he says: "I was cautioned not to speak of Socialism, as the subject was unpopular. The advice was good; Socialism was unpopular, and with good reason. The people had been wearied and disappointed by it; had been filled full with theories, until they were nauseated, and had made such miserable attempts at practice, that they seemed ashamed of what they had been doing. An enthusiastic socialist would soon be cooled down at New Harmony."

The strength of the reaction against Communism caused by Owen's failure, may be seen to this day in the sect devoted to "Individual Sovereignty." Josiah Warren, the leader of that sect, was a member of Owen's Community, and a witness of its confusions and downfall; from which he swung off into the extreme of anti-Communism. The village of "Modern Times," where all forms of social organization were scouted as unscientific, was the electric negative of New Harmony.

Macdonald thus moralizes over his master's failure:

"Mr. Owen said he wanted honesty of purpose, and he got dishonesty. He wanted temperance, and instead, he was continually troubled with the intemperate. He wanted industry, and he found idleness. He wanted cleanliness, and found dirt. He wanted carefulness, and found waste. He wanted to find desire for knowledge, but he found apathy. He wanted the principles of the formation of character understood, and he found them misunderstood. He wanted these good qualities combined in one and all the individuals of the Community, but he could not find them; neither could he find those who were self-sacrificing and enduring enough, to prepare and educate their children to possess these qualities. Thus it was proved that his principles were either entirely erroneous, or much in advance of the age in which he promulgated them. He seems to have forgotten, that if one and all the thousand persons assembled there, had possessed the qualities which he wished them to possess, there would have been no necessity for his vain exertions to form a Community; because there would of necessity be brotherly love, charity, industry and plenty. We want no more than these; and if this is the material to form Communities of, and we can not find it, we can not form Communities; and if we can not find parents who are ready and willing to educate their children, to give them these qualities for a Community life, then what hope is there of Communism in the future?"

Almost the only redeeming feature in or near this whole scene of confusion—which might well be called New Discord instead of New Harmony—was the silent retreat of the Rappite thousand, which was so orderly that it almost escaped mention. Remembering their obscure achievements and their persistent success, we can still be sure that the *idea* of Owen and his thousand was not a delusion, but an inspiration, that only needed wiser hearts, to become a happy reality.

8

Ascetics in New Eden

FRUITLANDS

Fruitlands could from one point of view be called the utopia of the absurd. Started in Harvard, Massachusetts, early in the summer of 1841, it was a little farm community dreamed up by two mystical intellectuals—an American, Bronson Alcott, and an Englishman, Charles Lane—who were much more adept at idealizing farm labor than in actually performing it. Believing that they should not exploit innocent animals in farming, they at first tried digging up lots and pulling a plow themselves, until backaches and exhaustion persuaded them to compromise their ideal. But even then they never ceased to exploit at least one innocent "beast of burden," poor hardworking Mrs. Alcott, without whose never-ceasing labors the experiment would never have survived as long as it did.

In the name of moral integrity, Alcott and Lane preached an asceticism which did not always jibe with moral or rational consistency. Milk was forbidden, for example, because the philosophers believed humans had no right to take what belonged to cows and their calves; yet they allowed their own children nearly to starve on a diet of berries, grains, fruit, and water.

To add to the absurd dimensions, the participants in the creation of the "New Eden" certainly seemed unlikely to contribute to the creation of a stable and harmonious paradise. There was Joseph Palmer with his famous beard, who had rather fight than shave. There was Samuel Bower, an "Adamite" who, despite the volatility of the New England weather, advocated nudism. Samuel Larned was an enthusiastic Transcendentalist who had already survived one year solely on crackers and another year on apples. Abram Wood achieved uniqueness by insisting that everyone call him Wood Abram. Certainly few outsiders were surprised when Fruitlands failed after only seven and a half months; most were surprised that it lasted as long as it did.

Yet despite its absurd aspects, Fruitlands should not be dismissed lightly, for it was one of the purest examples of what Joseph Wood Krutch called a noble utopia. Its ideal (unlike that of an ignoble utopia) required that man be more rather than less than he was. Its architect, Amos Bronson Alcott, (1799–1888) was not a fool but a genius, even though he was a genius at education rather than community planning. Emerson had remarked on his "beautiful susceptibility," his "extraordinary insight," and his "singular superiority." Unwilling to dream small dreams and endowed with the typical utopian's "nerve of failure," Alcott's purpose, as he briefly summed it up in a letter to a sympathetic friend a few months before the experiment at Fruitlands began, was "to live independently of foreign aids by being sufficiently elevated to procure all articles for subsistence in the productions of the spot, under a regimen of healthful labor and recreation; with benignity towards all creatures, human and inferior; with beauty and refinement in all economics; and the purest charity throughout our demeanor."[1] And he added before concluding, that "we are not without hope that Providence will use us progressively for beneficial effects in the great work of regeneration, and the restoration of the highest life on earth."[2]

After Alcott had undertaken to realize his Transcendental dream at Fruitlands and had faced the dismal results of his failure—the farm untended, his partner disgusted and gone over to the Shakers, his family reduced to abject poverty, and he himself an object of pity and ridicule—he was filled with such despair and grief that he came close to dying. But the constant love and devotion of his good wife and four little daughters (the future "Little Women") helped him to recover, and finally in January, 1844, he and his family left the dilapidated eighteenth-century farmhouse to start a new life somewhere else.

Much later, in writing of her father's utopian venture, Louisa May Alcott in *Transcendental Wild Oats* had this to say:

> He had tried, but it was a failure. The world was not ready for Utopia yet, and those who attempted to found it only got laughed at for their pains. In other days, men could sell all and give to the poor, lead lives devoted to holiness and high thought, and, after the persecution was over, find themselves honored as saints or martyrs. But in modern times these things are out of fashion. To live for one's principles, at all costs, is a dangerous speculation; and the failure of an ideal, no matter how humane and noble, is harder for the world to forgive and forget than bank robbery or the grand swindles of corrupt politicians.[3]

But as Bronson Alcott himself later began to realize, perhaps Fruitlands had not been as complete a failure as he had first imagined. The "Transcendental wild oats" he and his companions had "sown broadcast" during that golden summer continued to bear an "invisible harvest." Like his friend Henry David Thoreau, Alcott helped to create a wider interest in establish-

---

[1] Quoted by Clara Endicott Sears, *Bronson Alcott's Fruitlands* (Boston: Houghton Mifflin Co., 1915), p. 12.

[2] Ibid., p. 13.

[3] *Silver Pitchers and Independence* (Boston: Roberts Brothers, 1888), p. 97.

ing a social order in which *being* rather than *doing* would be emphasized, in which daily life and human relations were simplified, and in which man could feel at home again with nature. And, as Alcott confided to his diary after leaving Fruitlands:

> That is failure when a man's idea ruins him, when he is dwarfed and killed by it; but when he is ever growing by it, ever true to it, and does not lose it by any partial or immediate failures—that is success, whatever it seems to the world.[4]

Today the old house, now well restored and maintained as a summer museum, nestles on a hillside off Prospect Road near Harvard, Massachusetts.

The following letter describing the program which Alcott and Lane hoped to carry out at Fruitlands was written in 1843 by the two utopians to A. Brooke of Oakland, Ohio, and was published in an abolitionist newspaper, *Herald of Freedom*.

[4] Sears, *Fruitlands*, p. 127.

From Herald of Freedom *(Concord, N.H.), Sept. 8,*
1843, vol. 9, no. 29, pp. 113–14.

Dear Sir:

Having perused your several letters in the *Herald of Freedom*, and
finding, moreover, a general invitation to correspondence from "persons who feel prepared to cooperate in the work of reform upon principles" akin to those you have set forth, I take this public means of
communicating with one who seems to be really desirous of aiding
entire human regeneration.

After many years passed in admiration of a better order in human
society, with a constant expectation that some beginning would
shortly be made, and a continued reliance that some party would
make it, the idea has gradually gained possession of my mind, that it
is not right thus to linger for the leadings of other men, but that each
should at once proceed to live out the proposed life to the utmost
possible extent. Assured that the most potent hindrances to goodness
abide in the soul itself; next in the body; thirdly in the house and
family; and in the fourth degree only in our neighbors, or in society at
large; I have daily found less and less reason to complain of public
institutions, or of the dilatoriness of reformers and genetic minds.

Animated by pure reform principles, or rather by pure creative
spirit, I have not hesitated to withdraw as far and as fast as hopeful
prudence dictated from the practices and principles of the old world,
and acting upon the conviction that whatever others might do, or
leave undone, however others might fail in the realization of their
ideal good, I, at least, should advance, I have accordingly arrived in
that region where I perceive you theoretically, and I hope, actually
dwell. I agree with you that it would be well to cross the ocean of
life from the narrow island of selfishness to the broad continent of
universal love at one dash; but the winds are not always propitious,
and steam is only a recent invention. I cannot yet boast of a year's
emancipation from Old England. One free step leads to another; and
the third must necessarily precede the fourth, as the second was before
the third.

A. Bronson Alcott's visit to England last year opened to me some of the superior conditions for a pure life which this country offers compared to the land of my nativity and that of your ancestors. My love for purity and goodness was sufficiently strong it seems to loosen me from a position as regards pecuniary income, affectionate friends, and mental liberty, which millions there and thousands here might envy. It has happened however that of the many persons with whom Mr. Alcott hoped to act in [con]junction and concert, not one is yet fully liberated by Providence to that end. So that instead of forming items in a large enterprise, we are left to be the principal actors in promoting an idea less in extent, but greater in intent, than any yet presented to our observation. . . .

Our removal to this estate in humble confidence has drawn to us several practical coadjutors, and opened many inquiries by letter for a statement of our principles and modes of life. We cannot perhaps turn our replies to better account than to transcribe some portions of them for your information, and, we trust, for your sincere satisfaction.

You must be aware, however, that written words cannot do much towards the elucidation of principles comprehending all human relationships, and claiming an origin profound as man's inmost consciousness of the ever present Living Spirit. A dwelling together, a concert in soul, and a consorting in body, is a position needful to entire understanding, which we hope at no distant day to attain with yourself and many other sincere friends. We have not yet drawn out any preordained plan of daily operations, as we are impressed with the conviction that by a faithful reliance on the spirit which actuates us, we are sure of attaining to clear revelations of daily practical duties as they are to be daily done by us. Where the Spirit of Love and Wisdom abounds, literal forms are needless, irksome or hinderative; where the Spirit is lacking, no preconceived rules can compensate.

To us it appears not so much that improved circumstances are to meliorate mankind, as that improved men will originate the superior condition for themselves and others. Upon the Human Will, and not upon circumstances, as some philosophers assert, rests the function, power and duty, of generating a better social state. The human beings in whom the Eternal Spirit has ascended from low animal delights or mere human affections, to a state of spiritual chastity and intuition, are in themselves a divine atmosphere, they *are* superior circumstances, and are constant in endeavoring to create, as well as to modify, all other conditions, so that these also shall more and more conduce to the like consciousness in others.

Hence our perseverance in efforts to attain simplicity in diet, plain garments, pure bathing, unsullied dwellings, open conduct, gentle behavior, kindly sympathies, serene minds. These, and several other particulars needful to the true end of man's residence on earth, may be designated the Family Life. Our Happiness, though not the direct object in human energy, may be accepted as the conformation of rectitude, and this is not otherwise attainable than in the Holy Family. The Family in its highest, divinest sense is therefore our true position, our sacred earthly destiny. It comprehends every divine, every human relation consistent with universal good, and all others it rejects, as it disdains all animal sensualities. . . .

The evils of life are not so much social, or political, as personal, and a personal reform only can eradicate them.

Let the Family, furthermore, be viewed as the home of pure social affections, the school of expanding intelligence, the sphere of unbought art, the scene of joyous employment, and we feel in that single sentiment, a fulness of action, of life, of being, which no scientific social contrivance can ensure, nor selfish accident supply.

Family is not dependent upon members, nor upon skill, nor riches, but upon union in and with that spirit which alone can bless any enterprise whatever. . . .

On this topic of Family association, it will not involve an entire agreement with the Shakers to say they are at least entitled to deeper consideration than they yet appear to have secured. There are many important acts in their career worthy of observation. It is perhaps most striking that the only really successful extensive Community of interest, spiritual and secular, in modern times was established by A Woman. Again, we witness in this people the bringing together of the two sexes in a new relation, or rather with a new idea of the old relation. This has led to results more harmonic than anyone seriously believes attainable for the human race, either in isolation or association, so long as divided, conflicting family arrangements are permitted. . . . The great secular success of the Shakers; their order, cleanliness, intelligence and serenity are so eminent, that it is worthy of enquiry how far these are attributal to an adherence to their peculiar doctrine.

As to Property, we discover not its just disposal either in individual or social tenures, but in its entire absorption into the New Spirit, which ever gives and never grasps. . . . While we write, negotiations are entertained for our removal to a place of less inconvenience, by friends who have long waited for some proof of a determination to act up to the idea they have cherished. Many, no doubt, are yet unprepared "to give up all and follow him" (the Spirit) who can importantly aid in the New Advent, and conscientiously accomplish the legal processes needful under the present circumstances. We do not recognize the purchase of land; but its redemption from the debasing state of *proprium*, or property, to divine uses, we clearly understand where those whom the world esteems as owners are found yielding their individual rights to the Supreme Owner. Looking at the subject practically in relation to a climate in which a costly shelter is necessary, and where a family with many children has to be provided for, the possibility of at once stepping boldly out of the toils into which the errors of our predecessors have cast us, is not so evident as it is desirable.

Trade we hope entirely to avoid at an early day. As a nursery for many evil propensities it is almost universally felt to be a most undesirable course. Such needful articles as we cannot yet raise by our own hand labor from the soil, thus redeemed from human ownership, we shall endeavor to obtain by friendly exchanges, and, as nearly as possible, without the intervention of money.

Of all the traffic in which civilized society is involved, that of human labor is perhaps the most detrimental. From the state of serfdom to the receipt of wages may be a step in human progress; but it is certainly full time for taking a new step out of the hiring system.

Our outward exertions are in the first instance directed to the soil, and as our ultimate aim is to furnish an instance of self-sustaining cultivation without the subjugation of either men or cattle, or the use of foul animal manures, we have at the outset to encounter struggles and oppositions somewhat formidable. Until the land is restored to its pristine fertility by the annual return of its own green crops, as sweet and animating manures, the human hand and simple implement cannot wholly supersede the employment of machinery and cattle. So long as cattle are used in agriculture, it is very evident that man will remain a slave, whether he be proprietor or hireling. The driving of cattle beyond their natural and pleasurable exertion; the waiting upon them as cook and chambermaid three parts of the year; the excessive labor of mowing, curing, and housing hay, and of collecting other fodder, and the large extra quantity of land needful to keep up this system, forms a combination of unfavorable circumstances which must depress the human affections so long as it continues, and overlay them by the injurious and extravagant development of the animal and bestial natures in man. . . . It is calculated that if not animal food were consumed, one-fourth of the land now used would suffice for human sustenance. And the extensive tracts of country now appropriated to grazing, mowing, and other modes of animal provision, could be cultivated by and for intelligent and affectionate human neighbors. The sty and the stable too often secure more of the farmer's regard than he bestows on the garden and the children. No hope is there for humanity while Woman is withdrawn from the tender assiduities which adorn her and her household, to the servitudes of the dairy and the flesh pots. . . . If the beasts were wholly absent from man's neighborhood, the human population might be at least four times as dense as it now is without raising the price of land. This would give to the country all the advantages of concentration without the vices which always spring up in the dense city.

Debauchery of both the earthly soil and the human body is the result of this cattlekeeping. The land is scourged for crops to feed the animals, those filthy ordures are used under the erroneous supposition of restoring lost fertility; disease is thus infused into the human body; stimulants and medicines are resorted to for relief, which end in a precipitation of the original evil to a more disastrous depth. These misfortunes which affect not only the body, but by reaction rise to the sphere of the soul, would be avoided, or at least in part, by the disuse of animal food. Our diet is therefore strictly the pure and bloodless kind. No animal substances, neither flesh, butter, cheese, eggs, nor milk, pollute our table or corrupt our bodies. Neither tea, coffee, molasses, nor rice, tempts us beyond the bounds of indigenous productions. Our sole beverage is pure fountain water. The native grains, fruits, herbs, and roots, dressed with the utmost cleanliness and regard to their purpose of edifying a healthful body, furnish the pleasantest refections and in the greatest variety requisite to the supply of the various organs. The field, the orchard, the garden, in their bounteous products of wheat, rye, barley, maize, oats, buckwheats, apples, pears, peaches, plums, cherries, currants, berries, potatoes, peas, beans, beets, carrots, melons, and other vines, yield an ample store for human nutrition, without dependence on foreign climes, or the degeneration of shipping and trade. The almost inexhaustible variety which the several stages and sorts of vegetable growth, and the several modes of preparation afford are a full answer to the question which is often put by those who have never ventured into the region of a pure and chaste diet: "If you give up flesh meat, upon what then can you live?"

Our other domestic habits are in harmony with those of diet. We rise with early dawn, begin the day with cold bathing, succeeded by a music lesson, and then a chaste repast. Each one finds occupation until the meridian meal, when usually some interesting and deep-searching conversation gives rest to the body and development to the mind. Occupation, according to the season and the weather, engages us out of doors or within, until the evening meal,—when we again assemble in social communion, prolonged generally until sunset, when we resort to sweet repose for the next day's activity.

In these steps of reform we do not rely so much on scientific reasoning or physiological skill, as on the Spirit's dictates. The pure soul, by the law of its own nature, adopts a pure diet and cleanly customs; nor needs detailed instruction for daily conduct. On a revision of our proceedings it would seem, that if we were in the right course in our particular instance, the greater part of man's duty consists in leaving alone much that he is in the habit of doing. It is a fasting from the present activity, rather than an increased indulgence in it, which, with patient watchfulness tends to newness of life. "Shall I sip tea or coffee?" the inquiry may be. No; abstain from *all* ardent, as from alcoholic drinks. "Shall I consume pork, beef, or mutton?" Not if you value health or life. "Shall I warm my bathing water?" Not if cheerfulness is valuable. "Shall I clothe in many garments?" Not if purity is aimed at. "Shall I prolong my dark hours, consuming animal oil and losing bright daylight in the morning?" Not if a clear mind is an object. "Shall I teach my children the dogmas inflicted on myself, under the pretence that I am transmitting truth?" Nay, if you love them intrude not these between them and the Spirit of all Truth. "Shall I become a hireling or hire others?" "Shall I subjugate cattle?" "Shall I trade?" "Shall I claim property in any created thing?" "Shall I adopt a form of religion?" "Shall I become a parent?" "Shall I interest myself in politics?" To how many of these questions could we ask them deeply enough, could they be heard as having relation to our eternal welfare, would the response be "Abstain"? Be not so active to do, as sincere to BE. Being, in preference to doing, is the great aim, and this comes to us rather by a resigned willingness than a wilful activity;—which is indeed a check to all divine growth. Outward abstinence is a sign of inward fulness; and the only source of true progress is inward. We may occupy ourselves actively in human improvements;—but these, unless inwardly well-impelled, never attain to, but rather hinder, divine progress in man. During the utterance of this narrative it has undergone some change in its personal expression which might offend the hypercritical; but we feel assured that you will kindly accept it as unartful offering of both your friends in ceaseless aspiration.

Charles Lane,
A. Bronson Alcott

Harvard, Massachusetts
August, 1843

9

Poetic Phalanx

BROOK FARM

Brook Farm was the brainchild of a former Unitarian minister, George Ripley (1802–1880), who wanted to show that the quality of life could be improved by cooperative effort and communal sharing. To restore man's harmonious relations with nature, to reconcile intellectual creation with manual labor, and, in Ripley's words, "to establish a mode of life which shall combine the enchantments of poetry with the facts of daily experience"—these were some of the goals which Ripley and a group of New England intellectuals sought to achieve through establishing a rural association in West Roxbury, Massachusetts. This association was called "The Brook Farm Institute of Agriculture and Education."

Ripley's original plan for Brook Farm and his initial implementation of it in 1841 were described in his letter to Ralph Waldo Emerson (included in Part 1) and in the "Plan of the West Roxbury Community" by Elizabeth P. Peabody, which appeared early in 1842.[1] With Ripley's experiment obviously in mind, Miss Peabody had already written glowingly in *The Dial* (October 1841) of "little communities" which were "the embryo of the kingdom to come." Since these communities were attempts to conform to Christ's Idea of Society according to Miss Peabody's interpretation, they necessarily had as their "ground idea" the perfection of man through education. The belief that Brook Farm had at its center a religious orientation to life was also affirmed three years later by one of its leaders, Charles A Dana, in a lecture on "Association, in its Connection with Religion." "Our ulterior aim," Dana said, "is nothing less than Heaven on Earth,—the conversion of this globe, now exhaling pestilential vapors and possessed by unnatural climates, into the abode of beauty and health, and the restitution to Humanity of the Divine Image, now so long lost and forgotten."[2] By the

---

[1] *The Dial,* 2 (Jan. 1842): 361–72.

[2] *Association in its Connection with Education and Religion* (Boston: Benjamin H. Greene, 1844), p. 26.

time Dana spoke these words before the New England Fourier Society in Boston on March 7, 1844, Brook Farm had already turned from its original Unitarian and Transcendental inspiration toward Fourierism, having adopted a revised constitution according to which it could develop into a Fourierist Association and eventually expand into "a perfect Phalanx." The introductory statement to this constitution is given below.

With the conversion of the Brook Farmers to Charles Fourier's brand of socialism, a new stage began in the life of the community. A new faith to live by, a controversial cause to fight for, and a central role in a widespread social movement soon transformed an idyllic retreat for intellectuals into a forum for social reformers. The founder of the *New York Tribune*, Horace Greeley, took a keen personal interest in the Fourierist movement at Brook Farm and elsewhere in the country. Fourier's chief American disciple, Albert Brisbane, heartily approved of the direction Brook Farm was taking and allowed his Fourierist journal *Phalanx* to be replaced by Brook Farm's *Harbinger*. Almost everyone in the community began to use Fourierist jargon, discussing enthusiastically the nature of "Association," the means for achieving "Attractive Industry," and the new work plan according to which inhabitants of the community would be organized into "Groups" and "Series."

Although the Brook Farm Association was not officially transformed into the Brook Farm Phalanx (i.e. Fourierist utopian community) until the spring of 1845, Ripley and his companions had already begun before that to construct a "large unitary edifice" which was to become eventually a part of the community's envisaged "Phalanstery." On March 3, 1846, the unfinished building burned to the ground. As a large proportion of the community's money had been invested in the building, its loss was a shock from which Brook Farm never recovered. For a while longer the Farm survived as a center of Fourierist activities; then it folded. Ripley moved to New York and became a journalist and later, with Dana, an encyclopedia editor. In 1849 the city of Roxbury bought the Brook Farm property to use as a poorhouse. Of the buildings constructed by the Brook Farmers only the Cottage remains today.

The second selection pertaining to Brook Farm reprinted here is Ralph Waldo Emerson's account of the life of the community. Emerson had received a cordial invitation from Ripley to join in the utopian experiment at its very beginning. This invitation Emerson had politely refused. He wrote Ripley on December 15, 1840, that while he found the design to be "noble and generous," he believed that "it has little to offer me which, with resolution, I cannot procure for myself." He was quite content with his position and property in Concord, he added, and, furthermore, he and his wife and mother were already so set in their ways that it was too late for them to participate energetically in utopian reforms. Sounding like Thoreau, Emerson expressed a conviction "that all I shall solidly do, I must do alone." What Emerson failed to mention was his real reason for not joining the association: he was convinced that the whole enterprise would inevitably fail.

Nevertheless, Emerson remained an interested observer of the utopian experiment and remained on friendly terms with the Brook Farmers. If his account of the community reflects his own biases and blind spots, it also reflects his interest and detachment. Like his contemporaries Nathaniel Hawthorne and Margaret Fuller, Emerson was intellectually aware of the appeal of the Brook Farm idea, but unlike Hawthorne (and like Fuller), he was never, even temporarily, captivated emotionally by it.

From the introductory statement to the constitution,
Constitution of the Brook Farm Association for Industry and Education, West Roxbury, Massachusetts, with an Introductory Statement, *2nd ed. (Boston: I. R. Butts, 1844), pp. 6–10.*

The Association at Brook Farm has now been in existence upwards of two years. Originating in the thought and experience of a few individuals, it has hitherto worn, for the most part, the character of a private experiment, and has avoided rather than sought, the notice of the public. It has, until the present time, seemed fittest to those engaged in this enterprise to publish no statements of their purposes or methods, to make no promises or declarations, but quietly and sincerely to realise, as far as might be possible, the great ideas which gave the central impulse to their movement. It has been thought that a steady endeavor to embody these ideas more and more perfectly in life, would give the best answer, both to the hopes of the friendly and the cavils of the sceptical, and furnish in its results the surest grounds for any larger efforts.

Meanwhile every step has strengthened the faith with which we set out; our belief in a divine order of human society, has in our own minds become an absolute certainty; and considering the present state of humanity and of social science, we do not hesitate to affirm, that the world is much nearer the attainment of such a condition than is generally supposed.

The deep interest in the doctrine of Association, which now fills the minds of intelligent persons every where, indicates plainly that the time has passed when even initiative movements ought to be prosecuted in silence, and makes it imperative on all who have either a theoretical or practical knowledge of the subject to give their share to the stock of public information.

Accordingly, we have taken occasion at several public meetings recently held in Boston, to state some of the results of our studies and experience, and we desire here to say emphatically, that while on the one hand we yield an unqualified assent to that doctrine of universal unity which Fourier teaches, so on the other, our whole observation has shown us the truth of the practical arrangements which he deduces therefrom. The law of groups and series is, as we are convinced, the law of human nature, and when men are in true social relations their industrial organization will necessarily assume those forms.

121

But beside the demand for information respecting the principles of Association, there is a deeper call for action in the matter. We wish, therefore, to bring Brook Farm before the public, as a location offering at least as great advantages for a thorough experiment as can be found in the vicinity of Boston. It is situated in West Roxbury, three miles from the depot of the Dedham Branch Rail Road, and about eight miles from Boston, and combines a convenient nearness to the city with a degree of retirement and freedom from unfavorable influences, unusual even in the country. The place is one of great natural beauty, and indeed the whole landscape is so rich and various as to attract the notice even of casual visitors. The farm now owned by the Association contains two hundred and eight acres, of as good quality as any land in the neighborhood of Boston, and can be enlarged by the purchase of land adjoining to any necessary extent. The property now in the hands of the Association is worth nearly or quite thirty thousand dollars, of which about twenty-two thousand dollars is invested either in the stock of the company, or in permanent loans at six per cent, which can remain as long as the Association may wish.

The fact that so large an amount of capital is already invested and at our service as the basis of more extensive operations, furnishes a reason why Brook Farm should be chosen as the scene of that practical trial of association which the public feeling calls for in this immediate vicinity, instead of forming an entirely new organization for that purpose. The completeness of our educational department is also not to be overlooked. This has hitherto received our greatest care, and in forming it we have been particularly successful. In any new Association it must be many years before so many accomplished and skillful teachers in the various branches of intellectual culture could be enlisted. Another strong reason is to be found in the degree of order our organization has already attained, by the help of which a large Association might be formed without the losses and inconveniences which would otherwise necessarily occur. The experience of nearly three years in all the misfortunes and mistakes incident to an undertaking so new and so little understood, carried on throughout by persons not entirely fitted for the duties they have been compelled to perform, has, as we think, prepared us to assist in the safe conduct of an extensive and complete Association.

Such an institution, as will be plain to all, cannot by any sure means, be brought at once and full grown into existence. It must at least in the present state of society, begin with a comparatively small number of select and devoted persons, and increase by natural and gradual aggregations. With a view to an ultimate expansion into a perfect Phalanx, we desire without any delay to organize the three primary departments of labor, namely, Agriculture, Domestic Industry, and the Mechanic Arts.

For this purpose additional capital will be needed, which it is most desirable should be invested by those who propose to connect themselves personally with the institution. These should be men and women accustomed to labor, skilful, careful, in good health, and more than all imbued with the idea of Association, and ready to consecrate themselves without reserve to its realization. For it ought to be known that the work we propose is a difficult one, and except to the most entire faith and resolution will offer insurmountable obstacles and discouragements. Neither will it be possible to find in Association at the outset the great outward advantages it ultimately promises. The first few years must be passed in constant and unwearied labor, heightened chiefly by the consciousness of high aims and the inward content that devotion to a universal object cannot fail to bring. Still there are certain tangible compensations which Association guarantees immediately. These are freedom from pecuniary anxiety, and the evils of competitive industry, free and friendly society, and the education of children. How great these are, those who have felt the terrible burdens which the present civilized society imposes in these respects will not need to be informed.

Those who may wish to further this course by investments of money only will readily perceive that their end is not likely to be lost in an Association whose means are devoted mainly to productive industry, and where nothing will ever be risked in uncertain speculations.

The following Constitution is the same as that under which we have hitherto acted, with such alterations as on a careful revision seemed needful. All persons who are not familiar with the purposes of Association, will understand from this document that we propose a radical and universal reform, rather than to redress any particular wrong or to remove the sufferings of any single class of human beings. We do this in the light of universal principles, in which all differences, whether of religion, or politics, or philosophy, are reconciled, and the dearest and most private hope of every man has the promise of fulfilment. Herein, let it be understood, we would remove nothing that is truly beautiful or venerable; we reverence the religious sentiment in all its forms, the family, and whatever else has its foundation either in human nature or the Divine Providence. The work we are engaged in is not destruction, but true conservation: it is not a mere revolution, but, as we are assured, a necessary step in the course of social progress which no one can be blind enough to think has yet reached its limit. We believe that humanity, trained by these long centuries of suffering and struggle, led onward by so many saints and heroes and sages, is at length prepared to enter into that universal order, toward which it has perpetually moved. Thus we recognize the worth of the whole Past and of every doctrine and institution it has bequeathed us; thus also we perceive that the Present has its own high mission, and we shall only say what is beginning to be seen by all sincere thinkers, when we declare that the imperative duty of this time and this country, nay more, that its only salvation, and the salvation of all civilized countries, lies in the Reorganization of Society, according to the unchanging laws of human nature and of universal harmony.

We look, then, to the generous and hopeful of all classes for sympathy, for encouragement and for actual aid, not to ourselves only, but to all those who are engaged in this great work. And whatever may be the result of any special efforts, we can never doubt that the object we have in view will finally be attained; that human life shall yet be developed, not in discord and misery, but in harmony and joy, and that the perfected earth shall at last bear on her bosom a race of men worthy of the name.

> *George Ripley* ⎫
> *Minor Pratt* ⎬ Directors
> *Charles A. Dana* ⎭

Brook Farm, West Roxbury, Massachusetts
January 18, 1844

From The Complete Works of Ralph Waldo Emerson, *edited by* E. W. Emerson *(Boston: Houghton Mifflin & Co., 1904), vol. 10, pp. 359–69.*

The West Roxbury Association was formed in 1841, by a society of members, men and women, who bought a farm in West Roxbury, of about two hundred acres, and took possession of the place in April. Mr. George Ripley was the President, and I think Mr. Charles Dana (afterwards well known as one of the editors of the New York Tribune) was the Secretary. Many members took shares by paying money, others held shares by their labor. An old house on the place was enlarged, and three new houses built. William Allen was at first and for some time the head farmer, and the work was distributed in orderly committees to the men and women. There were many employments more or less lucrative found for, or brought hither by these members,—shoemakers, joiners, seamstresses. They had good scholars among them, and so received pupils for their education. The parents of the children in some instances wished to live there, and were received as boarders. Many persons, attracted by the beauty of the place and the culture and ambition of the community, joined them as boarders, and lived there for years. I think the numbers of this mixed community soon reached eighty or ninety souls.

It was a noble and generous movement in the projectors, to try an experiment of better living. They had the feeling that our ways of living were too conventional and expensive, not allowing each to do what he had a talent for, and not permitting men to combine cultivation of mind and heart with a reasonable amount of daily labor. At the same time, it was an attempt to lift others with themselves, and to share the advantages they should attain, with others now deprived of them.

There was no doubt great variety of character and purpose in the members of the community. It consisted in the main of young people, —few of middle age, and none old. Those who inspired and organized it were of course persons impatient of the routine, the uniformity, perhaps they would say the squalid contentment of society around them, which was so timid and skeptical of any progress. One would say then that impulse was the rule in the society, without centripetal balance; perhaps it would not be severe to say, intellectual sans-culottism, an impatience of the formal, routinary character of our educational, religious, social and economical life in Massachusetts. Yet there was immense hope in these young people. There was noble-ness; there were self-sacrificing victims who compensated for the levity and rashness of their companions. The young people lived a great deal in a short time, and came forth some of them perhaps with shattered constitutions. And a few grave sanitary influences of charac-ter were happily there, which I was assured, were always felt.

George W. Curtis of New York, and his brother, of English Oxford, were members of the family from the first. Theodore Parker, the near neighbor of the farm and the most intimate friend of Mr. Ripley, was a frequent visitor. Mr. Ichabod Morton of Plymouth, a plain man formerly engaged through many years in the fisheries with success, eccentric,—with a persevering interest in education, and of a very democratic religion, came and built a house on the farm, and he, or members of his family, continued there to the end. Margaret Fuller, with her joyful conversation and large sympathy, was often a guest, and always in correspondence with her friends. Many ladies, whom to name were to praise, gave character and varied attraction to the place.

In and around Brook Farm, whether as members, boarders or visi-tors, were many remarkable persons, for character, intellect or accom-plishments. I recall one youth of the subtlest mind, I believe I must say the subtlest observer and diviner of character I ever met, living, reading, writing, talking there, perhaps as long as the colony held to-gether; his mind fed and overfed by whatever is exalted in genius, whether in Poetry or Art, in Drama or Music, or in social accomplish-ment and elegancy; a man of no employment or practical aims, a stu-dent and philosopher, who found his daily enjoyment not with the elders or his exact contemporaries so much as with the fine boys who were skating and playing ball or bird-hunting; forming the closest friendships with such, and finding his delight in the petulant heroism of boys; yet was he the chosen counsellor to whom the guardians would repair on any hitch or difficulty that occurred, and draw from him a wise counsel. A fine, subtle, inward genius, puny in body and habit as a girl, yet with an *aplomb* like a general, never disconcerted. He lived and thought, in 1842, such worlds of life; all hinging on the thought of Being or Reality as opposed to consciousness; hating intel-lect with the ferocity of a Swedenborg. He was the Abbé or spiritual father, from his religious bias. His reading lay in Aeschylus, Plato, Dante, Calderon, Shakespeare, and in modern novels and romances of merit. There too was Hawthorne, with his cold yet gentle genius, if he failed to do justice to this temporary home. There was the accom-plished Doctor of Music [John S. Dwight], who has presided over its literature ever since in our metropolis. Rev. William Henry Channing, now of London, was from the first a student of Socialism in France and England, and in perfect sympathy with this experiment. An English baronet, Sir John Caldwell, was a frequent visitor, and more or less directly interested in the leaders and the success.

Hawthorne drew some sketches, not happily, as I think; I should rather say, quite unworthy of his genius. No friend who knew Margaret Fuller could recognize her rich and brilliant genius under the dismal mask which the public fancied was meant for her in that disagreeable story.

The Founders of Brook Farm should have this praise, that they made what all people try to make, an agreeable place to live in. All comers, even the most fastidious, found it the pleasantest of residences. It is certain that freedom from household routine, variety of character and talent, variety of work, variety of means of thought and instruction, art, music, poetry, reading, masquerade, did not permit sluggishness or despondency; broke up routine. There is agreement in the testimony that it was, to most of the associates, education; to many, the most important period of their life, the birth of valued friendships, their first acquaintance with the riches of conversation, their training in behavior. The art of letter-writing, it is said, was immensely cultivated. Letters were always flying not only from house to house, but from room to room. It was a perpetual picnic, a French Revolution in small, an Age of Reason in a patty-pan.

In the American social communities, the gossip found such vent and sway as to become despotic. The institutions were whispering galleries, in which the adored Saxon privacy was lost. Married women I believe uniformly decided against the community. It was to them like the brassy and lacquered life in hotels. The common school was well enough, but to the common nursery they had grave objections. Eggs might be hatched in ovens, but the hen on her own account much preferred the old way. A hen without her chickens was but half a hen.

It was a curious experience of the patrons and leaders of this noted community, in which the agreement with many parties was that they should give so many hours of instruction in mathematics, in music, in moral and intellectual philosophy, and so forth,—that in every instance the newcomers showed themselves keenly alive to the advantages of the society, and were sure to avail themselves of every means of instruction; their knowledge was increased, their manners refined,—but they became in that proportion averse to labor, and were charged by the heads of the departments with a certain indolence and selfishness.

In practice it is always found that virtue is occasional, spotty, and not linear or cubic. Good people are as bad as rogues if steady performance is claimed; the conscience of the conscientious runs in veins, and the most punctilious in some particulars are latitudinarian in others. It was very gently said that people on whom beforehand all persons would put the utmost reliance were not responsible. They saw the necessity that the work must be done, and did it not, and it of course fell to be done by the few religious workers. No doubt there was in many a certain strength drawn from the fury of dissent. Thus Mr. Ripley told Theodore Parker, "There is your accomplished friend—: he would hoe corn all Sunday if I would let him, but all Massachusetts could not make him do it on Monday."

Of course every visitor found that there was a comic side to this Paradise of shepherds and shepherdesses. There was a stove in every chamber, and every one might burn as much wood as he or she would saw. The ladies took cold on Washing-day; so it was ordained that the gentlemen-shepherds should wring and hang out clothes; which they punctually did. And it would sometimes occur that when they danced in the evening, clothespins dropped plentifully from their pockets. The country members naturally were surprised to observe that one man ploughed all day and one looked out of the window all day, and perhaps drew his picture, and both received at night the same wages. One would meet also some modest pride in their advanced condition, signified by a frequent phrase, "Before we came out of civilization."

The question which occurs to you had occurred much earlier to Fourier: "How in this charming Elysium is the dirty work to be done?" And long ago Fourier had exclaimed, "Ah! I have it," and jumped with joy. "Don't you see," he cried, "that nothing so delights the young Caucasian child as dirt? See the mud-pies that all children will make if you will let them. See how much more joy they find in pouring their pudding on the table-cloth than into their beautiful mouths. The children from six to eight, organized into companies with flags and uniforms, shall do this last function of civilization."

In Brook Farm was this peculiarity, that there was no head. In every family is the father; in every factory, a foreman; in a shop, a master; in a boat, the skipper; but in this Farm, no authority; each was master or mistress of his or her actions; happy, hapless anarchists. They expressed, after much perilous experience, the conviction that plain dealing was the best defence of manners and moral between the sexes. People cannot live together in any but necessary ways. The only candidates who will present themselves will be those who have tried the experiment of independence and ambition, and have failed; and none others will barter for the most comfortable equality the chance of superiority. Then all communities have quarrelled. Few people can live together on their merits. There must be kindred, or mutual economy, or a common interest in their business, or other external tie.

The society at Brook Farm existed, I think about six or seven years, and then broke up, the Farm was sold, and I believe all the partners came out with pecuniary loss. Some of them had spent on it the accumulations of years. I suppose they all, at the moment, regarded it as a failure. I do not think they can so regard it now, but probably as an important chapter in their experience which has been of life-long value. What knowledge of themselves and of each other, what various practical wisdom, what personal power, what studies of character, what accumulated culture many of the members owed to it! What mutual measure they took of each other! It was a close union, like that in a ship's cabin, of clergymen, young collegians, merchants, mechanics, farmers' sons and daughters, with men and women of rare opportunities and delicate culture, yet assembled there by a sentiment which all shared, some of them hotly shared, of the honesty of a life of labor and of the beauty of a life of humanity. The yeoman saw refined manners in persons who were his friends; and the lady or the romantic scholar saw the continuous strength and faculty in people who would have disgusted them but that these powers were now spent in the direction of their own theory of life. . . .

10

Cabet's "Pretty Dream"

ICARIA

The "Icaria" described below was one of seven attempts to realize the original "pretty dream" of the French utopian socialist Étienne Cabet (1788–1856). None of these ever achieved striking success, although some lasted longer than others.

The first attempt, made in 1848 by an avant-garde of Icarian enthusiasts who traveled all the way from France to Texas, after three months of struggle ended in dismal failure. Under the guidance of Cabet himself a second attempt, this time at Nauvoo, Illinois, finally succeeded in 1849, and this community survived for eleven years even though Cabet and a group of his followers were expelled after much political turmoil. With the blessing of the exiled leader, a third Icarian community was established at Cheltenham near St. Louis, Missouri, but this was the most short-lived of all Icarias, lasting only about six years. Corning, Iowa, was the locale of the fourth Icaria, which was the one visited by Charles Nordhoff, a nineteenth century observer of intentional communities. For many years this community remained stable and prospered, but finally the blight of schism hit the Icarians once again. A generation gap opened and widened; the younger communitarians claimed their elders had grown too conservative and individualistic, and demanded reforms. In 1878 the Corning community split, the young party forming "Young Icaria" and the elders, "New Icaria." The new (or old) Icarians eventually had the satisfaction of seeing their community outlast the young people's Icaria, which after planting a California community called Icaria Speranza (1881–86) soon expired.

Despite their rather disheartening history and meager achievement, the Icarian communities are of interest to students of utopian experimentation for several reasons. First, they represent a series of attempts to bring into actual existence a society based upon a literary utopia. For the Icarians, this was Cabet's *Voyage to Icaria* (1840) in which a complete vision of an ideal society had been presented. Although Cabet's original vision of a society in

130

which everyone lived by the motto "to each according to his need, from each according to his capacity" had to be radically modified in light of unanticipated obstacles and obvious impracticability, he and his followers never doubted the truth of his vision and remained convinced that someday it could and would be realized. Second, Icaria, unlike the majority of nineteenth-century American communitarian experiments, was not based on religious supernaturalism but sprang from a humanistic and rationalistic philosophy. To be sure, its citizens were at times imbued with a humanistic religious fervor, but their ideals were basically those of the French Enlightenment—liberty, equality, fraternity—and they hoped to achieve these through education, science, and reason rather than through faith and worship. Third, the history of the Icarian movement can be a valuable case study in why intentional communities fail. The liabilities inherent in a prefabricated "plan for utopia," the dangers of charismatic leadership without practical wisdom, and the pitfalls of both extreme individualism and extreme collectivism are some of the object lessons which are highlighted by Icaria's history. And, finally, the whole story of Icaria from its origin in France to its final extinction in California shows clearly and unforgettably the extent to which human beings will struggle, suffer, and sacrifice to promote a utopian ideal which captivates the imagination.

From *Charles Nordhoff*, The Communistic Societies of the United States (*New York: Harper and Brothers, 1875), pp. 333–39.*

Étienne Cabet had a pretty dream; this dream took hold of his mind, and he spent sixteen years of his life in trying to turn it into real life.

One can not help respecting the handful of men and women who, in the wilderness of Iowa, have for more than twenty years faithfully endeavored to work out the problem of Communism according to the system he left them; but Cabet's own writings persuade me that he was little more than a vain dreamer, without the grim patience and steadfast unselfishness which must rule the nature of one who wishes to found a successful communistic society.

Cabet was born at Dijon, in France, in 1788. He was educated for the bar, but became a politician and writer. He was a leader of the Carbonari; was a member of the French Legislature; wrote a history of the French Revolution of July; established a newspaper; was condemned to two year's imprisonment for an article in it, but evaded his sentence by flying to London; in 1839 returned to France, and published a history of the French Revolution in four volumes; and the next year issued a book somewhat famous in its day—the *Voyage to Icaria*. In this romance he described a communistic Utopia, whose terms he had dreamed out; and he began at once to try to realize his dream. He framed a constitution for an actual Icaria; sought for means and members to establish it; selected Texas as its field of operations, and early in 1848 actually persuaded a number of persons to set sail for the Red River country.

Sixty-nine persons formed the advance guard of his Utopia. They were attacked by yellow fever, and suffered greatly; and by the time next year when Cabet arrived at New Orleans with a second band, the first was already disorganized. He heard, on his arrival, that the Mormons had been driven from Nauvoo, in Illinois, leaving their town deserted; and in May, 1850, he established his followers there.

They bought at Nauvoo houses sufficient to accommodate them, but very little land, renting such farms as they needed. They lived there on a communal system, and ate in a great dining-room. But Cabet, I have been told, did not intend to form his colony perma-

132

nently there, but regarded Nauvoo only as a rendezvous for those who should join the community, intending to draft them thence to the real settlements, which he wished to found in Iowa.

If Cabet had been a leader of the right temper, he might, I believe, have succeeded; for he appears to have secured the only element indispensable to success—a large number of followers. He had at Nauvoo at one time not less than fifteen hundred people. With so many members, a wise leader with business skill ought to be able to accomplish very much in a single year; in ten years his commune, if he could keep it together, ought to be wealthy.

The Icarians labored and planted with success at Nauvoo; they established trades of different kinds, as well as manufactures; and Cabet set up a printing-office, and issued a number of books and pamphlets in French and German, intended to attract attention to the community. Among these, a pamphlet of twelve pages, entitled, "Wenn ich $500,000 hätte" ("If I had half a million dollars"), which bears date Nauvoo, 1854, gives in some detail his plans and desires. It is a statement of what he could and would achieve for a commune if some one would start him with a capital of half. a million; and the fact that four years after he came to Nauvoo he should still have spent his time in such an impracticable dream, shows, I think, that he was not a fit leader for the enterprise. For nothing appears to me more certain than that a communistic society, to be successful, needs above all things to have the training, mental and physical, which comes out of a life of privation, spent in the patient accumulation of property by the labors of the members.

Moreover, in Cabet's first paragraph he shows contempt for one of the vital principles of a communistic society. "If I had five hundred thousand dollars," he writes, "this would open to us an immense credit, and in this way vastly increase our means." But it is absolutely certain that debt is the bane of such societies; and the remnant of Icarians who have so tenaciously and bravely held together in Iowa would be the first to confess this, for they suffered hardships for years because of debt.

If he had half a million, Cabet goes on to say, he would be able to establish his commune upon a broad and generous scale; and he draws a pretty picture of dwellings supplied with gas and hot and cold water; of factories fitted up on the largest scale; of fertile farms under the best culture; of schools, high and elementary; of theatres, and other places of amusement; of elegantly kept pleasure-grounds, and so on. Alas for the dreams of a dreamer! I turned over the leaves of his pamphlet while wondering through the muddy lanes of the present Icaria, on one chilly Sunday in March, with a keen sense of pain at the contrast between the comfort and elegance he so glowingly described and the dreary poverty of the life which a few determined men and women have there chosen to follow, for the sake of principles which they hold both true and valuable.

I have heard that Cabet developed at Nauvoo a dictatorial spirit, and that this produced in time a split in the society. The leader and his adherents went off to St. Louis, where he died in 1856. Meantime some of the members were already settled in Iowa, and those who remained at Nauvoo after Cabet's desertion or flight dispersed; the property was sold, and the Illinois colony came to an end. The greater part of the members went off, more or less disappointed. Between fifty and sixty settled upon the Iowa estate, and here began life, very poor and with a debt of twenty thousand dollars in some way fixed upon their land.

Their narrow means allowed them to build at first only the meanest mud hovels. They thought themselves prosperous when they were able to build log-cabins, though these were so wretched that comfort must have been unknown among them for years. They were obliged to raise all that they consumed; and they lived, and indeed still live, in the narrowest way.

The Icarian Commune lies about four miles from Corning, a station on the Burlington and Missouri River Railroad, in Iowa. They began here with four thousand acres of land, pretty well selected, and twenty thousand dollars of debt. After some years of struggle they gave up the land to their creditors, with the condition that they might redeem one half of it within a certain stipulated time. This they were able to do by hard work and pinching economy; and they own at present one thousand nine hundred and thirty-six acres, part of which is in timber, and valuable on that account.

There are in all sixty-five members, and eleven families. The families are not large, for there are twenty children and only twenty-three voters in the community.

They possess a saw-mill and grist-mill, built out of their savings within five years, and now a source of income. They cultivate three hundred and fifty acres of land, and have one hundred and twenty head of cattle, five hundred head of sheep, two hundred and fifty hogs, and thirty horses. Until within three years the settlement contained only log-cabins, and these very small, and not commodiously arranged. Since then they have got entirely out of debt, and have begun to build frame houses. The most conspicuous of these is a two-story building, sixty by twenty-four feet in dimensions, which contains the common dining-room, kitchen, a provision cellar, and upstairs a room for a library, and apartments for a family. In the spring of 1874 they had nearly a dozen frame houses, which included the dining-hall, a wash-house, dairy, and school-house. All the dwellings are small and very cheaply built. They have small shops for carpentry, blacksmithing, wagonmaking, and shoemaking; and they make, as far as possible, all they use.

Most of the people are French, and this is the language mainly spoken, though I found that German was also understood. Besides the French, there are among the members one American, one Swiss, a Swede, and a Spaniard, and two Germans. The children look remarkably healthy, and on Sunday were dressed with great taste. The living is still of the plainest. In the common dining-hall they assemble in groups at the tables, which were without a cloth, and they drink out of tin cups, and pour their water from tin cans. "It is very plain," said one to me; "but we are independent—no man's servants—and we are content."

They sell about two thousand five hundred pounds of wool each year, and a certain number of cattle and hogs; and these, with the earnings of their mills, are the sources of their income.

Their number does not increase, though four or five years ago they were reduced to thirty members; but since then seven who went off have returned. I should say that they had passed over the hardest times, and that a moderate degree of prosperity is possible to them now; but they have waited long for it. I judge that they had but poor skill in management and no business talent; but certainly they had abundant courage and determination.

They live under a somewhat elaborate constitution, made for them by Cabet, which lays down with great care the equality and brotherhood of mankind, and the duty of holding all things in common; abolishes servitude and service (or servants); commands marriage, under penalties; provides for education; and requires that the majority shall rule. In practice they elect a president once a year, who is the executive officer, but whose powers are strictly limited to carrying out the commands of the society. "He could not even sell a bushel of corn without instructions," said one to me. Every Saturday evening they hold a meeting of all the adults, women as well as men, for the discussion of business and other affairs. Officers are chosen at every meeting to preside and keep the records; the president may present subjects for discussion; and women may speak, but have no vote. The conclusions of the meeting are to rule the president during the next week. All accounts are made up monthly, and presented to the society for discussion and criticism. Besides the president, there are four directors —of agriculture, clothing, general industry, and building. These carry on the necessary work, and direct the other members. They buy at wholesale twice a year, and just before these purchases are made each member in public meeting makes his or her wants known. Luxury is prohibited in the constitution, but they have not been much tempted in that direction so far. They use tobacco, however.

They have no religious observances. Sunday is a day of rest from labor, when the young men go with guns, and the society sometimes has theatrical representations, or music, or some kind of amusement. The principle is to let each one do as he pleases.

They employ two or three hired men to chop wood and labor on the farm.

They have a school for the children, the president being teacher.

The people are opposed to what is called a "unitary home," and prefer to have a separate dwelling for each family.

The children are kept in school until they are sixteen; and the people lamented their poverty, which prevented them from providing better education for them.

Members are received by a three-fourths' majority.

This is Icaria. It is the least prosperous of all the communities I have visited; and I could not help feeling pity, if not for the men, yet for the women and children of the settlement, who have lived through all the penury and hardship of these many years. A gentlemen who knew of my visit there writes me: "Please deal gently and cautiously with Icaria. The man who sees only the chaotic village and the wooden shoes, and only chronicles those, will commit a serious error. In that village are buried fortunes, noble hopes, and the aspiration of good and great men like Cabet. Fertilized by these deaths, a great and beneficent growth yet awaits Icaria. It has an eventful and extremely interesting history, but its future is destined to be still more interesting. It, and it alone, represents in America a great idea— rational democratic communism."

I am far from belittling the effort of the men of Icaria. They have shown, as I have said, astonishing courage and perseverance. They have proved their faith in the communistic idea by labors and suffering which seem to me pitiful. In fact, communism is their religion. But their long siege at fortune's door only shows how important, and indeed indispensable to the success of such an effort, it is to have an able leader, and to give to him almost unlimited power and absolute obedience.

11

Free Love and Bible Communism

ONEIDA

The founder of the Oneida Community, John Humphrey Noyes (1811–1886), liked to think of his utopia as a transmigration of Brook Farm, which had ceased to exist in 1847, the same year Oneida was born. "As Unitarianism ripened into Transcendentalism at Boston, and Transcendentalism produced Brook Farm," Noyes wrote, "so Orthodoxy ripened into Perfectionism at New Haven, and Perfectionism produced the Oneida Community."[1]

In the new earthly paradise, which was located in the very center of New York State not far from Utica, Noyes attempted to join the assets of revivalism with the advantages of socialism. He was convinced that the Second Coming of Christ had already occurred, and that consequently he and other genuine Christians could declare themselves to be liberated from sin; in a word, saved. Along with this "Perfectionism," Noyes preached "Bible Communism," the tenets of which he set down in a book by that name published a few months after he founded Oneida. The justification of Communism, he claimed, could readily be found in the Christian New Testament, which urged believers to be "of one heart and of one soul" and to live in a way that "they had all things common." As images of God, human beings should live in a unity like that of the Father and the Son: "All mine thine, and all thine mine."

But Noyes gave this doctrine a new and radical interpretation that separated him sharply from previous Christian socialists and led him and his followers to a practice that stirred up violent controversy with the outside world. He argued that as there was no real difference between owning things and owning persons, "the same spirit which abolished exclusiveness in regard to money, would abolish, if circumstances allowed full scope to it, exclusiveness in regard to women and children."[2] On supposedly Christian grounds,

[1] Noyes, *American Socialisms*, p. 614.
[2] Ibid., p. 625.

137

Noyes proceeded to take the step which Plato had proposed long before on philosophical grounds.

Common possession of women and children soon became a reality at Oneida in accordance with Noyes's unique plan of "Multiple Marriage." Loving one another, he taught, meant not loving by pairs but *en masse*. The new kind of group marriage, in which "each was married to all," would have, Noyes argued, several important advantages over the old. It would permit a wider and richer range of satisfaction for "amative" or love impulses. It would reduce rather than encourage adultery by not forcing incompatible persons to remain together. And finally, it would allow for young people to satisfy their sexual needs sooner than in conventional marriage.

The "free love" which was thus brought about by "reforming" the institution of marriage should not, Noyes contended, be confused with licentiousness. In his view, "Multiple Marriages," unlike licentious relations, were permanent unions; they were responsible relations based on love rather than on mere lust; and they provided for the support and education of any children which resulted from such unions.

> Free love with us does *not* mean freedom to love today and leave tomorrow; nor freedom to take a woman's person and keep our property to ourselves; nor freedom to freight a woman with her offspring and send her down stream without care or help; not to regret children and leave them to the street and the poorhouse. Our community are *families*, as distinctly bounded and separated from promiscuous society as ordinary households.[3]

Noyes was particularly concerned with restoring what he considered to be the "true relations" between the sexes because he believed this to be a matter "second in importance only to the reconciliation of man to God." Out of the first social relation, that of a male and female (i.e. Adam and Eve) sprang all other social relations. The original breach with God resulted in a derangement of the first as well as all other human relationships. As Noyes saw it, the problem of establishing the kingdom of God on earth was first one of religion and second one of sexual morality, both of which could be solved only through adherence to his gospel of Perfectionism and Bible Communism. "The true scheme of redemption," he preached, "begins with reconciliation with God, proceeds first to a restoration of true relations between the sexes, then to a reform of the industrial system, and ends with victory over death."[4] He criticized Fourierism for confining itself primarily to reforming the industrial system while neglecting or ignoring the other vital links of the interconnected social chain. Noyes was convinced that "the sin-system, the marriage system, the work-system, and the death-system, were all one, and must be abolished together."[5] For, as he put it, "holiness, free-love, association in labor, and immortality, constituted the chain of redemption, and must come together in their true order."[6]

---

[3] Ibid., p. 639.
[4] Ibid., p. 630.
[5] Ibid.
[6] Ibid., pp. 630–31.

Guided by the charismatic "Father" Noyes, the "family" of devout free lovers at Oneida enjoyed for over thirty years a life of secure happiness and peaceful prosperity in their "Heavenly Association." In helping his flock achieve the goals of his utopia—"Unity, Organization, and Self-Improvement"—Noyes found it necessary to introduce several novel social practices which, to his delight, the Oneidans enthusiastically adopted. The first of these was a self-imposed discipline which was called "Male Continence." This allowed men and women to enjoy "amative" or erotic love independently of "propagative love." In other words, it was a form of birth control. Later, however, they were asked by their leader to forgo continence in order to participate in "a planned scientific procreation" which he called "stirpiculture." Fifty-three young women volunteered for the experiment, and eventually fifty-eight "stirpiculture babies" were produced as a result of the careful matching of the supposedly best males with the best females by Dr. Noyes and a committee.

A third important innovation was "Mutual Criticism." This was the practice by which members criticized one another freely from time to time in order to correct everyone's faults and shortcomings. Noyes regarded this practice as an instrument of good government, a means for moral improvement and fellowship, and a substitute for backbiting. He and his fellow Oneidans also occasionally resorted to it as a kind of therapy, which Noyes labeled "krinopathy" and it was sometimes used to treat injuries, ailments, and disease.

The following firsthand account of Oneida, written by Charles Nordhoff, describes the community as it existed in the 1870's before it abandoned "Bible Communism" and transformed itself into a joint stock company, Oneida Community, Ltd. This transformation, which took place in 1881, was the result of both internal dissension and external pressure. By that time, Oneida's aged and ailing founder Noyes had already gone into exile to avoid persecution, but it was he who directed and approved from afar what he considered to be a necessary but disappointing change in his utopia's form and substance. Today Oneida, Ltd. still exists, and is well known as a manufacturer of silverware.

From Charles Nordhoff, The Communistic Societies of the United States *(New York: Harper and Brothers, 1875), pp. 277–87; 275–77, with omissions.*

The farm, or domain, as they prefer to call it, of the Oneida Community forms a part of the old Reservation of the Oneida Indians. It is a plain, the land naturally good and well watered; and it has been industriously improved by the communists. It lies four miles from Oneida on the New York Central Railroad, and the Midland Railroad passes through it.

The dwelling-house, a large brick building with some architectural pretensions, but no artistic merit, stands on the middle of a pleasant lawn, near the main road. It has some extensions in the rear, the chief of which is a large wing containing the kitchen and dining-room. The interior of the house is well arranged; the whole is warmed by steam; and there are baths and other conveniences. There is on the second floor a large hall, used for the evening gatherings of the community, and furnished with a stage for musical and dramatic performances, and with a number of round tables, about which they gather in their meetings. On the ground floor is a parlor for visitors; and a library-room, containing files of newspapers, and a miscellaneous library of about four thousand volumes.

There are two large family rooms, one on each story, around which a considerable number of sleeping-chambers are built; and the upper of these large rooms has two ranges of such dormitories, one above the other, the upper range being reached by a gallery.

All the rooms are plainly furnished, there being neither any attempt at costly or elegant furnishing, nor a striving for Shaker plainness.

Above the dining-room is the printing-office, where the *Circular* is printed, and some job printing is done.

Opposite the dwelling, and across the road, are offices, a school-building, a lecture-room with a chemical laboratory, and a room for the use of the daguerreotypist of the community; farther on to the right is a large carpenter's shop, and to the left are barns, stables, the silk-dye house, and a small factory where the children of the community at odd hours make boxes for the spool silk produced here. There is also a large and conveniently arranged laundry.

Somewhat over a mile from the home place are the factories of the community—consisting of trap works, silk works, a forge, and machine shops. These are thoroughly fitted with labor-saving machinery, and are extensive enough to produce three hundred thousand traps, and the value of over two hundred thousand dollars' worth of silk-twist in a year. Near these workshops is a dwelling inhabited by thirty or forty of the communists, who are particularly employed in the shops.

The farm has been put in excellent order: there are extensive orchards of large and small fruits; and plantations of ornamental trees shelter the lawn about the dwelling. This lawn is in summer a favorite resort for picnic parties from a distance. As Sunday-school picnics are also brought hither, I judge that the hostility which once existed in the neighborhood to the Oneida Communists has disappeared. Indeed, at Oneida all with whom I had occasion to speak concerning the communists praised them for honesty, fair dealing, a peaceable disposition, and great business capacity.

Their system of administration is perfect and thorough. Their book-keeping—in which women are engaged as well as men, a young woman being the chief—is so systematized that they are able to know the profit or loss upon every branch of industry they pursue, as well as the cost of each part of their living.

They have twenty-one standing committees: on finance; amusements; patent-rights; location of tenant houses; arbitration; rents; baths, walks, roads, and lawns; fire; heating; sanitary; education; clothing; real estate and tenant houses; water-works and their supplies; painting; forest; water and steam power; photographs; hair-cutting; arcade; and Joppa—the last being an isolated spot on Oneida Lake, to which they go to bathe, fish, shoot, and otherwise ruralize.

Besides these, they divide the duties of administration among forty-eight departments: *Circular*; publication; silk manufacture; hardware; fruit-preserving; paper-box; printing; dyeing; carpentry; business office; shoe shop; library; photographs; educational; science and art; laundry; furniture; legal; subsistence; Wallingford printing; agriculture; horticulture; medical; incidentals; dentistry; real estate; musical; amusements; quarry; housekeeping; repairs; traveling; watches; clocks; tin shop; porterage; lights; livery; clothing; stationery; floral; water-works; children's; landscape; forests; heating; bedding; coal.

At first view these many committees and departments may appear cumbrous; but in practice they work well.

Every Sunday morning a meeting is held of what is called a "Business Board." This consists of the heads of all the departments, and of whoever, of the whole community, chooses to attend. At this meeting the business of the past week is discussed; and a secretary notes down briefly any action deemed advisable. At the Sunday evening meeting the secretary's report is read to all, and thereupon discussed; and whatever receives general or unanimous approval is carried out.

Once a year, in the spring, there is a special meeting of the Business Board, at which the work of the year is laid out in some detail.

At the beginning of the year an inventory is taken of all the possessions of the community.

Once a month the heads of the departments send in their accounts to the book-keepers, and these are then posted in the ledgers.

It is a principle with them to attempt nothing without the general consent of all the people; and if there is objection made, the matter proposed is put off for further discussion.

Shortly after New-Year, the Finance Committee sits and receives estimates. This means that each department sends in an estimate of the money it will require for the coming year. At the same time any one who has a project in his head may propose it, with an estimate of its cost. Thereupon the Finance Committee makes the necessary appropriations, revising the estimates in accordance with the general total which the society can afford to spend for the year. At or before this meeting the returns for the past year have been scrutinized.

All appointments on committees are made for a year; but there is a committee composed of men and women whose duty it is to appoint different persons to their work; and these may change the employments at any time. In practice, the foremen of the manufacturing establishments are not frequently changed. In appointing the labor of the members, their tastes as well as abilities are consulted, and the aim is to make each one contented.

The appointment of so many committees makes some one responsible for each department, and when any thing is needed, or any fault is to be found, the requisition can be directed to a particular person. Women, equally with men, serve on the committees.

They rise in the morning between five and half-past seven; this depending somewhat upon the business each is engaged in. The children sleep as long as they like. Breakfast is from eight to nine, and dinner from three to four; and they retire from half-past eight to half-past ten. The members do not now work very hard, as will appear from these hours; but they are steadily industrious; and as most of them superintend some department, and all of them work cheerfully, the necessary amount of labor is accomplished. Mere drudgery they nowadays put upon their hired people.

A square board, placed in a gallery near the library, tells at a glance where every body is. It contains the names of the men and women at the side, and the places where they can be found at the head; and a peg, which each one sticks in opposite his name, tells his whereabouts for the day.

There is no bell or other signal for proceeding to work; but each one is expected to attend faithfully to that which is given him or her to do; and here, as in other communities, no difficulty is found about idlers. Those who have disagreeable tasks are more frequently changed than others. Thus the women who superintend in the kitchen usually serve but a month, but sometimes two months at a time.

Children are left to the care of their mothers until they are weaned; then they are put into a general nursery under the care of special nurses or care-takers, who are both men and women. There are two of these nurseries, one for the smaller children, the other for those above three or four years of age, and able somewhat to help themselves. These eat at the same time with the older people, and are seated at tables by themselves in the general dining-room. The children I saw were plump, and looked sound; but they seemed to me a little subdued and desolate, as though they missed the exclusive love and care of a father and mother. This, however, may have been only fancy; though I should grieve to see in the eyes of my own little ones an expression which I thought I saw in the Oneida children, difficult to describe—perhaps I might say a lack of buoyancy, or confidence and gladness. A man or woman may not find it disagreeable to be part of a great machine, but I suspect it is harder for a little child. However, I will not insist on this, for I may have been mistaken. I have seen, with similar misgivings, a lot of little chickens raised in an egg-hatching machine, and having a blanket for shelter instead of the wing of a mother: I thought they missed the cluck and the vigilant if sometimes severe care of the old hen. But after all they grew up to be hearty chickens, as zealous and greedy, and in the end as useful as their more particularly nurtured fellows.

In the dining-hall I noticed an ingenious contrivance to save trouble to those who wait on the table. The tables are round, and accommodate ten or twelve people each. There is a stationary rim, having space for the plates, cups, and saucers; and within this is a revolving disk, on which the food is placed, and by turning this about each can help himself.

They do not eat much meat, having it served not more than twice a week. Fruits and vegetables make up the greater part of their diet. They use tea, and coffee mixed with malt, which makes an excellent beverage. They use no tobacco, nor spirituous liquors.

The older people have separate sleeping-chambers; the younger usually room two together.

The men dress as people in the world do, but plainly, each one following his own fancy. The women wear a dress consisting of a bodice, loose trousers, and a short skirt falling to just above the knee. Their hair is cut just below the ears, and I noticed that the younger women usually gave it a curl. The dress is no doubt extremely convenient: it admits of walking in mud or snow, and allows freedom of exercise; and it is entirely modest. But it was to my unaccustomed eyes totally and fatally lacking in grace and beauty. The present dress of women, prescribed by fashion, and particularly the abominable false hair and the preposterously ugly hats, are sufficiently barbarous; but the Oneida dress, which is so scant that it forbids any graceful arrangement of drapery, seemed to me no improvement.

As they have no sermons nor public prayers, so they have no peculiar mode of addressing each other. The men are called Mr., and the women Miss, except when they were married before they entered the society. It was somewhat startling to me to hear Miss ——— speak about her baby. Even the founder is addressed or spoken of simply as Mr. Noyes.

At the end of every year each person gives into the Finance Board a detailed statement of what clothing he or she requires for the coming year, and upon the aggregate sum is based the estimate for the next year for clothing. . . .

When a man needs a suit of clothes, he goes to the tailor and is measured, choosing at the same time the stuff and the style or cut.

There is a person called familiarly "Incidentals." To him is intrusted a fund for incidental and unforeseen expenses; and when a young woman wants a breast-pin—the only ornament worn—she applies to "Incidentals." When any one needs a watch, he makes his need known to the committee on watches.

For the children they have a sufficiently good school, in which the Bible takes a prominent part as a text-book. The young people are encouraged to continue their studies, and they have two or three classes in history, one in grammar, and several in French, Latin, geology, etc. These study and recite at odd times; and it is their policy not to permit the young men and women to labor too constantly. The Educational Committee superintends the evening classes.

They also cultivate vocal and instrumental music; and have several times sent one or two of their young women to New York to receive special musical instruction. Also for some years they have kept several of their young men in the Yale scientific school, and in other departments of that university. Thus they have educated two of their members to be physicians; two in the law; one in mechanical engineering; one in architecture; and others in other pursuits. Usually these have been young men from twenty-two to twenty-five years of age, who had prepared themselves practically beforehand.

It is their habit to change their young people from one employment to another, and thus make each master of several trades. The young women are not excluded from this variety; and they have now several girls learning the machinists' trade, in a building appropriated to this purpose; and their instructor told me they were especially valuable for the finer and more delicate kinds of lathework. A young man whom they sent to the Sheffield scientific school to study mechanical engineering had been for a year or two in the machine shop before he went to Yale; he is now at the head of the silk works. Their student in architecture had in the same way prepared himself in their carpenter's shop.

No one who visits a communistic society which has been for some time in existence can fail to be struck with the amount of ingenuity, inventive skill, and business talent developed among men from whom, in the outer world, one would not expect such qualities. This is true, too, of the Oneida Communists. They contrived all the machinery they use for making traps—one very ingenious piece making the links for the chains. They had no sooner begun to work in silk than they invented a little toy which measures the silk thread as it is wound on spools, and accurately gauges the number of yards; and another which tests the strength of silk; and these have come into such general use that they already make them for sale.

So, too, when they determined to begin the silk manufacture, they sent one of their young men and two women to work as hands in a well-managed factory. In six months these returned, having sufficiently mastered the business to undertake the employment and instruction of hired operatives. Of the machinery they use, they bought one set and made all the remainder upon its pattern, in their own foundry and shops. A young man who had studied chemistry was sent out to a dye-house, and in a few months made himself a competent dyer. In all this complicated enterprise they made so few mistakes that in six months after they began to produce silk-twist their factory had a secure reputation in the market.

It is their custom to employ their people, where they have responsible places, in couples. Thus there are two house stewards, two foremen in a factory, etc.; both having equal knowledge, and one always ready to take the other's place if he finds the work wearing upon him.

They seemed to me to have an almost fanatical horror of forms

Thus they change their avocations frequently; they remove from Oneida to Willow Place, or to Wallingford, on slight excuses; they change the order of their evening meetings and amusements with much care; and have changed even their meal hours. One said to me, "We used to eat three meals a day—now we eat but two; but we may be eating five six months from now."

Very few of their young people have left them; and some who have gone out have sought to return. They have expelled but one person since the community was organized. While they received members, they exacted no probationary period, but used great care before admission. Mr. Noyes said on this subject:

> There has been a very great amount of discrimination and vigilance exercised by the Oneida Community from first to last in regard to our fellowships, and yet it seems to me it is one of the greatest miracles that this community has succeeded as it has. Notwithstanding our discrimination and determination to wait on God in regard to those we receive, we scarcely have been saved.

New members sign a paper containing the creed, and also an agreement to claim no wages or other reward for their labor while in the community. . . .

Concerning their management of the intercourse of the sexes, so much has been written, by themselves and by others, that I think I need say only that—

1st. They regard their system as part of their religion. Noyes said, in a "Home Talk," reported in the *Circular*, February 2, 1874: "Woe to him who abolishes the law of the apostasy before he stands in the holiness of the resurrection. The law of the apostasy is the law of marriage; and it is true that whoever undertakes to enter into the liberty of the resurrection without the holiness of the resurrection, will get woe and not happiness. It is as important for the young now as it was for their fathers then, that they should know that holiness of heart is what they must have before they get liberty in love. They must put the first thing first, as I did and as their parents did; they must be *Perfectionists* before they are *Communists.*" He seems to see, too, that "complex marriage," as he calls it, is not without grave dangers to the community, for he added, in the same "Home Talk": "We have got into the position of Communism, where without genuine salvation from sin our passions will overwhelm us, and nothing but confusion and misery can be expected. On the other hand, we have got into a position where, if we do have the grace of God triumphant in our hearts and flowing through all our nature, there is an opportunity for harmony and happiness beyond all that imagination has conceived. So it is hell behind us, and heaven before us, and a necessity that we should *march!*"

2nd. "Complex marriage" means, in their practice: that, within the limits of the community membership, any man and woman may and do freely cohabit, having first gained each other's consent, not by private conversation or courtship, but through the intervention of some third person or persons; that they strongly discourage, as an evidence of sinful selfishness, what they call "exclusive and idolatrous attachment" of two persons for each other, and aim to break up by "criticism" and other means every thing of this kind in the community; that they teach the advisability of pairing persons of different ages, the young of one sex with the aged of the other, and as the matter is under the control and management of the more aged members it is thus arranged; that "persons are not obliged, under any circumstances, to receive the attentions of those whom they do not like;" and that the propagation of children is controlled by the society, which pretends to conduct this matter on scientific principles: "Previous to about two and a half years ago we refrained from the usual rate of child-bearing, for several reasons, financial and otherwise. Since that time we have made an attempt to produce the usual number of offspring to which people in the middle classes are able to afford judicious moral and spiritual care, with the advantage of a liberal education. In this attempt twenty-four men and twenty women have been engaged, selected from among those who have most thoroughly practiced our social theory."[1]

Finally, they find in practice a strong tendency toward what they call "selfish love"—that is to say, the attachment of two persons to each other, and their desire to be true to each other; and there are here and there in their publications signs that there has been suffering among their young people on this account. They rebuke this propensity, however, as selfish and sinful, and break it down rigorously.

[1] "Essay on Scientific Propagation," by John Humphrey Noyes (Oneida, New York: The Oneida Community, n.d.).

12

Why Utopias Fail

A SURVEY AND AN EXAMPLE, MORNING STAR

In the following selections the question crucial both to planners of utopias or "intentional communities" and to their critics is raised: Why have such experiments so often ended in failure?

John Humphrey Noyes, founder of Oneida, calls attention primarily to one factor—the supposed imperfection of human nature—which to him accounts for the transitoriness of most of the communities he studied. His position entails an assumption about human nature, that it is "depraved"; as well as an oversimplification, that one factor alone can bring about the failure of a community.

There are numerous other factors which undoubtedly have played a part in bringing about the failure of various utopian experiments. Some of these factors have already been mentioned in considering specific utopias. The hostility of the outside world or surrounding society to a new and perhaps controversial communal experiment such as the one described below by Kenneth Lamott can lead to strong economic, political, or even military sanctions upon the community, which make it difficult if not impossible for it to survive. An unexpected disaster, such as the burning of the Brook Farm phalanstery, can produce an economic or moral crisis which can bring a utopian experiment to an abrupt end. A failure to select members with the financial, physical, intellectual, moral, or other attributes necessary for a certain type of utopian experiment, or (what amounts to the same thing) the indiscriminate admission of all comers by a new community, can lead to its deterioration and destruction. Incompetent leadership, the loss of an able or charismatic leader, or the failure to make provisions for transferring or perpetuating the power of leadership can also contribute to the eventual extinction of a once flourishing utopian community. Sometimes the society in which a utopian community exists may "catch up" with or even surpass the quality of life prevalent in the utopia, thus rendering it obsolete. Or, a sudden or radical change—a war, an economic crisis, a new invention, the passage of a new law—can wreak havoc in the life of a utopia. Utopias have also gone out of existence because older members have lost their original zeal, or because younger members have left to seek money or adventure in the outside world, or simply because the whole membership for some reason has decided to disperse. And these reasons by no means exhaust the possibilities in explaining the failure of utopian experiments.

But what of the successes? How are they to be accounted for? Why did some utopias last longer than others and some even achieve relatively long-lasting success (e.g. the Shakers)? Noyes believed that religion was always the key integrating force in every successful utopian experiment. Other students of successful utopian communities have discussed the importance of one or more of these additional factors: charismatic leadership, sound economic planning, careful selection and thorough indoctrination of new members of a community, skillful public relations with the outside world, and provisions for innovation and change.

More recently, scholars with a knowledge of sociology have centered their attention on the kind of commitment characteristic in successful utopian experiments and have attempted to discover the mechanisms by means of which this commitment to the basic ideals or value system of the utopia has been achieved, sustained, and perpetuated.

From John Humphrey Noyes, History of American Socialisms *(Philadelphia: J. B. Lippincott, 1870), pp. 646–57.*

Looking back now over the entire course of this history, we discover a remarkable similarity in the symptoms that manifested themselves in the transitory Communities, and almost entire unanimity in the witnesses who testify as to the causes of their failure. GENERAL DEPRAVITY, all say, is the villain of the whole story.

In the first place Macdonald himself, after "seeing stern reality," confesses that in his previous hopes of Socialism he "had imagined mankind better than they are."

Then Owen, accounting for the failure at New Harmony, says, "he wanted honesty, and he got dishonesty; he wanted temperance, and instead he was continually troubled with the intemperate; he wanted cleanliness, and he found dirt," and so on.

The Yellow Spring Community, though composed of "very superior class," found in the short space of three months, that "self-love was a spirit that would not be exorcised. Individual happiness was the law of nature, and it could not be obliterated; and before a single year had passed, this law had scattered the members of that society which had come together so earnestly and under such favorable circumstances, back into the selfish world from which they came."

The trustees of the Nashoba Community, in aband ning Frances Wright's original plan of common property, acknowledge their conviction that such a system can not succeed "without the members composing it are superior beings. That which produces in the world only commonplace jealousies and every-day squabbles, is sufficient to destroy a Community."

The spokesman of the Haverstraw Community at first attributes their failure to the "dishonesty of the managers"; but afterward settles down into the more general complaint that they lacked "men and women of skillful industry, sober and honest, with a knowledge of themselves and a disposition to command and be commanded," and intimates that "the sole occupation of the men and women they had, was parade and talk."

The historian of the Coxsackie Community says "they had many

150

persons engaged in talking and law-making, who did not work at any useful employment. The consequences were, that after struggling on for between one and two years, the experiment came to an end. There were few good men to steer things right."

Warren found that the friction that spoiled his experiments was "the want of common honesty."

Ballou complained that "the timber he got together was not suitable for building a Community. The men and women that joined him were very enthusiastic and commenced with great zeal; their devotion to the cause seemed to be sincere; but they did not know themselves."

At the meetings that dissolved the Northampton Community, "some spoke of the want of that harmony and brotherly feeling, which were indispensable to success; others spoke of the unwillingness to make sacrifices on the part of some of the members; also of the lack of industry and the right appropriation of time."

Collins lived in a quarrel with a rival during nearly the whole life of his Community, and finally gave up the experiment from "a conviction that the theory of Communism could not be carried out in practice; that the attempt was premature, the time had not yet arrived, and the necessary conditions did not yet exist." His experience led him to the conclusion that "there is floating upon the surface of society, a body of restless, disappointed, jealous, indolent spirits, disgusted with our present social system, not because it enchains the masses to poverty, ignorance, vice, and endless servitude; but because they can not render it subservient to their private ends. Experience shows that this class stands ready to mount every new movement that promises ease, abundance, and individual freedom; and that when such an enterprise refuses to interpret license for freedom, and insists that every member shall make their strength, skill and talent, subservient to the movement, then the cry of tyranny and oppression is raised against those who advocate such industry and self-denial; then the enterprise must become a scape-goat, to bear the fickleness, indolence, selfishness, and envy of this class."

The testimony in regard to the Sylvania Association is, that "young men wasted the good things at the commencement of the experiment; and besides victuals, dry-goods supplied by the Association were unequally obtained. Idle and greedy people find their way into such attempts, and soon show forth their character by burdening others with too much labor, and, in times of scarcity, supplying themselves with more than their allowance of various necessaries, instead of taking less."

The failure of the One Mentian Community is attributed to "ignorance and disagreements," and that of the Social Reform Unity to "lack of wisdom and general preparation."

The Leraysville Phalanx went to pieces in a grumble about management.

Of the Clarkson Association a writer in the *Phalanx* says that they were "ignorant of Fourier's principles, and without plan or purpose, save to fly from the ills they had already experienced in civilization. Thus they assembled together such elements of discord, as naturally in a short time led to their dissolution."

The Sodus Bay Socialists quarreled about religion, and when they broke up, some decamped in the night, with as much of the common property as they could lay hands on. Whereupon Macdonald sententiously remarks—"The fact that mankind do not like to have their faults and failings made public, will probably account for the difficulty in obtaining particulars of such experiments."

The Bloomfield Association went to wreck in a quarrel about land-titles.

Of the Jefferson County Association, Macdonald says, "After a few months, disagreements became general. Their means were totally inadequate; they were too ignorant of the principles of Association; were too much crowded together, and had too many idlers among them. There was bad management on the part of the officers, and some were suspected of dishonesty."

The Moorhouse Union appears to have been almost wholly a gathering of worthless adventurers.

Mr. Moore, in his *Post Mortem* on the Marlboro Association, very delicately observes that "the failure of the experiment may be traced to the fact that the minds of its originators were not homogeneous."

Macdonald, after studying the Prairie Home Community, says, "From all I saw I judged that it was too loosely put together, and that the members had not entire confidence in each other."

The malcontent who gives an account of the Trumbull Phalanx says: "Some came with the idea that they could live in idleness at the expense of the purchasers of the estate, and these ideas they practically carried out; while others came with good hearts for the cause. There were one or two designing persons, who came with no other intent than to push themselves into situations in which they could impose upon their fellow members; and this, to a certain extent, they succeeded in doing." And again: "I think most persons came there for a mere shift. Their poverty and their quarreling about what they called religion (for there were many notions as to which was the right way to heaven), were great drawbacks to success."

There were rival leaders in the Ohio Phalanx, and their respective parties quarreled about constitutions till they got into a lawsuit which broke them up. The member who gave the account of this Association says: "The most important causes of failure were said to be the deficiency of wealth, wisdom and goodness."

The Clermont Phalanx had jealousies among its women that led to a lawsuit; and a difficulty with one of its leading members about land-titles.

The story of the Alphadelphia Phalanx is briefly told thus: "The disagreement with Mr. Tubbs about a mill-race at the commencement of the experiment, threw a damper on it, from which it never recovered. All lived in clover so long as a ton of sugar or any other such luxury lasted. The officers made bad bargains. Laborers became discouraged. In the winter some of the influential members went away temporarily, and thus left the real friends of the Association in the minority; and when they returned after two or three months absence, every thing was turned upside-down. There was a manifest lack of good management and foresight. The old settlers accused the majority of this, and were themselves elected officers; but they managed no better, and finally broke up the concern."

The Wisconsin Phalanx kept its quarrels below lawsuit point, but the leading member who gives account of it, says that the habit of the members was to "scold and work, and work and scold"; and that "they had among their number a few men of leading intellect who always doubted the success of the experiment, and hence determined to accumulate property individually by any and every means called fair in competitive society. These would occasionally gain some important positions in the society, and representing it in part at home and abroad, caused much trouble. By some they were accounted the principal cause of the final failure."

Mr. Daniels, a gentleman who saw the whole progress of the Wisconsin Phalanx, says that "the cause of its breaking up was speculation, the love of money and the want of love for Association. Their property becoming valuable, they sold it for the purpose of making money out of it."

The North American was evidently shattered by secessions, resulting partly from religious dissensions and partly from differences about business.

Brook Farm alone is reported as harmonious to the end.

It should be observed that the foregoing disclosures of disintegrating infirmities were generally made reluctantly, and are necessarily very imperfect. Large departments of dangerous passion are entirely ignored. For instance, in all the memoirs of the Owen and Fourier Associations, not a word is said on the "Woman Question"! Among all the disagreements and complaints, not a hint occurs of any jealousies and quarrels about love matters. In fact women are rarely mentioned; and the terrible passions connected with distinction of sex, which the

Shakers, Rappites, Oneidians, and all the rest of the religious Communities have had so much trouble with, and have taken so much pains to provide for or against, are absolutely left out of sight. Owen, it is true, named marriage as one of the trinity of man's oppressors: and it is generally understood that Owenism and Fourierism both gave considerable latitude to affinities and divorces; but this makes it all the more strange that there was no trouble worth mentioning, in any of these Communities, about crossing love-claims. Can it be, we ask ourselves, that Owen had such conflicts with whiskey-tippling, but never a fight with the love-mania? that all through the Fourier experiments, men and women, young men and maidens, by scores and hundreds were tumbled together into unitary homes, and sometimes into log-cabins seventeen feet by twenty-five, and yet no sexual jostlings of any account disturbed the domestic circle? The only conclusion we can come to is, that some of the most important experiences of the transitory Communities have not been surrendered to history.

Nevertheless the troubles that do come to the surface show, as we have said, that human depravity is the dread "Dweller of the Threshold," that lies in wait at every entrance to the mysteries of Socialism. . . .

From Kenneth Lamott, "Doing Their Thing at Morning Star," Horizon 10 (Spring 1968): 14–19. Copyright 1968 by Kenneth Lamott. Reprinted by permission of Harold Matson Company, Inc.

I have become a Harmonite and mean to spend the remainder of my days in this abode of peace and quietness . . . I am at length free—my body is at my command, and I enjoy mental liberty, after having long been deprived of it.

—William Pelham, Letter from
New Harmony, 1825

Why do I live at Morning Star? I groove here. I feel myself at peace. I feel empathy.

—A Resident of Morning Star, 1967

Within a half-hour after I had walked up a steep hill and through a grove of redwoods into the Morning Star Ranch, a rural commune of hippies north of San Francisco, I found myself stripped down to my shorts, attempting to hold a Yoga position called the Thunderbolt. There were six of us in the hillside clearing: Sandy, a Negro who had been protesting that he wanted no part of Yoga and was now complaining that it had given him a Charley horse; a young Mexican-American who was already quite expert; an army veteran with his name tattooed on his shoulder; a boy I shall call Milt, who, with his ragged black beard, his mop of long frizzly hair, and his thick glasses mended with adhesive tape, looking the epitome of the hippie; myself, white of skin and stiff of muscle; and Lou Gottlieb, a reformed forty-four-year-old folk singer and musicologist as well as the owner of the Morning Star property and the spiritual and temporal leader of the community.

"Man, that bumblebee's bothering me," Sandy said, swatting at an insect that was hovering over his back.

"Leave him alone, he's just trying to make friends," Gottlieb said. "You're probably the first spook he's ever seen."

Sandy grunted and tried an exercise called the Cobra, while Gottlieb exhorted us to stretch our necks backward until we could feel the flash of enlightenment that is said to come to the adept. While the rest of us were straining, Sandy suddenly stood up and, pulling on his clothes, announced "I got to call my wife."

"You have to do *what?*" Gottlieb demanded.

"Call my wife, man."

Gottlieb laughed.

"I mean it," Sandy said desperately. "I got to call the old lady."

Gottlieb laughed again, and Sandy loped off into the trees, presumably heading toward the glass-and-aluminum pay booth that stands like a relic of a departed alien civilization in the midst of the shacks and wigwams of Morning Star. Gottlieb instructed us to lay ourselves out in a position called the Corpse and count our breathing to fifty. When I finished and sat up, he was striding away toward the woods, a tall, dark, rather gaunt man with an authoritative manner and a full black beard like a prophet's.

After we had put on our clothes, the veteran bummed a cigarette from me, pinched out some of the tobacco at the end, and mixed a "cocktail," using the cigarette and the remains of a joint of marijuana that he produced from his pocket. Milt, the bearded one, told me he had recently found Yoga a great comfort while he was doing five days in the county jail. When I asked what he had been arrested for, he said that he had been caught stealing $1.26 worth of food in a chain grocery.

"You really got to do this Yoga every day," the Mexican-American boy told me.

Most of those who come to look at us seem highly pleased, but they see only the outside.
—Thomas Pears, Letter from New Harmony, 1826

I don't believe in nudism myself; I'd be uncomfortable. And I think everyone should be clothed at the dinner table.
—Lou Gottlieb, 1967

Apart from certain details of style (drugs, primarily), the thirty or more rural communes that have sprung up over the country during the past year or so call strongly to mind the classic American utopias that flourished during the last century. Utopias were then, as they are becoming now, a considerable movement; writing in 1870, John Humphrey Noyes, the historian of early American socialism, counted forty-seven colonies that had already come and gone, a list that ran from the Alphadelphia Phalanx to the Peace Union settlement.

The great majority of these utopias, to be sure, consisted of farming colonies of pious German immigrants such as made up the Shaker and the Rappist groups, drawn together by a common regard for the virtues of hard work and the more radical forms of evangelical Christianity. Other roads to salvation, however, were sought by the colonists at Brook Farm (Massachusetts), the Oneida community (New York), and New Harmony (Indiana). Parallels that bridge a century and a half are not hard to find between these older colonies and the new. The transcendental world view of Brook Farm, the free love at Oneida, the constant dissonance between the ideal and the practical at New Harmony, are all echoed to some extent at such latter-day utopias as Timothy Leary's Millbrook colony in rural New York; Drop City, which is a village of geodesic domes built from junk automobile tops near Trinidad, Colorado; the Tolstoy colony near Davenport, Washington, and, of course, Morning Star itself.

Morning Star, in fact, lies within a few miles of the sites of three utopian communes that flourished in the latter part of the nineteenth century. (The longest-lived of these was the Brotherhood of the New Life, founded by the mystic and poet Thomas Lake Harris at Fountain Grove, California, in 1875. It lasted as a utopia until 1892 but survived as a commercial vineyard for forty-two years more.) The guiding principles of Morning Star are not easy to classify, but if I were to try, I should describe its operative principles as an amalgam of primitive Christianity, Zen, Yoga, social nudism, and philosophical anarchism.

"Everybody's free to do his own thing," I was told by a red-bearded man I found sitting in the sun on the porch of what is called the Upper House. "Everybody's welcome here, everybody who wants to get away from that Great Society down there. Lou has only one strict rule: no camp-fires. I guess there are about sixty or seventy people here during the week and twice that on weekends. If you want to work, you can. If you don't want to, you don't have to. As I say, everybody's free to do his own thing."

The climate here is warm and easy in the summer, without a drop of rain falling from June to September. In the apple orchard and among the redwood groves that cover Morning Star's thirty-one acres, mobile youngsters from San Francisco and New York and Vancouver and Louisville and Chicago have erected their pads, which range from conventional campers' tents and solid wooden huts to tepees and brushwood hogans. One resident was discovered in a hollowed-out redwood stump, which he had equipped with a flat roof. He was chewing redwood bark: he said it gave him a feeling of closeness to his home. Another settler is building a substantial three-room house. Many of the pads are decorated with the iconography of the 1960's— the nuclear disarmament symbol, LOVE, and "god's eyes" of brightly colored yarn—but there are also a couple of life-sized crosses and a sign with the legend JESUS IS THE WAY.

In the winter it rains often, and the nights grow cold to the freezing point, but on a pleasant summer's day it is not hard to become convinced that this *is* the great good place, the New Jerusalem. The charm is so powerful that even Paul Stefani, a narcotics investigator in the local district attorney's office, confessed after his first visit that "I came back to the office and kidded the guys that I wouldn't be around much longer, that I was going to defect."

For the weekend tourists there is at least one clear attraction. Casual nudism is endemic, and on a Sunday ranchers in sombreros, the local gentry in golf caps, and high-school boys in crew cuts stalk the hills and groves with their Polaroids. They don't have to look far, for the whole point of going around naked, of course, is to celebrate the innocent glory of the flesh. For what it is worth, let me add the observation that nudism at Morning Star, as elsewhere, seems generally antierotic in tendency, with none of the nuzzling, groping, and covert probing that goes on in every corner of the best-regulated beach.

I am come to this country to introduce an entire new state of society; to change it from an ignorant, selfish system to an enlightened social system which shall gradually unite all interests into one, and remove all causes for contests between individuals.
            —Robert Owen, Founder of New Harmony, 1825

We are running a pilot study in survival. The hippies are the first wave of the technological unemployed. Continuing the tradition of the intentional community—Brook Farm, Oneida, New Harmony—the problem is to get a piece of land and see who it attracts. We are attempting a definition of a style of life.
            —Lou Gottleib, Founder of Morning Star, 1967

New Harmony, which lasted from 1825 to 1830, was founded by Robert Owen, a self-made English textile magnate who sank some two hundred thousand dollars into his unsuccessful socialist experiment on the banks of the Wabash but who is remembered chiefly as a pioneer of the British Labor movement. Lou Gottlieb, the founder and patron of Morning Star, is as diverse in his interests as Owen, although in a considerably different style. The last time I'd seen Gottlieb had been many years ago at the San Francisco night club called the hungry i, where he had been plucking a double bass with the Gateway Singers and singing urban folk songs of his own composition. (One of these, as I recall, began, "Oh, Doctor Freud, oh, Doctor Freud,/How I wish you had been differently employed. . . .") Since then he has led another trio called the Limeliters, while earning a Ph.D. in musicology at Berkeley.

In the late spring of 1966 he moved out to Morning Star. As the word spread that settlers were welcome, other people joined him, including some Diggers—members of the internal Salvation Army of the hippie movement, which feeds the mind-blown hungry and clothes the naked. Although Morning Star has been identified as a Digger community, this was never strictly true. Some food grown at Morning Star went to Haight-Ashbury by way of the Diggers, but the alliance was in the nature of things a loose one.

When I first walked up the hill into Morning Star, I was met by the sound of a Mozart sonata being played by a performer of obviously professional caliber. It was Gottlieb, of course, practicing in his cabin, which is just large enough for a piano, a bed, some books, and Gottlieb himself. I later discovered he practiced six or seven hours a day, for a concert debut to take place when he turns fifty, he said. Not wanting to disturb him, I walked on up to the Upper House, where I was shortly to be recruited for the Yoga session, and it wasn't until well into the afternoon that I returned to the cabin.

The daily regime at Morning Star is hard to describe in any convincing detail, for its pure and literal anarchy outrages all one's middle-class bias in favor of order and organization. The style of life here has pushed permissiveness to its outer limits. Work does manage to get done—meals are cooked, dishes are washed, the tomatoes, cabbages, pumpkins, and beans in the garden somehow get tended—but nobody has been assigned to any particular duty. People sleep, talk, smoke pot, talk, lie in the sun, talk, meditate, talk, sing, and talk.

In the afternoon, I joined six or seven other people, both hippie and straight, who had gathered outside Gottlieb's cabin to listen to him practice. I fell into conversation with a San Franciscan named Karl, whom I guessed to be in his seventies—a short, compact man in golden corduroys, who wore his hair and beard in the classic style of Buffalo Bill Cody. He told me that although he doesn't live at Morning Star he comes up on weekends to refresh his spirit. Among the others were a pleasant, round-faced Negro boy and a spare, deeply tanned man whom I had already noticed several times because he had a habit of keeping his face, eyes closed, lifted directly into the sun.

There was also a pretty college-age girl I shall call Karen, who had come up with a bearded boy to visit Morning Star for the day. They were both holding flowers and looking a little self-conscious. Karen burbled on and on, while Karl patiently and courteously fielded her observations that it was all so wonderful that it was hard to believe, that it was awfully pretty up here, that it must be a wonderful place to live, and so on and so on. Then, with a burst of Beethoven, the piano stopped, and Gottlieb came out to join us, dressed conventionally in a dark sport shirt, slacks, white athletic socks, and an old pair of loafers.

"I just want to tell you how pretty that was," Karen exclaimed. "You're a *good* piano player."

"Oh, God," Gottlieb said quitely and retreated a step.

Karen forged on remorselessly. "It's such a beautiful place I wouldn't mind living here myself. Don't you love it?"

Gottlieb, who is a highly articulate and even voluble man, disappeared silently. He returned with a paper sign that read: THIS BODY HAS ALREADY TALKED WAY TOO MUCH. He sat on the bench, pulled up his legs Yoga fashion, placed the sign on his lap, looked into trees, and said nothing. A black and white puppy approached. Undismayed, Karen exclaimed, "What a cute puppy! What's its name?"

"God," somebody on the other side of Gottlieb said.

"What a funny name for a puppy!" Karen cried. "Here, God! Come here, God!"

Looking rather nervously over its shoulder, the puppy departed at a fast trot. After a moment of blessed silence, Karen said, crestfallen. "Oh! I didn't realize I was being put down."

She recovered in a moment, however, and dashed off in high spirits to show a newly arrived friend around Morning Star. Looking after her, Gottlieb said mildly, "And to think that's exactly the sort of girl I used to run around after."

He closed his eyes and folded his hands in an attitude of meditation. I found a comfortable place on the deck and dozed in the warm sun with my back against the cabin. The others did likewise or wandered away. It was very pleasant.

Suddenly a car erupted on the narrow dirt road that comes up from the parking lot and ground to a dusty halt a few feet from me. A deputy sheriff was at the wheel, a young, beefy man wearing a spanking fresh khaki uniform. He put his head out of the window—dark glasses, square teeth, carefully combed wavy yellow hair—and said, "Hi, Lou."

"Hello," Gottlieb said courteously.

"Can we have a word with you?"

"Of course."

The deputy churned the car up the gravel a few extra feet toward the cabin and got out with his passenger. The second man was older, a graying crew-cut type wearing a sport shirt with the tails out and sharply pressed slacks. The bottom of a well-worn woven leather pistol holster protruded from under his shirt.

"I wonder if we could talk privately," the uniformed deputy said. "Certainly," Gottlieb said. I reluctantly walked away.

> *Now Vice and Crime no more shall stalk*
> *Unseen in open day,*
> *To cross our silent, peaceful walk*
> *Through life's enchanting way....*
> —A New Harmony Song

> *If they find any evidence of organization here, I wish they would show it to me.*
> —Lou Gottleib (After having been charged with operating an organized camp in violation of State Health Regulations)

A tall girl who appeared to be wearing nothing except a long brown T shirt was strumming a guitar and singing to an audience of a dozen or so people in the Lower House. Some of them were sitting on a ratty sofa and a couple of overstuffed chairs. On a mattress on the floor sat a young fellow wearing a marine private's tunic and blue jeans. A thin girl in a granny dress was curled up on the other mattress. A cotton spread had been thrown over her, and a half-eaten apple lay near her mouth. Because she looked withdrawn and glassy-eyed, I assumed she was on an acid trip, but when I looked closer, she seemed merely sick and unhappy. A car had just come back from town with groceries, and out in the kitchen several people were getting dinner together.

I decided to go to the well, which occupies a strategic position between the Upper House, the Lower House, and Gottlieb's cabin. I found Milt at the well and asked him if he knew what was on the minds of the deputies, still talking earnestly to Gottlieb, who looked completely undisturbed.

"Somebody in a sheriff's car comes up here about twice a week," Milt said. "Usually it's about illegal camp-fires or underage runaways or sanitation." Milt went on, grinning cheerfully, "The cops aren't very high on my list of worries. Not having a warm place to sleep comes first. Then comes going hungry. Cops are third."

I asked if the sheriff had ever made any trouble about drugs.

"Not yet," he said, "but we don't have any guarantee about the future. I make sure I'm never carrying any pot on me. I do my best to smoke only other people's pot. It's pretty hard for them to bust you just for smoking. Usually they have to prove possession." As far as I could tell, marijuana was smoked freely, but there was not much visible evidence of LSD use. One boy whom I asked said, "Oh, hell, who wants to get on acid and go around all stinking with sweat?"

Karl, the elderly man with flowing gray hair, came up to the well to say good-bye. He was going back to the city, he said, to take a sick girl to the hospital.

I asked if this was the girl I'd seen in the Lower House.

He nodded. "I don't know if you noticed, but her face is all swollen up. She's been on speed [methedrine]. It rots out the teeth, and she's a pretty sick girl." We shook hands, and he walked over to his camper truck. The girl was already lying on a bunk in the back, and a boy got in to keep her company, shutting the door behind him.

By this time the deputies had disappeared, and a number of people had drifted back toward Gottlieb's cabin. Milt, who had taken off his clothes, which he was now holding in one hand, was telling an inquisitive tourist that he had gone to Hebrew school for six years. Gottlieb had resumed his position of meditation.

I walked through the orchard and back through the redwoods. As I came out of the woods, I stepped almost into the middle of a quiet group of two bearded men and two girls, who were sitting in the shade. None of them were wearing clothes, although the men had straw hats on. As I looked back at them, it struck me that they had fallen almost precisely into the easy postures of the picnicking bohemians in Manet's *Le Déjeuner sur l'Herbe*.

Gottlieb was looking somewhat more convivial when I returned to his cabin. A disciple was sitting at his feet, a muscular man in shorts and sandals, with long reddish hair and a beard. He was rocking back and forth on his heels, staring unblinkingly at Gottlieb and, when I stopped, at me. I thanked Gottlieb for his hospitality, and he invited me to come back; I said I thought I would.

It wasn't until I was sitting in my car that I realized I hadn't found out what the sheriff had come for this time.

Oh, if you could see some of the rough uncouth creatures here, I think you would find it rather hard to look upon them exactly in the light of brothers and sisters.
—Sarah Pears, Letter from New Harmony, 1826

It's not like it used to be. Too many outsiders have been coming up here during the summer—Hell's Angels, tourists, people who come up for the wrong reasons. I don't know if Lou's right, letting everybody in.
—A resident of Morning Star, 1967

By the time I returned to Morning Star a few days later, the community had suffered an act of violence that demonstrated the impossibility of a utopia's cutting itself off entirely from the dominant pressures of the world outside. A fight had broken out one night between

Negroes and whites, apparently over a white girl. Some of the Negroes had retrieved guns that they had hidden in the bushes and had fired several shots. Nobody had been hit, but another Negro, angry and frightened, had called the cops. (It wasn't, in fact, the first incident of the sort. Earlier in the summer a crowd of Gypsy Jokers—an "outlaw" motorcycle gang—had violently dispossessed some Negro residents from their sleeping bags.)

Although the county authorities seem to have endured Morning Star with quite remarkable forbearance up to this point, the shooting crystallized the local sentiment hostile to Gottlieb. (It is not, I think, irrelevant to note that the most emotional arguments were directed against "nudity visible from the highway." Ah, America!) The district attorney announced his intention of closing the place down, and a judge enjoined Gottlieb and a hundred John Does from running an organized camp, from parading their nudity, from building camp-fires, and from letting the public onto the property. A safari of officials tramped up the hill from the parking lot: the sheriff and eight deputies, a half-dozen building inspectors, FBI agents, a country supervisor, the chief probation officer, a municipal court judge, and even border patrolmen looking for Canadians.

I had, as it happened, talked to two of the Canadians on the day after the gunplay. I found them lying out in the orchard, sunning themselves in the buff. "When we get back to Canada we're going to start a place like this ourselves," a boy from British Columbia told me. When I asked what the trouble was with Morning Star, a boy from Montreal who'd been living at Morning Star since early spring said, "Before the summer everything was different. Everybody turned out for Yoga, everybody worked in the vegetable fields, everybody was on the macrobiotic diet—you know, brown rice and stuff like that. Then these outsiders moved into the Upper House and began playing the record player loud and drinking and eating meat."

He bummed a cigarette from me and lay back in the sun for a few minutes. Then he sat up and asked, "Say, have you ever heard of a place called Tolstoy?"

I said I'd heard of it but that was all.

"It's a groovy place. They don't let *everybody in*—just people who really believe in it. They've got some organization there. Everybody knows what he's supposed to be doing."

I said it sounded somewhat different from Morning Star.

"It is," he said. "It sure is." He sounded wistful.

When I walked back to the center of the community, a series of arpeggios from the cabin told me that Gottlieb had come back. A good-looking white girl and the round-faced Negro boy were sitting on the bench outside. I knew I ought to stop and talk to Gottlieb, but the questions I thought of sounded a little fatuous now ("Mr. Gottlieb, do you think Morning Star has a future?"), and besides, I didn't want to interrupt his practicing. And besides that, I felt more than a little depressed about the whole scene already.

Whatever the immediate causes of my depression, it turned out to be fully and unhappily justified by what happened next. After some legal backing and filling, the judge who had issued the injunction gave Gottlieb four days to bring Morning Star up to the standards of an organized camp. At the end of the four days he found Gottlieb in contempt of court and fined him five hundred dollars, with an additional five hundred to be levied for every day that any guests remained on his property.

The next day a posse of deputies arrived and pointed out to Gottlieb that the fourteen young people who had insisted on staying would cost him another five hundred dollars. Gottlieb asked his friends to leave. His friends declined. Gottlieb asked the deputies to remove his friends. The deputies declined. Gottlieb asked what he should do. The deputies suggested that he make a citizen's arrest. Reluctantly, Gottlieb went from one person to the next, asking each one to leave and, when he wouldn't, arresting him for trespass. Then the deputies put the hippies in their cars and carted them off to jail.

A couple of days later, hearing that Gottlieb was visiting each one of the 396 citizens who had signed a petition that had helped bring on the injunction ("I'm going to try to look into their hearts"), I dialed the number of the phone booth near the well. A long time went by, there was some electronic clicking, and then a recorded female voice told me that the number was no longer in service.

QUESTIONS ON PART II

COMMUNITY OF CELIBATES (THE SHAKERS)

1. Give examples of how everyday activities were managed in such a way among the Shakers that ideal or spiritual goals were promoted.
2. By what devices was social cohesion or group unity sustained by the Shakers?
3. In planning a contemporary intentional community, what lessons might be gained from studying the Shaker experiment?

OWENITES IN INDIANA (NEW HARMONY)

4. What were some of the administrative decisions made by Robert Owen which were crucial in the rise and fall of New Harmony? What is your impression of the wisdom of these decisions?
5. What major factors contributed to the failure of the New Harmony experiment? Refer to specific events whenever possible.
6. What factors which might have been conducive to successful community life were present in the Shaker experiment but lacking in the New Harmony experiment?

ASCETICS IN NEW EDEN (FRUITLANDS)

7. Contrast Lane's and Alcott's attitude toward daily practical duties in communal living with that of the Shakers. Why did they admire the Shakers?
8. Do you agree with the Fruitlanders' belief that improved circumstances will not meliorate mankind, but "improved men will originate the superior condition for themselves and others"? Why or why not?
9. Explain how the Fruitlanders planned to achieve their aim of "being in preference to doing."

Poetic Phalanx (Brook Farm)

10. Explain the original Brook Farm view of labor. Do you think this is still a defensible view? Why or why not?
11. By what ultimate principles did the Brook Farmers attempt to justify their proposed "radical and universal reform" of society?
12. How were the activities at Brook Farm unified and varied?

Cabet's "Pretty Dream" (Icaria)

13. Despite the apparent disadvantages of living in Icaria, what advantages did Icaria provide for its inhabitants?

Free Love and Bible Communism (Oneida)

14. To what extent was life at Oneida regimented and to what extent unregimented?
15. How did the communitarianism practiced at Oneida differ from that practiced by the Shakers?

Why Utopias Fail

16. Assuming you were asked to design a utopian community which avoided the pitfalls discussed by Noyes and Lamott, what measures would you propose?

SUPPLEMENTARY READINGS

(Works marked * are available in paperbound editions.)

Armytage, W. H. G. *Heavens Below: Utopian Experiments in England, 1560–1960.* Toronto: University of Toronto Press, 1961.

Andrews, Edward D. **The Gift to be Simple: Songs, Dances and Rituals of the American Shakers.* New York: Dover Publications, 1940.

———. **The People Called Shakers.* New York: Oxford University Press, 1953.

Bestor, Arthur E. *Backwoods Utopias: The Sectarian and Owenite Phases of Communitarian Socialism in America: 1663–1829.* Philadelphia: University of Pennsylvania Press, 1950.

Calverton, V. F. *Where Angels Dared to Tread.* Indianapolis: Bobbs-Merrill, 1941.

Clark, Elmer T. *The Small Sects in America.* New York: Abington-Cokesbury, 1949.

Codman, John Thomas. *Brook Farm, Historical and Personal Memoirs.* Boston: Arena Publishing Co., 1894.

Conkin, Paul K. *Two Paths to Utopia, the Hutterites and the Llano Colony.* Lincoln, Nebraska: University of Nebraska Press, 1964.

Crowe, Charles. *George Ripley: Transcendentalist and Utopian Socialist.* Athens, Ga.: University of Georgia Press, 1967.

Curtis, Edith R. *A Season in Utopia, the Story of Brook Farm.* New York: Thomas Nelson and Sons, 1941.

Egbert, Donald D., and Stow Persons, eds., and T. D. Seymour Bassett, bibliographer. *Socialism and American Life.* 2 vols. Princeton: Princeton University Press, 1952. Vol. I.

Gide, Charles, *Communist and Cooperative Colonies,* translated by E. R. Row. New York: Thomas Y. Crowell Co., 1930.

Harrison, John F. C. *Quest for the New Moral World: Robert Owen and the Owenites in Britain and America.* New York: Charles Scribner's Sons, 1969.

Hawthorne, Nathaniel. **The Blithedale Romance.* New York: W. W. Norton, 1958.

Hedgepeth, William, and Dennis Stock. *The Alternative: Communal Life in New America.* New York: Collier Books, Collier-Macmillan, Ltd., London, 1970.

Heilbroner, Robert L. *The Worldly Philosophers*. New York: Simon & Schuster, 1953. Chap. 5 ("Utopian Socialists").

Hillquit, Morris. *History of Socialism in the United States*. New York: Funk and Wagnalls, 1903.

Hinds, William A. *American Communities and Cooperative Colonies*, 2nd rev. ed. Chicago: Charles H. Kerr and Company, 1908.

Hine, Robert V. *California's Utopian Colonies*. New Haven: Yale University Press, 1966. Chap. 4 ("Icaria Speranza").

Hochfield, George, ed. *Selected Writings of the American Transcendentalists*. New York: New American Library, 1966.

Holloway, Mark, *Heavens on Earth: Utopian Communities in America, 1680–1880*. New York: Dover Publications, 1966.

Kanter, Rosabeth M., "Commitment and Social Organization: A Study of Commitment Mechanisms in Utopian Communities." *American Sociological Review* 33 (August 1968): 499–517.

———. "Communes." *Psychology Today*. 4 (July 1970) 53–78.

Laidler, Harry W. *Social-Economic Movements*. New York: Thomas Y. Crowell Company, 1944. Part I.

Lockwood, George B. *The New Harmony Movement*. New York: Appleton and Company, 1905.

Manuel, Frank E., and Fritzie P., eds. *French Utopias: An Anthology of Ideal Societies*. New York: The Free Press, 1966. (Contains selections from Saint-Simon, Fourier, and Cabet.)

Melcher, Marguerite F. *The Shaker Adventure*. Princeton: Princeton University Press, 1941.

Nordhoff, Charles. *The Communistic Societies of the United States*. New York: Schocken Books, 1965.

Noyes, John Humphrey. *History of American Socialisms*. New York: Dover Publications, 1966.

Noyes, Pierrepont B. *My Father's House, an Oneida Boyhood*. New York: Farrar and Rinehart, 1937.

Parker, Robert A. *A Yankee Saint, John Humphrey Noyes and the Oneida Community*. New York: G. P. Putnam's Sons, 1935.

Pease, William H., and Jane. *Black Utopias: Negro Communal Experiments in America*. Madison, Wisconsin: The State Historical Society of Wisconsin, 1963.

Perkins, William R., and B. L. Wick. *History of the Amana Society*. Iowa City: University of Iowa, 1891.

Sams, Henry W., ed. *Autobiography of Brook Farm*. Englewood Cliffs, N. J.: Prentice-Hall, 1958.

Sanborn, Frank B., and William T. Harris. *A. Bronson Alcott: His Life and Philosophy*, 2 vols. Boston: Roberts, 1893.

Sears, Clara Endicott. *Bronson Alcott's Fruitlands*. Boston: Houghton Mifflin & Co., 1915.

Shambaugh, Bertha M. H. *Amana That Was and Amana That Is.* Iowa City: State Historical Society of Iowa, 1932.

Shaw, Albert. *Icaria: A Study in Communistic History.* New York: Putnam, 1884.

Spiro, Melford E. **Kibbutz, Venture in Utopia.* New York: Schocken Books, 1956.

Swift, Lindsay. *Brook Farm, Its Members, Scholars, and Visitors.* New York: Macmillan Co., 1900.

Webber, Everett. *Escape to Utopia, the Communal Movement in America.* New York: Hastings House, 1959.

Wilson, William E. *The Angel and the Serpent.* Bloomington, Indiana: Indiana University Press, 1964. (On Rapp's Harmony and Owen's New Harmony).

Note: For references to several of the more recent utopian experiments see note 5 on page 2.

III

Contra Utopia

Friendship and association are very fine things, and a grand phalanx of the best of the human race, banded for some catholic object; yes, excellent; but remember that no society can ever be so large as one man. He, in his friendship, in his natural and momentary associations, doubles or multiplies himself; but in the hour in which he mortgages himself to two or ten or twenty, he dwarfs himself below the stature of one.

Ralph Waldo Emerson

13

Utopia Under Scrutiny

ARISTOTLE'S CRITICISMS OF
PLATO'S COMMUNITARIANISM

Indebted though he was to the philosophy of his teacher Plato, Aristotle (384–322 B.C.) found much to object to in Plato's conception of utopia. This does not mean, however, that Aristotle himself hesitated to engage in utopian speculation; to the contrary, a considerable part of his *Politics*, especially Book Seven, is devoted to speculation about the nature of an ideal city-state —its location, size, government, educational system, and other such topics. Nevertheless Aristotle found several of the proposals set forth in Plato's *Republic* far too radical for his conservative tastes. He therefore attempted to show in Book Two of his *Politics* that these proposals were not only contrary to common sense but, if put into practice, would in all likelihood lead to disastrous consequences for a state.

Presupposed in Aristotle's discussion is his view that a state is a plurality, a collection of individuals organized under a certain constitution in order to meet certain needs, not an organism in which individual parts lose their identity by being fused together into an undifferentiated and unified whole. To be sure, man is by nature a social animal and cannot achieve the good life apart from a politically constituted community; but this does not mean, Aristotle held, that a man must give up all sense of individual difference and independence in becoming part of and playing the role of good citizen in the ideal city-state.

Aristotle also objected to Plato's communism and his abolition of the family as an institution—measures which, Plato had made clear, however, were to apply only to the guardians (including philosopher-rulers and soldiers) and not to the artisans and husbandmen. He based his objections upon his desire to achieve social harmony without robbing individuals of the gratification they might have in the possession and use of private property and in personal relationships which, he believed, a good state is set up to protect and foster rather than to abolish.

Despite his criticisms of Plato's utopia, Aristotle showed in other parts of his writings on politics that he also found much to admire and emulate in Plato's community design. His discussions of education and art especially show how deeply influenced he was by his great teacher's views. In Aristotle's utopia, as in Plato's, gymnastics and music would form the basis of public education. Further, Aristotle shares Plato's concern that education should make citizens loyal to the state. Whatever be the form of government, there is little hope for its survival if its future citizens are not early molded to suit its demands. In Aristotle's opinion, it would be as foolish to instill aristocratic virtues in citizens who are to live in a democracy as to instill democratic values in those who will live under a monarchy. He also shares Plato's (and the typical Greek's) prejudice against those who made their living with their hands. Both of the utopian thinkers would place thinkers at the apex of the human hierarchy; the best kind of life would bring leisure for the continued cultivation of reason. Intellectual contemplation, not sense pleasure or political success, brings the highest human self-realization.

But despite their similarities, Aristotle parts company with Plato when he finds that Plato's proposals violate reason, experience, or common sense. Although he undoubtedly realized the nature of Plato's radicalism, which sprang from that philosopher's profoundly conservative desire to arrest change and to achieve a dictatorship of those best qualified to rule, Aristotle rejected it in favor of a more open kind of society. He remained relatively flexible in his views of the comparative advantages of different kinds of government. The forms of government he preferred were monarchy, aristocracy, and constitutional democracy ("polity"). These were less likely to be overthrown by revolution, which to the utopian conservative is the chief danger to be avoided once the ideal government has been set up. The wise statesman, Aristotle advises, will vigilantly guard against the beginning of undesirable changes, especially when they relate to laws. The statesman should remind the people of what they stand to lose if they disturb the status quo; he should make sure that citizens loyal to the state are always stronger (i.e. more powerfully represented) than those disloyal to it; and he should see to it that the form of education is adapted to the form of government. To the utopian of more liberal or radical faith, Aristotle's pronouncements on revolution place him among the enemies of utopias of reconstruction. And his belief that existing evils do not arise from private property but from the wickedness of human nature separates him from those utopians who believe that either human nature is basically good or at least is malleable.

From Aristotle, Politica, *translated by Benjamin Jowett, revised by W. D. Ross (Oxford: The Clarendon Press, 1921), bk. 2, chaps. 1–5. Reprinted by permission of The Clarendon Press, Oxford. Footnotes have been omitted.*

1

Our purpose is to consider what form of political community is best of all for those who are most able to realize their ideal of life. We must therefore examine not only this but other constitutions, both such as actually exist in well-governed states, and any theoretical forms which are held in esteem; that what is good and useful may be brought to light. And let no one suppose that in seeking for something beyond them we are anxious to make a sophistical display at any cost; we only undertake this inquiry because all the constitutions with which we are acquainted are faulty.

We will begin with the natural beginning of the subject. Three alternatives are conceivable: The members of a state must either have (1) all things or (2) nothing in common, or (3) some things in common and some not. That they should have nothing in common is clearly impossible, for the constitution is a community, and must at any rate have a common place—one city will be in one place, and the citizens are those who share in that one city. But should a well-ordered state have all things, as far as may be, in common, or some only and not others? For the citizens might conceivably have wives and children and property in common, as Socrates proposes in the *Republic* of Plato. Which is better, our present condition, or the proposed new order of society?

2

There are many difficulties in the community of women. And the principle on which Socrates rests the necessity of such an institution evidently is not established by his arguments. Further, as a means to the end which he ascribes to the state, the scheme, taken literally, is impracticable, and how we are to interpret it is nowhere precisely

175

stated. I am speaking of the premise from which the argument of Socrates proceeds, 'that the greater the unity of the state the better'. Is it not obvious that a state may at length attain such a degree of unity as to be no longer a state?—since the nature of a state is to be a plurality, and in tending to greater unity, from being a state, it becomes a family, and from being a family, an individual; for the family may be said to be more one than the state, and the individual than the family. So that we ought not to attain this greatest unity even if we could, for it would be the destruction of the state. Again, a state is not made up only of so many men, but of different kinds of men; for similars do not constitute a state. It is not like a military alliance. The usefulness of the latter depends upon its quantity even where there is no difference in quality (for mutual protection is the end aimed at), just as a greater weight of anything is more useful than a less (in like manner, a state differs from a nation, when the nation has not its population organized in villages, but lives an Arcadian sort of life); but the elements out of which a unity is to be formed differ in kind. Wherefore the principle of compensation, as I have already remarked in the *Ethics*, is the salvation of states. Even among freemen and equals this is a principle which must be maintained, for they cannot all rule together, but must change at the end of a year or some other period of time or in some order of succession. The result is that upon this plan they all govern; just as if shoemakers and carpenters were to exchange their occupations, and the same persons did not always continue shoemakers and carpenters. And since it is better that this should be so in politics as well, it is clear that while there should be continuance of the same persons in power where this is possible, yet where this is not possible by reason of the natural equality of the citizens, and at the same time it is just that all should share in the government (whether to govern be a good thing or a bad), an approximation to this is that equals should in turn retire from office and should, apart from official position, be treated alike. Thus the one party rule and the others are ruled in turn, as if they were no longer the same persons. In like manner when they hold office there is a variety in the offices held. Hence it is evident that a city is not by nature one in that sense which some persons affirm; and that what is said to be the greatest good of cities is in reality their destruction; but surely the good of things must be that which preserves them. Again, in another point of view, this extreme unification of the state is clearly not good; for a family is more self-sufficing than an individual, and a city than a family, and a city only comes into being when the community is large enough to be self-sufficing. If then self-sufficiency is to be desired, the lesser degree of unity is more desirable than the greater.

3

But, even supposing that it were best for the community to have the greatest degree of unity, this unity is by no means proved to follow from the fact 'of all men saying "mine" and "not mine" at the same instant of time', which, according to Socrates, is the sign of perfect unity in a state. For the word 'all' is ambiguous. If the meaning be that every individual says 'mine' and 'not mine' at the same time, then perhaps the result at which Socrates aims may be in some degree accomplished; each man will call the same person his own son and the same person his own wife, and so of his property and of all that falls to his lot. This, however, is not the way in which people would speak who had their wives and children in common; they would say 'all' but not 'each'. In like manner their property would be described as belonging to them, not severally but collectively. There is an obvious fallacy in the term 'all': like some other words, 'both', 'odd', 'even', it is ambiguous, and even in abstract argument becomes a source of logical puzzles. That all persons call the same thing mine in the sense in which each does so may be a fine thing, but it is impracticable; or if the words are taken in the other sense, such a unity in no way conduces to harmony. And there is another objection to the proposal. For that which is common to the greatest number has the least care bestowed upon it. Every one thinks chiefly of his own, hardly at all of the common interest; and only when he is himself concerned as an individual. For besides other considerations, everybody is more inclined to neglect the duty which he expects another to fulfil; as in families many attendants are often less useful than a few. Each citizen will have a thousand sons who will not be his sons individually, but anybody will be equally the son of anybody, and will therefore be neglected by all alike. Further, upon this principle, every one will use the word 'mine' of one who is prospering or the reverse, however small a fraction he may himself be of the whole number; the same boy will be 'my son', 'so and so's son', the son of each of the thousand, or whatever be the number of the citizens; and even about this he will not be positive; for it is impossible to know who chanced to have a child, or whether, if one came into existence, it has survived. But which is better—for each to say 'mine' in this way, making a man the same relation to two thousand or ten thousand citizens, or to use the word 'mine' in the ordinary and more restricted sense? For usually the same person is called by one man his own son whom another calls his own brother or cousin or kinsman—blood relation or connexion by marriage either of himself or of some relation of his, and yet another his clansman or tribesman; and how much better it is to be the real cousin of somebody than to be a son after Plato's fashion! Nor is there any way of preventing brothers and children and fathers and mothers from sometimes recognizing one another; for children are born like their parents, and they will necessarily be finding indications of their relationship to one another. Geographers declare such to be the fact; they say that in part of Upper Libya, where the women are common, nevertheless the children who are born are assigned to their respective fathers on the ground of their likeness. And some women, like the females of other animals—for example, mares and cows—have a strong tendency to produce offspring resembling their parents, as was the case with the Pharsalian mare called Honest.

4

Other evils, against which it is not easy for the authors of such a community to guard, will be assaults and homicides, voluntary as well as involuntary, quarrels and slanders, all which are most unholy acts when committed against fathers and mothers and near relations, but not equally unholy when there is no relationship. Moreover, they are much more likely to occur if the relationship is unknown, and, when they have occurred, the customary expiations of them cannot be made. Again, how strange it is that Socrates, after having made the children common, should hinder lovers from carnal intercourse only, but should permit love and familiarities between father and son or between brother and brother, than which nothing can be more unseemly, since even without them love of this sort is improper. How strange, too, to forbid intercourse for no other reason than the violence of the pleasure, as though the relationship of father and son or of brothers with one another made no difference.

This community of wives and children seems better suited to the husbandmen than to the guardians, for if they have wives and children in common, they will be bound to one another by weaker ties, as a subject class should be, and they will remain obedient and not rebel. In a word, the result of such a law would be just the opposite of that which good laws ought to have, and the intention of Socrates in making these regulations about women and children would defeat itself. For friendship we believe to be the greatest good of states and the preservative of them against revolutions; neither is there anything which Socrates so greatly lauds as the unity of the state which he and all the world declare to be created by friendship. But the unity which he commends would be like that of the lovers in the *Symposium*, who, as Aristophanes says, desire to grow together in the excess of their affection, and from being two to become one, in which case one or both would certainly perish. Whereas in a state having women and children common, love will be watery; and the father will certainly not say 'my son', or the son 'my father'. As a little sweet wine mingled with a great deal of water is imperceptible in the mixture, so, in this sort of community, the idea of relationship which is based upon these names will be lost; there is no reason why the so-called father should care about the son, or the son about the father, or brothers about one another. Of the two qualities which chiefly inspire regard and affection—that a thing is your own and that it is your only one—neither can exist in such a state as this.

Again, the transfer of children as soon as they are born from the rank of husbandmen or of artisans to that of guardians, and from the rank of guardians into a lower rank, will be very difficult to arrange; the givers or transferrers cannot but know whom they are giving and transferring, and to whom. And the previously mentioned evils, such as assaults, unlawful loves, homicides, will happen more often amongst those who are transferred to the lower classes, or who have a place assigned to them among the guardians; for they will no longer call the members of the class they have left brothers, and children, and fathers, and mothers, and will not, therefore, be afraid of committing any crimes by reason of consanguinity. Touching the community of wives and children, let this be our conclusion.

5

Next let us consider what should be our arrangements about property: should the citizens of the perfect state have their possessions in common or not? This question may be discussed separately from the enactments about women and children. Even supposing that the women and children belong to individuals, according to the custom which is at present universal, may there not be an advantage in having and using possessions in common? Three cases are possible: (1) the soil may be appropriated, but the produce may be thrown for consumption into the common stock; and this is the practice of some nations. Or (2), the soil may be common, and may be cultivated in common, but the produce divided among individuals for their private use; this is a form of common property which is said to exist among certain barbarians. Or (3), the soil and the produce may be alike common.

When the husbandmen are not the owners, the case will be different and easier to deal with; but when they till the ground for themselves the question of ownership will give a world of trouble. If they do not share equally in enjoyments and toils, those who labour much and get little will necessarily complain of those who labour little and receive or consume much. But indeed there is always a difficulty in men living together and having all human relations in common, but especially in their having common property. The partnerships of fellow-travellers are an example to the point; for they generally fall out over everyday matters and quarrel about any trifle which turns up. So with servants: we are most liable to take offense at those with whom we most frequently come into contact in daily life.

These are only some of the disadvantages which attend the community of property; the present arrangement, if improved as it might be by good customs and laws, would be far better, and would have the advantages of both systems. Property should be in a certain sense common, but, as a general rule, private; for, when everyone has a distinct interest, men will not complain of one another, and they will make more progress, because every one will be attending to his own business. And yet by reason of goodness, and in respect of use, 'Friends', as the proverb says, 'will have all things common.' Even now there are traces of such a principle, showing that it is not impracticable, but, in well-ordered states, exists already to a certain extent and may be carried further. For, although every man has his own property, some things he will place at the disposal of his friends, while of others he shares the use with them. The Lacedaemonians, for example, use one another's slaves, and horses, and dogs, as if they were their own; and when they lack provisions on a journey, they appropriate what they find in the fields throughout the country. It is clearly better that property should be private, but the use of it common; and the special business of the legislator is to create in men this benevolent disposition. Again, how immeasurably greater is the pleasure, when a man feels a thing to be his own; for surely the love of self is a feeling implanted by nature and not given in vain, although selfishness is rightly censured; this, however, is not the mere love of self, but the love of self in excess, like the miser's love of money; for all, or almost all, men love money and other such objects in a measure. And further, there is the greatest pleasure in doing a kindness or service to friends or guests or companions, which can only be rendered when a man has private property. These advantages are lost by excessive unification of the state. The exhibition of two virtues, besides, is visibly annihilated in such a state: first, temperance towards women (for it is an honourable action to abstain from another's wife for temperance sake); secondly, liberality in the matter of property. No one, when men have all things in common, will any longer set an example of liberality or do any liberal action; for liberality consists in the use which is made of property.

Such legislation may have a specious appearance of benevolence; men readily listen to it, and are easily induced to believe that in some wonderful manner everybody will become everybody's friend, especially when some one is heard denouncing the evils now existing in states, suits about contracts, convictions for perjury, flatteries of rich men and the like, which are said to arise out of the possession of private property. These evils, however, are due to a very different cause —the wickedness of human nature. Indeed, we see that there is much more quarrelling among those who have all things in common, though there are not many of them when compared with the vast numbers who have private property.

Again, we ought to reckon, not only the evils from which the citizens will be saved, but also the advantages which they will lose. The life which they are to lead appears to be quite impracticable. The error of Socrates must be attributed to the false notion of unity from which he starts. Unity there should be both of the family and of the state, but in some respects only. For there is a point at which a state may attain such a degree of unity as to be no longer a state, or at which, without actually ceasing to exist, it will become an inferior state, like harmony passing into unison, or rhythm which has been reduced to a single foot. The state, as I was saying, is a plurality, which should be united and made into a community by education; and it is strange that the author of a system of education which he thinks will make the state virtuous, should expect to improve his citizens by regulations of this sort, and not by philosophy or by customs and laws, like those which prevail at Sparta and Crete respecting common meals, whereby the legislator has made property common. Let us remember that we should not disregard the experience of ages; in the multitude of years these things, if they were good, would certainly not have been unknown; for almost everything has been found out, although sometimes they are not put together; in other cases men do not use the knowledge which they have. Great light would be thrown on this subject if we could see such a form of government in the actual process of construction; for the legislator could not form a state at all without distributing and dividing its constituents into associations for common meals, and into phratries and tribes. But all this legislation ends only in forbidding agriculture to the guardians, a prohibition which the Lacedaemonians try to enforce already.

But, indeed, Socrates has not said, nor is it easy to decide, what in such a community will be the general form of the state. The citizens who are not guardians are the majority, and about them nothing has been determined: are the husbandmen, too, to have their property in common? Or is each individual to have his own? and are their wives and children to be individual or common? If, like the guardians, they are to have all things in common, in what do they differ from them, or what will they gain by submitting to their government? Or, upon what principle would they submit, unless indeed the governing class adopt the ingenious policy of the Cretans, who give their slaves the same institutions as their own, but forbid them gymnastic exercises and the possession of arms. If, on the other hand, the inferior classes are to be like other cities in respect of marriage and property, what will be the form of the community? Must it not contain two states in one, each hostile to the other? He makes the guardians into a mere occupying garrison, while the husbandmen and artisans and the rest are the real citizens. But if so the suits and quarrels, and all the evils which Socrates affirms to exist in other states, will exist equally among them. He says indeed that, having so good an education, the citizens will not need many laws, for example laws about the city or about the markets; but then he confines his education to the guardians. Again, he makes the husbandmen owners of the property upon condition of their paying a tribute. But in that case they are likely to be much more unmanageable and conceited than the Helots, or Penestae, or slaves in general. And whether community of wives or property be necessary for the lower equally with the higher class or not, and the questions akin to this, what will be the education, form of government, laws of the lower class, Socrates has nowhere determined: neither is it easy to discover this, nor is their character of small importance if the common life of the guardians is to be maintained.

Again, if Socrates makes the women common, and retains private property, the men will see to the fields, but who will see to the house? And who will do so if the agricultural class have both their property and their wives in common? Once more: it is absurd to argue, from the analogy of the animals, that men and women should follow the same pursuits, for animals have not to manage a household. The government, too, as constituted by Socrates, contains elements of danger; for he makes the same persons always rule. And if this is often a cause of disturbance among the meaner sort, how much more among high-spirited warriors? But that the persons whom he makes rulers must be the same is evident; for the gold which the God mingles in the souls of men is not at one time given to one, at another time to another, but always to the same; as he says, 'God mingles gold in some, and silver in others, from their very birth; but brass and iron in those who are meant to be artisans and husbandmen.' Again, he deprives the guardians even of happiness, and says that the legislator ought to make the whole state happy. But the whole cannot be happy unless most, or all, or some of its parts enjoy happiness. In this respect happiness is not like the even principle in numbers, which may exist only in the whole, but in neither of the parts; not so happiness. And if the guardians are not happy, who are? Surely not the artisans, or the common people. The Republic of which Socrates discourses has all these difficulties, and others quite as great.

14

Non-Conformity and Utopia

FEODOR DOSTOYEVSKY'S UNDERGROUND MAN
AS CRITIC OF UTOPIA

A utopian socialist in his youth, the Russian novelist Feodor Dostoyevsky (1821–1881) became a supporter of Russian orthodoxy and autocracy after spending four years in a Siberian prison because of his liberal beliefs and associations. His later literary works, including his greatest works, *Notes from Underground* (1864), *Crime and Punishment* (1866), *The Idiot* (1868), *The Possessed* (1871), and *The Brothers Karamazov* (1881), transcend his essential conservatism and speak in universal terms to the human condition. They are products of a searching imagination, a profound understanding of human nature, and an uncompromising love of goodness and truth.

In *Notes from Underground* Dostoyevsky created a fascinating antihero, a man fraught with self-contradictions and tormented by uncertainty and guilt. Through this character's recording of his impassioned but sometimes incoherent thoughts and feelings Dostoyevsky gave credibility and form to what the Russian critic D. S. Mirsky says deserves a place "among the great mystical revelations of mankind."[1]

The whole novel must be read in order to appreciate fully the nature of this revelation, but essentially it is a profound insight into the nature of man. Here is man speaking of his incurable passion for freedom at any price, even at the price of creating a hell rather than a heaven—"a Crystal Palace"—on earth. Here is a perspective on man quite unlike that given by a utopian socialist such as Edward Bellamy or a utopian neo-behaviorist such as B. F. Skinner. It is the portrait of a man who will sabotage plans for his salvation, who will throw a monkey-wrench in the gleaming utopian machinery, who will stick out his tongue and thumb his nose at perfection. It is the man for whom the anti-utopians Zamiatin, Huxley, and Orwell later spoke, following in the path blazed by Dostoyevsky. Zamiatin's nameless (but numbered) rebel

---

[1] D. S. Mirsky, *A History of Russian Literature from its Beginnings to 1900*, ed. Francis J. Witfield (New York: Random House, Vintage Books, 1958), p. 286.

in *We*, Huxley's John Savage in *Brave New World*, Orwell's Winston Smith in *1984* are all offspring of Dostoyevsky's Underground Man. In our time he has become the hero or antihero of existentialist novels and the Theatre of the Absurd. Whatever be his destiny, whatever be his chances for self-realization and happiness, he will never choose to join a utopia, certainly not one designed by a rationalistic, scientifically oriented socialist who naively overlooks the mysterious depths of human nature and is willing to enslave men in order to control them and force them to be happy.

The answers to man's problems, when and if they come, will not come, Dostoyevsky believed, from applying the organizational schemes of a Saint-Simon or a Fourier or the revolutionary zeal of a Belinsky or a Chernyshevsky. Rather the answers will come, he believed, from applying the self-abjuration, compassion, and forgiveness taught by Jesus Christ. This message of redemption and salvation through suffering and loving-kindness is expressed by Dostoyevsky in his novels *Crime and Punishment* and *The Idiot* and in his famous tribute to Pushkin at the poet's tomb in 1880, a year before his own death. In this tribute we find one of the clearest and last statements of Dostoyevsky's own utopian ideal—a world restored to peace, united through Russian influence, and watched over by the Greek Orthodox Church, the unique preserver, in his view, of "the Divine Image of Christ."

But if Dostoyevsky did occasionally envisage a utopia in his speeches, articles, and letters, the characters in his novels usually speak with the greatest power of conviction as critics rather than as proponents of utopianism. After reading the following selections from *Notes from Underground*, the reader who wants to explore further Dostoyevsky's anti-utopianism should turn to *The Possessed* and *The Brothers Karamazov*.

In the former work (Part II, Chapter 7), is found among the gathering of nihilists the utopian Shigalov who is working out the solution to the social problem but is perplexed because his conclusion contradicts his original idea. Starting out to achieve unlimited freedom, he ends up proposing unlimited despotism. He has been reduced to despair when he realizes that a paradise on earth could only be achieved by having a powerful dictatorship of free men rule a mass of enslaved but happy human beings.

In *The Brothers Karamazov*, Dostoyevsky's last novel, is the famous legend of the Grand Inquisitor (Book V, Chapter 5), another of the novelist's creations worthy of being called one of "the great mystical revelations of mankind." This legend of Jesus come to earth again and accused and denounced by the director of the Spanish Inquisition is recounted movingly by the searcher Ivan Karamazov to his saintly brother Alyosha. It lends itself to numerous interpretations, no one of which can possibly exhaust its complex and subtle meaning. One interpretation, relevant to Dostoyevsky's negative view of utopianism, is that men are frightened by the freedom which Jesus holds out to them and flee from it into the arms of despots, such as the Inquisitor, who, in exchange for men's compliancy, offer them what they crave and what apparently will satisfy them—authority, miracle, and mystery. However, the happiness they thus gain is unworthy of men, for without freedom, the highest human values cannot be realized.

Even if this interpretation of Dostoyevsky's meaning is correct, that man is often willing to sell his birthright of freedom for the security he craves, there remains the hope which the novelist had held out earlier through his Underground Man—that man will not be content for long in any utopia that demands of him unthinking conformity and relinquishment of his freedom of choice.

From Notes from Underground, *pt. 1, pp. 64–78.*
Reprinted with permission of The Macmillan Company from White Nights and Other Stories *by Fyodor Dostoyevsky, translated from the Russian by Constance Garnett. Printed in Great Britain. Reprinted also with permission of William Heinemann, Ltd.*

. . . Gentlemen, you must excuse me for being over-philosophical; it's the result of forty years underground! Allow me to indulge my fancy. You see, gentlemen, reason is an excellent thing, there's no disputing that, but reason is nothing but reason and satisfies only the rational side of man's nature, while will is a manifestation of the whole life, that is, of the whole human life including reason and all the impulses. And although our life, in this manifestation of it, is often worthless, yet it is life and not simply extracting square roots. Here I, for instance, quite naturally want to live, in order to satisfy all my capacities for life, and not simply my capacity for reasoning, that is, not simply one twentieth of my capacity for life. What does reason know? Reason only knows what it has succeeded in learning (some things, perhaps, it will never learn; this is a poor comfort, but why not say so frankly?) and human nature acts as a whole, with everything that is in it, consciously or unconsciously, and, even if it goes wrong, it lives. I suspect, gentlemen, that you are looking at me with compassion; you tell me again that an enlightened and developed man, such, in short, as the future man will be, cannot consciously desire anything disadvantageous to himself, that that can be proved mathematically. I thoroughly agree, it can—by mathematics. But I repeat for the hundredth time, there is one case, one only, when man may consciously, purposely, desire what is injurious to himself, what is stupid, very stupid—simply in order to have the right to desire for himself even what is very stupid and not to be bound by an obligation to desire only what is sensible. Of course, this very stupid thing, this caprice of ours, may be in reality, gentlemen, more advantageous for us than anything else on earth, especially in certain cases. And in particular it may be more advantageous than any advantage even when it does us obvious harm, and contradicts the soundest conclusions of our reason concerning our advantage—for in any circumstances it preserves for us what is most precious and most important—that is, our personality, our individuality. Some, you see, maintain that this really is the most precious thing for mankind; choice can, of course, if it chooses, be in agreement with reason; and especially if this be not abused but kept within bounds. It is profitable and sometimes even praiseworthy. But very often and even most often, choice is utterly and stubbornly opposed to reason . . . and . . . and . . . do you know that that, too, is profitable, sometimes even praiseworthy? Gentlemen, let us suppose that man is not stupid. (Indeed one cannot refuse to suppose that, if only from the one consideration, that, if man is stupid, then who is wise?) But if he is not stupid, he is monstrously ungrateful! Phenomenally ungrateful. In fact, I believe that the best definition of man is the ungrateful biped. But that is not all, that is not his worst defect; his worst defect is his perpetual moral obliquity, perpetual—from the days of the Flood to the Schleswig-Holstein period. Moral obliquity and consequently lack of good sense; for it has long been accepted that lack of good sense is due to no other cause than moral obliquity. Put it to the test and cast your eyes upon the history of mankind. What will you see? Is it a grand spectacle? Grand, if you like. Take the Colossus of Rhodes, for instance, that's worth something. With good reason Mr. Anaevsky testifies of it that some say that it is the work of man's hands, while others maintain that it has been created by nature herself. Is it many-coloured? May be it is many-coloured, too: if one takes the dress uniforms, military and civilian, of all peoples in all ages—that alone is worth something, and if you take the undress uniforms you will never get to the end of it; no historian would be equal to the job. Is it monotonous? May be it's monotonous too: it's fighting and fighting; they are fighting now, they fought first and they fought last—you will admit, that it is almost too monotonous. In short, one may say anything about the history of the world—anything that might enter the most disordered imagination. The only thing one can't say is that it's rational. The very word sticks in one's throat. And, indeed, this is the odd thing that is continually happening: there are continually turning up in life moral and rational persons, sages and lovers of humanity who make it their object to live all their lives as morally and rationally as possible, to be, so to speak, a light to their neighbours simply in order to show them that it is possible to live morally and rationally in this world. And yet we all know that those very people sooner or later have been false to themselves, playing some queer trick, often a most unseemly one. Now I ask you: what can be expected of man since he is a being endowed with such strange qualities? Shower upon him every earthly blessing, drown him in a sea of happiness, so that nothing but bubbles of bliss can be seen on the surface; give him economic prosperity, such that he should have nothing else to do but sleep, eat cakes and busy himself with the continuation of his species, and even then out of sheer ingratitude, sheer spite, man would play you some nasty trick. He would even risk his cakes and would deliberately desire the most fatal rubbish, the most uneconomical absurdity, simply to introduce into all this positive good sense his fatal fantastic element. It is just his fantastic dreams, his vulgar folly that he will desire to retain, simply in order to prove to himself—as though that were so necessary—that men still are men and not the keys of a piano, which the laws of nature threaten to control so completely that soon one will be able to desire nothing but by the calendar. And that is not all: even if man really were nothing but a piano-key, even if this were proved to him by natural science and mathematics, even then he would not become reasonable, but would purposely do something perverse out of simple ingratitude, simply to gain his point. And if he does not find means he will contrive destruction and chaos, will contrive sufferings of all sorts, only to gain his point! He will launch a curse upon the world, and as only man can curse (it is his privilege, the primary distinction between him and other animals), may be by his curse alone he will attain his object—that is, convince himself that he is a man and not a piano-key! If you say that all this, too, can be calculated and tabulated—chaos and darkness and curses, so that the mere possibility of calculating it all beforehand would stop it all, and reason would reassert itself, then man would purposely go mad in order to be rid of reason and gain his point! I believe in it, I answer for it, for the whole work of man really seems to consist in nothing but proving to himself every minute that he is a man and not a piano-key! It may be at the cost of his skin, it may be by cannibalism! And this being so, can one help being tempted to rejoice that it has not yet come off, and that desire still depends on something we don't know?

You will scream at me (that is, if you condescend to do so) that no one is touching my free will, that all they are concerned with is that my will should of itself, of its own free will, coincide with my own normal interests, with the laws of nature and arithmetic.

Good Heavens, gentlemen, what sort of free will is left when we come to tabulation and arithmetic, when it will all be a case of twice two make four. Twice two makes four without my will. As if free will meant that! . . .

Gentlemen, I am joking, and I know myself that my jokes are not brilliant, but you know one can't take everything as a joke. I am, perhaps, jesting against the grain. Gentlemen, I am tormented by questions; answer them for me. You, for instance, want to cure men of their old habits and reform their will in accordance with science and good sense. But how do you know, not only that it is possible, but also that it is *desirable*, to reform man in that way? And what leads you to the conclusion that man's inclinations *need* reforming? In short, how do you know that such a reformation will be a benefit to man? And to go to the root of the matter, why are you so positively convinced that not to act against his real normal interests guaranteed by the conclusions of reason and arithmetic is certainly always advantageous for man and must always be a law for mankind? So far, you know, this is only your supposition. It may be the law of logic, but not the law of humanity. You think, gentlemen, perhaps that I am mad? Allow me to defend myself. I agree that man is pre-eminently a creative animal, predestined to strive consciously for an object and to engage in engineering—that is, incessantly and eternally to make new roads, *wherever they may lead*. But the reason why he wants sometimes to go off at a tangent may just be that he is *predestined* to make the road, and perhaps, too, that however stupid the "direct" practical man may be, the thought sometimes will occur to him that the road almost always does lead *somewhere*, and that the destination it leads to is less important than the process of making it, and that the chief thing is to save the well-conducted child from despising engineering, and so giving way to the fatal idleness, which, as we all know, is the mother of all the vices. Man likes to make roads and to create, that is a fact beyond dispute. But why has he such a passionate love for destruction and chaos also? Tell me that! But on that point I want to say a couple of words myself. May it not be that he loves chaos and destruction (there can be no disputing that he does sometimes love it) because he is instinctively afraid of attaining his object and completing the edifice he is constructing? Who knows, perhaps he only loves that edifice from a distance, and is by no means in love with it at close quarters; perhaps he only loves building it and does not want to live in it, but will leave it, when completed, for the use of *les animaux domestiques* —such as the ants, the sheep, and so on. Now the ants have quite a different taste. They have a marvellous edifice of that pattern which endures for ever—the ant-heap.

With the ant-heap the respectable race of ants began and with the ant-heap they will probably end, which does the greatest credit to their perseverance and good sense. But man is a frivolous and incongruous creature, and perhaps, like a chess player, loves the process of the game, not the end of it. And who knows (there is no saying with certainty), perhaps the only goal on earth to which mankind is striving lies in this incessant process of attaining, in other words, in life itself, and not in the thing to be attained, which must always be expressed as a formula, as positive as twice two makes four, and such positiveness is not life, gentlemen, but is the beginning of death. Any-

way, man has always been afraid of this mathematical certainty, and I
am afraid of it now. Granted that man does nothing but seek that
mathematical certainty, he traverses oceans, sacrifices his life in the
quest, but to succeed, really to find it, he dreads, I assure you. He
feels that when he has found it there will be nothing for him to look
for. When workmen have finished their work they do at least receive
their pay, they go to the tavern, then they are taken to the police-
station—and there is occupation for a week. But where can man go?
Anyway, one can observe a certain awkwardness about him when he
has attained such objects. He loves the process of attaining, but does
not quite like to have attained, and that, of course, is very absurd. In
fact, man is a comical creature; there seems to be a kind of jest in it
all. But yet mathematical certainty is, after all, something insuffer-
able. Twice two makes four seems to me simply a piece of insolence.
Twice two makes four is a pert coxcomb who stands with arms akimbo
barring your path and spitting. I admit that twice two makes four is
an excellent thing, but if we are to give everything its due, twice two
makes five is sometimes a very charming thing too.

And why are you so firmly, so triumphantly, convinced that only
the normal and the positive—in other words, only what is conducive
to welfare—is for the advantage of man? Is not reason in error as
regards advantage? Does not man, perhaps, love something besides
well-being? Perhaps he is just as fond of suffering? Perhaps suffering
is just as great a benefit to him as well-being? Man is sometimes
extraordinarily, passionately, in love with suffering, and that is a fact.
There is no need to appeal to universal history to prove that; only ask
yourself, if you are a man and have lived at all. As far as my personal
opinion is concerned, to care only for well-being seems to me positively ill-bred. Whether it's good or bad, it is sometimes very pleasant,
too, to smash things. I hold no brief for suffering nor for well-being
either. I am standing for . . . my caprice, and for its being guaranteed
to me when necessary. Suffering would be out of place in vaudevilles,
for instance; I know that. In the "Palace of Crystal" it is unthinkable;
suffering means doubt, negation, and what would be the good of a
"palace of crystal" if there could be any doubt about it? And yet I
think man will never renounce real suffering, that is, destruction and
chaos. Why, suffering is the sole origin of consciousness. Though I did
lay it down at the beginning that consciousness is the greatest misfortune for man, yet I know man prizes it and would not give it up
for any satisfaction. Consciousness, for instance, is infinitely superior
to twice two makes four. Once you have mathematical certainty there
is nothing left to do or to understand. There will be nothing left but
to bottle up your five senses and plunge into contemplation. While if

you stick to consciousness, even though the same result is attained, you can at least flog yourself at times, and that will, at any rate, liven you up. Reactionary as it is, corporal punishment is better than nothing. . . .

You believe in a palace of crystal that can never be destroyed—a palace at which one will not be able to put out one's tongue or make a long nose on the sly. And perhaps that is just why I am afraid of this edifice, that it is of crystal and can never be destroyed and that one cannot put one's tongue out at it even on the sly.

You see, if it were not a palace, but a hen-house, I might creep into it to avoid getting wet, and yet I would not call the hen-house a palace out of gratitude to it for keeping me dry. You laugh and say that in such circumstances a hen-house is as good as a mansion. Yes, I answer, if one had to live simply to keep out of the rain.

But what is to be done if I have taken it into my head that is not the only object in life, and that if one must live one had better live in a mansion. That is my choice, my desire. You will only eradicate it when you have changed my preference. Well, do change it, allure me with something else, give me another ideal. But meanwhile I will not take a hen-house for a mansion. The palace of crystal may be an idle dream, it may be that it is inconsistent with the laws of nature and that I have invented it only through my own stupidity, through the old-fashioned irrational habits of my generation. But what does it matter to me that it is inconsistent? That makes no difference since it exists in my desires, or rather exists as long as my desires exist. Perhaps you are laughing again? Laugh away; I will put up with any mockery rather than pretend that I am satisfied when I am hungry. I know, anyway, that I will not be put off with a compromise, with a recurring zero, simply because it is consistent with the laws of nature and actually exists. I will not accept as the crown of my desires a block of buildings with tenements for the poor on a lease of a thousand years, and perhaps with a sign-board of a dentist hanging out. Destroy my desires, eradicate my ideals, show me something better, and I will follow you. You will say, perhaps, that it is not worth your trouble; but in that case I can give you the same answer. We are discussing things seriously; but if you won't deign to give me your attention, I will drop your acquaintance. I can retreat into my underground hole.

But while I am alive and have desires I would rather my hand were withered off than bring one brick to such a building! Don't remind me that I have just rejected the palace of crystal for the sole reason that one cannot put out one's tongue at it. I did not say because I am so fond of putting my tongue out. Perhaps the thing I resented was, that of all your edifices there has not been one at which one could not put out one's tongue. On the contrary, I would let my tongue be cut off out of gratitude if things could be so arranged that I should lose all desire to put it out. It is not my fault that things cannot be so arranged, and that one must be satisfied with model flats. Then why am I made with such desires? Can I have been constructed simply in order to come to the conclusion that all my construction is a cheat? Can this be my whole purpose? I do not believe it.

But do you know what: I am convinced that we underground folk ought to be kept on a curb. Though we may sit forty years underground without speaking, when we do come out into the light of day and break out we talk and talk and talk. . . .

15

Over-Organization and Dystopia

ALDOUS HUXLEY'S REFLECTIONS ON TRENDS
TOWARD A BRAVE NEW WORLD

In his famous satirical utopia *Brave New World* (1932), Aldous Huxley (1894–1967) delineated what was to him a horrendous society of the distant future in which science and technology had been applied to the solution of all natural and human problems, making possible at last a happy, tranquil, and prosperous world. God was dead, but in his place reigned the spirit of "Our Ford" who, as the father of mass-production, had been the chief inspiration for the new order. People were no longer conceived by parents and born; they were hatched in test tubes, having been predestined scientifically to play their appropriate economic roles. From childhood everyone was conditioned to stay happily in his place, and to enjoy rather than to question. Sexual promiscuity had replaced love; soma, a drug with almost miraculous properties, had removed frustrations and boredom along with personal and political restlessness; old age had been made beautiful; even death had lost its sting.

This world seems to Huxley's hero John Savage, who is cast into it completely unprepared to meet its demands and expectations, to be a hell rather than a heaven on earth. Before he acts at the end of the novel to escape from the nightmarish "utopia," the noble savage has declared his right to have God and poetry, danger and freedom, goodness and sin; in brief, as Mustapha Mond, the World Controller, interprets his words, "the right to be unhappy."

In looking back at *Brave New World* in *Brave New World Revisited* (1958), Huxley was appalled by the swiftness with which the prophecies he had made in the earlier book were coming true. Although he had imagined the society depicted in *Brave New World* as existing in the twenty-sixth century (or the sixth century After Ford), within his own lifetime it was apparent that the drift of forces was such that humanity was being carried in the present century toward the realization of the ideals of *Brave New World* —community, identity, and stability. What had previously seemed utterly fantastic, highly improbable, and downright absurd in the novel no longer

194

seemed so in light of what had taken place since the novel was written. The population explosion and the economic insecurity and unrest of masses of people had contributed to the creation of stronger and more centralized governments with almost dictatorial powers. Larger and more tightly knit bureaucratic organizations were increasingly taking over the management and control of every aspect of individual lives for the sake of collective happiness. Security was far more widely accepted than freedom as an important value by the majority of men. Persuasion through irrational propaganda techniques, both overt and hidden, was being more widely used to manipulate the minds of people under democracies as well as under dictatorships. Mass media were nurturing a passive herd mentality and generating masses of compliant consumers. While brainwashing had been developed to a fine art by the middle of the twentieth century, more advanced and "humane" (i.e. less unpleasant) modes of changing, conditioning, and controlling behavior were being advocated and perfected by "behavioral engineers." Research in the use of drugs to control behavior was widespread and promised fruitful results before long. Perhaps "soma" had not yet been discovered, but there were chemical tranquilizers, stimulants, and hallucinants readily available. In addition, techniques of subliminal projection and hypnopaedia ("sleep teaching") were being developed and could conceivably be perfected and widely used in our time. These and other developments convinced Huxley that a *Brave New World* society would become more feasible as the twentieth century "progressed" and would perhaps become a reality, unless something were done to check the push of powerful impersonal forces.

What, if anything, can be done to preserve the advantages of individualism and to promote the cause of freedom? Huxley considered it crucial for us to answer this question if we are to avoid a collective, scientifically controlled paradise. He suggested the direction in which his answer would proceed in the last two sections of *Brave New World Revisited*, especially in Section XI, "Education for Freedom," and earlier in his preface to *Brave New World*. Also, he adumbrated his answer in another novel, *Island* (1962), which as a constructive utopia provides an alternative to the dystopia of *Brave New World*. The contentment of the inhabitants of Pala (Huxley's imaginary island utopia), their synthesis of the wisdom of East and West, their drug-induced mysticism, their uninhibited love-making, their continuous attention to the immediate, their willingness to work hard may be more appealing than the hedonistic nightmare of *Brave New World*, but suggest an escapism which to some readers is no less disturbing. Pala, betrayed from within, fades away like a beautiful dream, and we wake to find the day of *Brave New World* still dawning.

The shortest and broadest road to the nightmare of Brave New World leads, as I have pointed out, through over-population and the accelerating increase of human numbers—twenty-eight hundred millions today, fifty-five hundred millions by the turn of the century, with most of humanity facing the choice between anarchy and totalitarian control. But the increasing pressure of numbers upon available resources is not the only force propelling us in the direction of totalitarianism. This blind biological enemy of freedom is allied with immensely powerful forces generated by the very advances in technology of which we are most proud. Justifiably proud, it may be added; for these advances are the fruits of genius and persistent hard work, of logic, imagination and self-denial—in a word, of moral and intellectual virtues for which one can feel nothing but admiration. But the Nature of Things is such that nobody in this world ever gets anything for nothing. These amazing and admirable advances have had to be paid for. Indeed, like last year's washing machine, they are still being paid for—and each installment is higher than the last. Many historians, many sociologists and psychologists have written at length, and with a deep concern, about the price that Western man has had to pay and will go on paying for technological progress. They point out, for example, that democracy can hardly be expected to flourish in societies where political and economic power is being progressively concentrated and centralized. But the progress of technology has led and is still leading to just such a concentration and centralization of power. As the machinery of mass production is made more efficient it tends to become more complex and more expensive—and so less available to the enterpriser of limited means. Moreover, mass production cannot work without mass distribution; but mass distribution raises problems which only the largest producers can satisfactorily solve. In a world of mass production and mass distribution the Little Man, with his inadequate stock of working capital, is at a grave disadvantage. In competition with the Big Man, he loses his money and finally his very existence as an independent producer; the Big

Man has gobbled him up. As the Little Men disappear, more and more economic power comes to be wielded by fewer and fewer people. Under a dictatorship the Big Business, made possible by advancing technology and the consequent ruin of Little Business, is controlled by the State—that is to say, by a small group of party leaders and the soldiers, policemen and civil servants who carry out their orders. In a capitalist democracy, such as the United States, it is controlled by what Professor C. Wright Mills has called the Power Elite. This Power Elite directly employs several millions of the country's working force in its factories, offices and stores, controls many millions more by lending them the money to buy its products, and, through its ownership of the media of mass communication, influences the thoughts, the feelings and the actions of virtually everybody. To parody the words of Winston Churchill, never have so many been manipulated so much by so few. We are far indeed from Jefferson's ideal of a genuinely free society composed of a hierarchy of self-governing units—"the elementary republics of the wards, the county republics, the State republics and the Republic of the Union, forming a gradation of authorities."

We see, then, that modern technology has led to the concentration of economic and political power, and to the development of a society controlled (ruthlessly in the totalitarian states, politely and inconspicuously in the democracies) by Big Business and Big Government. But societies are composed of individuals and are good only insofar as they help individuals to realize their potentialities and to lead a happy and creative life. How have individuals been affected by the technological advances of recent years? Here is the answer to this question given by a philosopher-psychiatrist, Dr. Erich Fromm:

> Our contemporary Western society, in spite of its material, intellectual and political progress, is increasingly less conducive to mental health, and tends to undermine the inner security, happiness, reason and the capacity for love in the individual; it tends to turn him into an automaton who pays for his human failure with increasing mental sickness, and with despair hidden under a frantic drive for work and so-called pleasure.

Our "increasing mental sickness" may find expression in neurotic symptoms. These symptoms are conspicuous and extremely distressing. But "let us beware," says Dr. Fromm, "of defining mental hygiene as the prevention of symptoms. Symptoms as such are not our enemy, but our friend; where there are symptoms there is conflict, and conflict always indicates that the forces of life which strive for integration and happiness are still fighting." The really hopeless victims of mental illness are to be found among those who appear to be most normal. "Many of them are normal because they are so well adjusted to our mode of existence, because their human voice has been silenced so early in their lives, that they do not even struggle or suffer or develop symptoms as the neurotic does." They are normal not in what may be called the absolute sense of the word; they are normal only in relation to a profoundly abnormal society. Their perfect adjustment to that abnormal society is a measure of their mental sickness. These millions of abnormally normal people, living without fuss in a society to which, if they were fully human beings, they ought not to be adjusted, still cherish "the illusion of individuality," but in fact they have been to a great extent deindividualized. Their conformity is developing into something like uniformity. But "uniformity and freedom are incompatible. Uniformity and mental health are incompatible too. . . . Man is not made to be an automaton, and if he becomes one, the basis for mental health is destroyed."

In the course of evolution nature has gone to endless trouble to see that every individual is unlike every other individual. We reproduce our kind by bringing the father's genes into contact with the mother's. These hereditary factors may be combined in an almost infinite number of ways. Physically and mentally, each one of us is unique. Any culture which, in the interests of efficiency or in the name of some political or religious dogma, seeks to standarize the human individual, commits an outrage against man's biological nature.

Science may be defined as the reduction of multiplicity to unity. It seeks to explain the endlessly diverse phenomena of nature by ignoring the uniqueness of particular events, concentrating on what they have in common and finally abstracting some kind of "law," in terms of which they make sense and can be effectively dealt with. For examples, apples fall from the tree and the moon moves across the sky. People had been observing these facts from time immemorial. With Gertrude Stein they were convinced that an apple is an apple is an apple, whereas the moon is the moon is the moon. It remained for Isaac Newton to perceive what these very dissimilar phenomena had in common, and to formulate a theory of gravitation in terms of which certain aspects of the behavior of apples, of the heavenly bodies and indeed of everything else in the physical universe could be explained and dealt with in terms of a single system of ideas. In the same spirit the artist takes the innumerable diversities and uniquenesses of the outer world and his own imagination and gives them meaning within an orderly system of plastic, literary or musical pattern. The wish to impose order upon confusion, to bring harmony out of dissonance and unity out of multiplicity is a kind of intellectual instinct, a primany and fundamental urge of the mind. Within the realms of science, art and philosophy the workings of what I may call this "Will to Order" are mainly beneficent. True, the Will to Order has produced many premature syntheses based upon insufficient evidence, many absurd systems of metaphysics and theology, much pedantic mistaking of notions for realities, of symbols and abstractions for the data of immediate experience. But these errors, however regrettable, do not do much harm, at any rate directly—though it sometimes happens that a bad philosophical system may do harm indirectly, by being used as a justification for senseless and inhuman actions. It is in the social sphere, in the realm of politics and economics, that the Will to Order becomes really dangerous.

Here the theoretical reduction of unmanageable multiplicity to comprehensible unity becomes the practical reduction of human diversity to subhuman uniformity, of freedom to servitude. In politics the equivalent of a fully developed scientific theory or philosophical system is a totalitarian dictatorship. In economics, the equivalent of a beautifully composed work of art is the smoothly running factory in which the workers are perfectly adjusted to the machines. The Will to Order can make tyrants out of those who merely aspire to clean up a mess. The beauty of tidiness is used as a justification for despotism.

Organization is indispensable; for liberty arises and has meaning only within a self-regulating community of freely co-operating individuals. But, though indispensable, organization can also be fatal. Too much organization transforms men and women into automata, suffocates the creative spirit and abolishes the very possibility of freedom. As usual, the only safe course is in the middle, between the extremes of *laissez-faire* at one end of the scale and of total control at the other.

During the past century the successive advances in technology have been accompanied by corresponding advances in organization. Complicated machinery has had to be matched by complicated social arrangements, designed to work as smoothly and efficiently as the new instruments of production. In order to fit into these organizations, individuals have had to deindividualize themselves, have had to deny their native diversity and conform to a standard pattern, have had to do their best to become automata.

The dehumanizing effects of over-organization are reinforced by the dehumanizing effects of over-population. Industry, as it expands, draws an ever greater proportion of humanity's increasing numbers into large cities. But life in large cities is not conducive to mental health (the highest incidence of schizophrenia, we are told, occurs among the swarming inhabitants of industrial slums); nor does it foster the kind of responsible freedom within small self-governing groups, which is the first condition of a genuine democracy. City life is anonymous and, as it were, abstract. People are related to one another, not as total personalities, but as the embodiments of economic functions or, when they are not at work, as irresponsible seekers of entertainment. Subjected to this kind of life, individuals tend to feel lonely and insignificant. Their existence ceases to have any point or meaning.

Biologically speaking, man is a moderately gregarious, not a completely social animal—a creature more like a wolf, let us say, or an elephant, than like a bee or an ant. In their original form human societies bore no resemblance to the hive or the ant heap; they were merely packs. Civilization is, among other things, the process by which primitive packs are transformed into an analogue, crude and mechanical, of the social insects' organic communities. At the present time the pressures of over-population and technological change are accelerating this process. The termitary has come to seem a realizable and even, in some eyes, a desirable ideal. Needless to say, the ideal will never in fact be realized. A great gulf separates the social insect from the not too gregarious, big-brained mammal; and even though the mammal should do his best to imitate the insect, the gulf would remain. However hard they try, men cannot create a social organism, they can only create an organization. In the process of trying to create an organism they will merely create a totalitarian despotism.

Brave New World presents a fanciful and somewhat ribald picture of a society, in which the attempt to re-create human beings in the likeness of termites has been pushed almost to the limits of the possible. That we are being propelled in the direction of Brave New World is obvious. But no less obvious is the fact that we can, if we so desire, refuse to co-operate with the blind forces that are propelling us. For the moment, however, the wish to resist does not seem to be very strong or very widespread. As Mr. William Whyte has shown in his remarkable book, *The Organization Man*, a new Social Ethic is replacing our traditional ethical system—the system in which the individual is primary. The key words in this Social Ethic are "adjustment," "adaptation," "socially oriented behavior," "belongingness," "acquisition of social skills," "team work," "group living," "group loyalty," "group dynamics," "group thinking," "group creativity." Its basic assumption is that the social whole has greater worth and significance than its individual parts, that inborn biological differences should be sacrificed to cultural uniformity, that the rights of the collectivity take precedence over what the eighteenth century called the Rights of Man. According to the Social Ethic, Jesus was completely wrong in asserting that the Sabbath was made for man. On the contrary, man was made for the Sabbath, and must sacrifice his inherited idiosyncrasies and pretend to be the kind of standardized good mixer that organizers of group activity regard as ideal for their purposes. This ideal man is the man who displays "dynamic conformity" (delicious phrase!) and an intense loyalty to the group, an unflagging desire to subordinate himself, to belong. And the ideal man must have an ideal wife, highly gregarious, infinitely adaptable and not merely resigned to the fact that her husband's first loyalty is to the Corporation, but actively loyal on her own account. "He for God only," as Milton said of Adam and Eve, "she for God in him." And in one important respect the wife of the ideal organization man is a good deal worse off than our First Mother. She and Adam were permitted by the Lord to be completely uninhibited in the matter of "youthful dalliance."

> Nor turned, I ween,
> Adam from his fair spouse, nor Eve the rites
> Mysterious of connubial love refused

Today, according to a writer in the *Harvard Business Review*, the wife of the man who is trying to live up to the ideal proposed by the Social Ethic, "must not demand too much of her husband's time and interest. Because of his single-minded concentration on his job, even his sexual activity must be relegated to a secondary place." The monk makes vows of poverty, obedience and chastity. The organization man is allowed to be rich, but promises obedience ("he accepts authority without resentment, he looks up to his superiors"—*Mussolini ha sempre ragione*) and he must be prepared, for the greater glory of the organization that employs him, to forswear even conjugal love.

It is worth remarking that, in *1984*, the members of the Party are compelled to conform to a sexual ethic of more than Puritan severity. In *Brave New World*, on the other hand, all are permitted to indulge their sexual impulses without let or hindrance. The society described in Orwell's fable is a society permanently at war, and the aim of its rulers is first, of course, to exercise power for its own delightful sake, and, second, to keep their subjects in that state of constant tension which a state of constant war demands of those who wage it. By crusading against sexuality the bosses are able to maintain the required tension in their followers and at the same time can satisfy their lust for power in a most gratifying way. The society described in *Brave New World* is a world-state, in which war has been eliminated and where the first aim of the rulers is at all costs to keep their subjects from making trouble. This they achieve by (among other methods) legalizing a degree of sexual freedom (made possible by the abolition of the family) that practically guarantees the Brave New

Worlders against any form of destructive (or creative) emotional tension. In *1984* the lust for power is satisfied by inflicting pain; in *Brave New World*, by inflicting a hardly less humiliating pleasure.

The current Social Ethic, it is obvious, is merely a justification after the fact of the less desirable consequences of over-organization. It represents a pathetic attempt to make a virtue of necessity, to extract a positive value from an unpleasant datum. It is a very unrealistic, and therefore very dangerous, system of morality. The social whole, whose value is assumed to be greater than that of its component parts, is not an organism in the sense that a hive or a termitary may be thought of as an organism. It is merely an organization, a piece of social machinery. There can be no value except in relation to life and awareness. An organization is neither conscious nor alive. Its value is instrumental and derivative. It is not good in itself; it is good only to the extent that it promotes the good of the individuals who are the parts of the collective whole. To give organizations precedence over persons is to subordinate ends to means. What happens when ends are subordinated to means was clearly demonstrated by Hitler and Stalin. Under their hideous rule personal ends were subordinated to organizational means by a mixture of violence and propaganda, systematic terror and the systematic manipulation of minds. In the more efficient dictatorships of tomorrow there will probably be much less violence than under Hitler and Stalin. The future dictator's subjects will be painlessly regimented by a corps of highly trained social engineers. "The challenge of social engineering in our time," writes an enthusiastic advocate of this new science, "is like the challenge of technical engineering fifty years ago. If the first half of the twentieth century was the era of the technical engineers, the second half may well be the era of social engineers"—and the twenty-first century, I suppose, will be the era of World Controllers, the scientific caste system and Brave New World. To the question *quis custodiet custodes?* —Who will mount guard over our guardians, who will engineer the engineers?—the answer is a bland denial that they need any supervision. There seems to be a touching belief among certain Ph.D.'s in sociology that Ph.D.'s in sociology will never be corrupted by power. Like Sir Galahad's, their strength is as the strength of ten because their heart is pure—and their heart is pure because they are scientists and have taken six thousand hours of social studies.

Alas, higher education is not necessarily a guarantee of higher virtue, or higher political wisdom. And to these misgivings on ethical and psychological grounds must be added misgivings of a purely scientific character. Can we accept the theories on which the social engineers base their practice, and in terms of which they justify their manipulations of human beings? For example, Professor Elton Mayo tells us categorically that "man's desire to be continuously associated in work with his fellows is a strong, if not the strongest human characteristic." This, I would say, is manifestly untrue. Some people have the kind of desire described by Mayo; others do not. It is a matter of temperament and inherited constitution. Any social organization based upon the assumption that "man" (whoever "man" may be) desires to be continuously associated with his fellows would be, for many individual men and women, a bed of Procrustes. Only by being amputated or stretched upon the rack could they be adjusted to it.

Again, how romantically misleading are the lyrical accounts of the Middle Ages with which many contemporary theorists of social relations adorn their works! "Membership in a guild, manorial estate or village protected medieval man throughout his life and gave him peace and serenity." Protected him from what, we may ask. Certainly not from remorseless bullying at the hands of his superiors. And along with all that "peace and serenity" there was, throughout the Middle Ages, an enormous amount of chronic frustration, acute unhappiness and a passionate resentment against the rigid, hierarchical system that permitted no vertical movement up the social ladder and, for those who were bound to the land, very little horizontal movement in space. The impersonal forces of over-population and over-organization, and the social engineers who are trying to direct these forces, are pushing us in the direction of a new medieval system. This revival will be made more acceptable than the original by such Brave-New-Worldian amenities as infant conditioning, sleep-teaching and drug-induced euphoria; but, for the majority of men and women, it will still be a kind of servitude.

16

Utopia and the Coming Slavery

HERBERT SPENCER'S CRITIQUE OF THE WELFARE STATE

In a collection of essays entitled *The Man Versus the State* (1884), the well-known English philosopher and sociologist Herbert Spencer (1820–1903) delivered one of the most forceful attacks on socialism and cogent defenses of individualism of the late nineteenth century. Although Spencer's primary aim in his essays was to show the defects and dangers of state socialism, several of his criticisms would seem to apply as well to utopianism.

Spencer's basic position on socialism may be summarized best in his own words: "All socialism involves slavery." In reaching this conclusion he argued that in order for the socialist machine to perform its functions, there had to be strict regimentation, hierarchical organization, and authoritarian administration. In the name of greater efficiency, this regulation and organization would inevitably develop into what Spencer termed "the tyranny of organization" and "the despotism of a graduated and centralized officialism." Under a triumph of socialism, this official authority would be granted (or would certainly gain) the power to enforce its decrees upon the workers and to maintain order. Although the workers would not realize it until it was too late to do anything about it, they would stand toward their government agencies or administrators in the relation of slaves to masters.

Moreover, it would soon be glaringly evident to all concerned that the socialistic administration was not as altruistic in practice as it had been envisaged in theory. Defects in human nature—love of power, selfishness, injustice, greed—would, Spencer held, manifest themselves in and through the social order, bringing inevitably public misconduct and corruption. "There is no political alchemy," as he put it, "by which you can get golden conduct out of leaden instincts." Finally, confronted by internal pressure (e.g. an economic crisis) or by external threat (e.g. a war), the socialistic administration could quickly and efficiently transform itself into "a grinding tyranny".

Thus Spencer saw the dangers inherent in an impersonal bureaucratic management of human affairs and criticized the conception of a wholly planned and controlled welfare state half a century before Orwell and Huxley wrote their famous dystopias. Spencer showed that he was well aware of the logic (or illogic) by which freedom can be identified with slavery and by which "Big Brother," even if he did not exist, would have to be invented. He also saw clearly and warned against the tendencies which were leading mankind toward the "Brave New World" of "Community, Identity, and Stability."

If Spencer was sceptical of socialistic regimes, he was also sceptical of utopian thinking. He rejected the belief, often accepted by utopians, that an imperfect humanity can be made perfect by reconstructed social institutions. He argued, as suggested above, that the defects in human nature would appear no matter under which social system people live. Further, he was unconvinced that the often expressed utopian aim of removing all pain and suffering from life would be a desirable aim, even if it were a possible one to achieve. In adjusting to his environment, in learning, in growing, and in evolving to a higher level of achievement, man cannot avoid suffering and experiencing unhappiness and misery, which result inevitably "from incongruity between constitution and conditions." And like Freud, Spencer recognized that man as a civilized creature must learn and practice "the ability to sacrifice a small immediate gratification for a future great one." Spencer, therefore, would certainly find serious fault with those utopians who sought to realize a hedonistic paradise on earth, just as he would have criticized utopians such as Edward Bellamy who failed to see the dangers inherent in a bureaucratic organization or an "industrial army" which supposedly would make possible a socialistic "Commonwealth of the Golden Rule."

It would be a mistake to conclude in light of Spencer's position so far set forth, however, that he was a reactionary opposed to all progressive reforms and a defender of the status quo. To the contrary, he claimed that he was opposed to socialism primarily because he favored progress and believed that socialism would block it. Whether or not we agree with Spencer's strictures, we should not overlook the fact that he, like John Stuart Mill and Henry David Thoreau, though on different grounds, was attempting to defend rationally and fairly the individual's claim for self-determination and freedom of choice against bureaucratic and authoritarian control.

From Herbert Spencer, "From Freedom to Bondage,"
Essays, scientific, political, and speculative, *vol. 3*
(New York: D. Appleton & Co., 1892), pp. 456–70.

. . . Iron and brass are simpler things than flesh and blood, and dead wood than living nerve; and a machine constructed of the one works in more definite ways than an organism constructed of the other,—especially when the machine is worked by the inorganic forces of steam or water, while the organism is worked by the forces of living nerve-centres. Manifestly, then, the ways in which the machine will work are much more readily calculable than the ways in which the organism will work. Yet in how few cases does the inventor foresee rightly the actions of his new apparatus! Read the patent-list, and it will be found that not more than one device in fifty turns out to be of any service. Plausible as his scheme seemed to the inventor, one or other hitch prevents the intended operation, and brings out a widely different result from that which he wished.

What, then, shall we say of these schemes which have to do not with dead matters and forces, but with complex living organisms working in ways less readily foreseen, and which involve the co-operation of multitudes of such organisms? Even the units out of which this rearranged body politic is to be formed are often incomprehensible. Everyone is from time to time surprised by others' behavior, and even by the deeds of relatives who are best known to him. Seeing, then, how uncertainly any one can foresee the actions of an individual, how can he with any certainty foresee the operation of a social structure? He proceeds on the assumption that all concerned will judge rightly and act fairly—will think as they ought to think, and act as they ought to act; and he assumes this regardless of the daily experiences which show him that men do neither the one nor the other, and forgetting that the complaints he makes against the existing system show his belief to be that men have neither the wisdom nor the rectitude which his plan requires them to have.

Paper constitutions raise smiles on the faces of those who have observed their results; and paper social systems similarly affect those who have contemplated the available evidence. How little the men who wrought the French revolution and were chiefly concerned in

206

setting up the new governmental apparatus, dreamt that one of the early actions of this apparatus would be to behead them all! How little the men who drew up the American Declaration of Independence and framed the republic, anticipated that after some generations the legislature would lapse into the hands of wire-pullers; that its doings would turn upon the contests of office-seekers; that political action would be everywhere vitiated by the intrusion of a foreign element holding the balance between parties; that electors, instead of judging for themselves, would habitually be led to the polls in thousands by their "bosses;" and that respectable men would be driven out of public life by the insults and slanders of professional politicians. Nor were there better previsions in those who gave constitutions to the various other states of the New World, in which unnumbered revolutions have shown with wonderful persistence the contrasts between the expected results of political systems and the achieved results. It has been no less thus with proposed systems of social re-organization, so far as they have been tried. Save where celibacy has been insisted on, their history has been everywhere one of disaster; ending with the history of Cabet's Icarian colony lately given by one of its members, Madame Fleury Robinson, in *The Open Court*—a history of splittings, re-splittings, and re-re-splittings, accompanied by numerous individual secessions and final dissolution. And for the failure of such social schemes, as for the failure of the political schemes, there has been one general cause.

Metamorphosis is the universal law, exemplified throughout the Heavens and on the Earth: especially throughout the organic world; and above all in the animal division of it. No creature, save the simplest and most minute, commences its existence in a form like that which it eventually assumes; and in most cases the unlikeness is great—so great that kinship between the first and the last forms would be incredible were it not daily demonstrated in every poultry-yard and every garden. More than this is true. The changes of form are often several: each of them being an apparently complete transformation—egg, larva, pupa, imago, for example. And this universal metamorphosis, displayed alike in the development of a planet and of every seed which germinates on its surface, holds also of societies, whether taken as wholes or in their separate institutions. No one of them ends as it begins; and the difference between its original structure and its ultimate structure is such that, at the outset, change of the one into the other would have seemed incredible. In the rudest tribe the chief, obeyed as leader in war, loses his distinctive position when the fighting is over; and even where continued warfare has produced permanent chieftainship, the chief, building his own hut, getting his own food, making his own implements, differs from others only by his predominant influence. There is no sign that in course of time, by conquests and unions of tribes, and consolidations of clusters so formed with other such clusters, until a nation has been produced, there will originate from the primitive chief, one who, as czar or emperor, surrounded with pomp and ceremony, has despotic power over scores of millions, exercised through hundreds of thousands of soldiers and hundreds of thousands of officials. When the early Christian missionaries, having humble externals and passing self-denying lives, spread over pagan Europe, preaching forgiveness of injuries and the returning of good for evil, no one dreamt that in course of time their representatives would form a vast hierarchy, possessing everywhere a large part of the land, distinguished by the haughtiness of its members grade above grade, ruled by military bishops who led their retainers to battle, and headed by a pope exercising supreme power over kings. So, too, has it been with that very industrial system which many are now so eager to replace. In its original form there was no prophecy of the factory-system or kindred organizations of workers. Differing from them only as being the head of his house, the master worked along with his apprentices and a journeyman, or two, sharing with them his table and accommodation, and himself selling their joint produce. Only with industrial growth did there come employment of a larger number of assistants, and a relinquishment, on the part of the master, of all other business than that of superintendence. And only in the course of recent times did there evolve the organizations under which the labors of hundreds and thousands of men receiving wages, are regulated by various orders of paid officials under a single or multiple head. These originally small, semi-socialistic, groups of producers, like the compound families or house-communities of early ages, slowly dissolved because they could not hold their ground: the larger establishments, with better subdivision of labor, succeeded because they ministered to the wants of society more effectually. But we need not go back through the centuries to trace transformations sufficiently great and unexpected. On the day when £30,000 a year in aid of education was voted as an experiment, the name of idiot would have been given to an opponent who prophesied that in 50 years the sum spent through imperial taxes and local rates would amount to £10,000,000 or who said that the aid to education would be followed by aids to feeding and clothing, or who said that parents and children, alike deprived of all option, would, even if starving, be compelled by fine or imprisonment to conform, and receive that which, with papal assumption, the State calls education. No one, I say, would have dreamt that out of so innocent-looking a germ would have so quickly evolved this tyrannical system, tamely submitted to by people who fancy themselves free.

Thus in social arrangements, as in all other things, change is inevitable. It is foolish to suppose that new institutions set up, will long retain the character given them by those who set them up. Rapidly or slowly they will be transformed into institutions unlike those intended —so unlike as even to be unrecognizable by their devisers. And what, in the case before us, will be the metamorphosis? The answer pointed to by instances above given, and warranted by various analogies, is manifest.

A cardinal trait in all advancing organization is the development of the regulative apparatus. If the parts of a whole are to act together, there must be appliances by which their actions are directed; and in proportion as the whole is large and complex, and has many requirements to be met by many agencies, the directive apparatus must be extensive, elaborate, and powerful. That it is thus with individual organisms needs no saying; and that it must be thus with social organisms is obvious. Beyond the regulative apparatus such as in our own society is required for carrying on national defence and maintaining public order and personal safety, there must, under the *régime* of socialism, be a regulative apparatus everywhere controlling all kinds of production and distribution, and everywhere apportioning the shares of products of each kind required for each locality, each working establishment, each individual. Under our existing voluntary co-operation, with its free contracts and its competition, production and distribution need no official oversight. Demand and supply, and the desire of each man to gain a living by supplying the needs of his fellows, spontaneously evolve that wonderful system whereby a great city has its food daily brought round to all doors or stored at adjacent shops; has clothing for its citizens everywhere at hand in multitudinous varieties; has its houses and furniture and fuel ready made or stocked in each locality; and has mental pabulum from halfpenny papers hourly hawked round, to weekly shoals of novels, and less abundant books of instruction, furnished without stint for small payments. And throughout the kingdom, production as well as distribution is similarly carried on with the smallest amount of superintendence which proves efficient; while the quantities of the numerous commodities required daily in each locality are adjusted without any other agency than the pursuit of profit. Suppose now that this industrial *régime* of willinghood, acting spontaneously, is replaced by a *régime* of industrial obedience, enforced by public officials. Imagine the vast administration required for that distribution of all commodities to all people in every city, town and village, which is now effected by traders! Imagine, again, the still more vast administration required for doing all that farmers, manufacturers, and merchants do; having not only its various orders of local superintendents, but its sub-centres and chief centres needed for apportioning the quantities of each thing everywhere needed, and the adjustment of them to the requisite times. Then add the staffs wanted for working mines, railways, roads, canals; the staffs required for conducting the importing and exporting businesses and the administration of mercantile shipping; the staffs required for supplying towns not only with water and gas but with locomotion by tramways, omnibuses, and other vehicles, and for the distribution of power, electric and other. Join with these the existing postal, telegraphic, and telephonic administrations; and finally those of the police and army, by which the dictates of this immense consolidated regulative system are to be everywhere enforced. Imagine all this and then ask what will be the position of the actual workers! Already on the continent, where governmental organizations are more elaborate and coercive than here, there are chronic complaints of the tyranny of bureaucracies—the *hauteur* and brutality of their members. What will these become when not only the more public actions of citizens are controlled, but there is added this far more extensive control of all their respective daily duties? What will happen when the various divisions of this vast army of officials, united by interests common to officialism—the interests of the regulators *versus* those of the regulated—have at their command whatever force is needful to suppress insubordination and act as "saviours of society"? Where will be the actual diggers and miners and smelters and weavers, when those who order and superintend, everywhere arranged class above class, have come, after some generations, to inter-marry with those of kindred grades, under feelings such as are operative in existing classes: and when there have been so produced a series of castes rising in superiority; and when all these, having everything in their own power, have arranged modes of living for their own advantage: eventually forming a new aristocracy far more elaborate and better organized than the old? How will the individual worker fare if he is dissatisfied with his treatment—thinks that he has not an adequate share of the products, or has more to do than can rightly be demanded, or wishes to undertake a function for which he feels himself fitted but which is not thought proper for him by his superiors, or desires to make an independent career for himself? This dissatisfied unit in the immense machine will be told he must submit or go. The mildest penalty for disobedience will be industrial excommunication. And if an international organization of labor is formed as proposed, exclusion in one country will mean exclusion in all others—industrial excommunication will mean starvation.

That things must take this course is a conclusion reached not by deduction only, nor only by induction from those experiences of the past instanced above, nor only from consideration of the analogies furnished by organisms of all orders; but it is reached also by observation of cases daily under our eyes. The truth that the regulative structure always tends to increase in power, is illustrated by every established body of men. The history of each learned society, or society for other purpose, shows how the staff, permanent or partially permanent, sways the proceedings and determines the actions of the society with but little resistance, even when most members of the society disapprove: the repugnance to anything like a revolutionary step being ordinarily an efficient deterrent. So it is with joint-stock companies—those owning railways for example. The plans of a board of directors are usually authorized with little or no discussion; and if there is any considerable opposition, this is forthwith crushed by an overwhelming number of proxies sent by those who always support the existing administration. Only when the misconduct is extreme does the resistance of shareholders suffice to displace the ruling body. Nor is it otherwise with societies formed of working men and having the interests of labor especially at heart—the trades-unions. In these, too, the regulative agency becomes all powerful. Their members, even when they dissent from the policy pursued, habitually yield to the authorities they have set up. As they cannot secede without making enemies of their fellow workmen, and often losing all chance of employment, they succumb. We are shown, too, by the late congress, that already, in the general organization of trade-unions so recently formed, there are complaints of "wire-pullers" and "bosses" and "permanent officials." If, then, this supremacy of the regulators is seen in bodies of quite modern origin, formed of men who have, in many of the cases instanced, unhindered powers of asserting their independence, what will the supremacy of the regulators become in long-established bodies, in bodies which have become vast and highly organized, and in bodies which, instead of controlling only a small part of the unit's life, control the whole of his life?

Again there will come the rejoinder—"We shall guard against all that. Everybody will be educated; and all, with their eyes constantly open to the abuse of power, will be quick to prevent it." The worth of these expectations would be small even could we not identify the causes which will bring disappointment; for in human affairs the most promising schemes go wrong in ways which no one anticipated. But in this case the going wrong will be necessitated by causes which are conspicuous. The working of institutions is determined by men's characters; and the existing defects in their characters will inevitably bring about the results above indicated. There is no adequate endowment of those sentiments required to prevent the growth of a despotic bureaucracy.

Were it needful to dwell on indirect evidence, much might be made of that furnished by the behavior of the so-called Liberal party—a party which, relinquishing the original conception of a leader as a mouthpiece for a known and accepted policy, thinks itself bound to accept a policy which its leader springs upon it without consent or warning—a party so utterly without the feeling and idea implied by liberalism, as not to resent this tramping on the right of private judgment, which constitutes the root of liberalism—nay, a party which vilifies as renegade liberals, those of its members who refuse to surrender their independence! But without occupying space with indirect proofs that the mass of men have not the natures required to check the development of tyrannical officialism, it will suffice to contemplate the direct proofs furnished by those classes among whom the socialistic idea most predominates, and who think themselves most interested in propagating it—the operative classes. These would constitute the great body of the socialistic organization, and their characters would determine its nature. What, then, are their characters as displayed in such organizations as they have already formed?

Instead of the selfishness of the employing classes and the selfishness of competition, we are to have the unselfishness of a mutually-aiding system. How far is this unselfishness now shown in the behavior of working men to one another? What shall we say to the rules limiting the numbers of new hands admitted into each trade, or to the rules which hinder ascent from inferior classes of workers to superior classes? One does not see in such regulations any of that altruism by which socialism is to be pervaded. Contrariwise, one sees a pursuit of private interests no less keen than among traders. Hence, unless we suppose that men's natures will be suddenly exalted, we must conclude that the pursuit of private interests will sway the doings of all the component classes in a socialistic society.

With passive disregard of others' claims goes active encroachment on them. "Be one of us or we will cut off your means of living," is the usual threat of each trades-union to outsiders of the same trade. While their members insist on their own freedom to combine and fix the rates at which they will work (as they are perfectly justified in doing), the freedom of those who disagree with them is not only denied but the assertion of it is treated as a crime. Individuals who maintain their rights to make their own contracts are vilified as "blacklegs" and "traitors," and meet with violence which would be merciless were there no legal penalties and no police. Along with this trampling on the liberties of men of their own class, there goes peremptory dictation to the employing class: not prescribed terms and working arrangements only shall be conformed to, but none save those belonging to their body shall be employed—nay, in some cases, there shall be a strike if the employer carries on transactions with trading bodies that give work to non-union men. Here, then, we are variously shown by trades-unions, or at any rate by their newer trades-unions, a determination to impose their regulations without regard to the rights of those who are to be coerced. So complete is the inversion of ideas and sentiments that maintenance of these rights is regarded as vicious and trespass upon them as virtuous.

Along with this aggressiveness in one direction there goes submissiveness in another direction. The coercion of outsiders by unionists is paralleled only by their subjection to their leaders. That they may conquer in the struggle they surrender their individual liberties and individual judgments, and show no resentment however dictatorial may be the rule exercised over them. Everywhere we see such subordination that bodies of workmen unanimously leave their work or return to it as their authorities order them. Nor do they resist when taxed all round to support strikers whose acts they may or may not approve, but instead, ill-treat recalcitrant members of their body who do not subscribe.

The traits thus shown must be operative in any new social organization, and the question to be asked is—What will result from their operation when they are relieved from all restraints? At present the separate bodies of men displaying them are in the midst of a society partially passive, partially antagonistic; are subject to the criticisms and reprobations of an independent press; and are under the control of law, enforced by police. If in these circumstances these bodies habitually take courses which override individual freedom, what will happen when, instead of being only scattered parts of the community, governed by their separate sets of regulators, they constitute the whole community, governed by a consolidated system of such regulators; when functionaries of all orders, including those who officer the press, form parts of the regulative organization; and when the law is both enacted and administered by this regulative organization? The fanatical adherents of a social theory are capable of taking any measures, no matter how extreme, for carrying out their views: holding, like the merciless priesthoods of past times, that the end justifies the means.

And when a general socialistic organization has been established, the vast, ramified, and consolidated body of those who direct its activities, using without check whatever coercion seems to them needful in the interests of the system (which will practically become their own interests) will have no hesitation in imposing their rigorous rule over the entire lives of the actual workers; until, eventually, there is developed an official oligarchy, with its various grades, exercising a tyranny more gigantic and more terrible than any which the world has seen.

Let me again repudiate an erroneous inference. Any one who supposes that the foregoing argument implies contentment with things as they are, makes a profound mistake. The present social state is transitional, as past social states have been transitional. There will, I hope and believe, come a future social state differing as much from the present as the present differs from the past with its mailed barons and defenceless serfs. In *Social Statics*, as well as in *The Study of Sociology* and in *Political Institutions*, is clearly shown the desire for an organization more conducive to the happiness of men at large than that which exists. My opposition to socialism results from the belief that it would stop the progress to such a higher state and bring back a lower state. Nothing but the slow modification of human nature by the discipline of social life, can produce permanently advantageous changes.

A fundamental error pervading the thinking of nearly all parties, political and social, is that evils admit of immediate and radical remedies. "If you will but do this, the mischief will be prevented." "Adopt my plan and the suffering will disappear." "The corruption will unquestionably be cured by enforcing this measure." Everywhere one meets with beliefs, expressed or implied, of these kinds. They are all ill-founded. It is possible to remove causes which intensify the evils; it is possible to change the evils from one form into another; and it is possible, and very common, to exacerbate the evils by the efforts made to prevent them; but anything like immediate cure is impossible. In the course of thousands of years mankind have, by multiplication, been forced out of that original savage state in which small numbers supported themselves on wild food, into the civilized state in which the food required for supporting great numbers can be got only by continuous labor. The nature required for this last mode of life is widely different from the nature required for the first; and long-continued pains have to be passed through in remoulding the one into the other. Misery has necessarily to be borne by a constitution out of harmony with its conditions; and a constitution inherited from primitive men is out of harmony with the conditions imposed on existing men. Hence it is impossible to establish forthwith a satisfactory social state. No such nature as that which has filled Europe with millions of armed men, here eager for conquest and there for revenge—no such nature as that which prompts the nations called Christian to vie with one another in filibustering expeditions all over the world, regardless of the claims of aborigines, while their tens of thousands of priests of the religion of love look on approvingly—no such nature as that which, in dealing with weaker races, goes beyond the primitive rule of life for life, and for one life takes many lives—no such nature, I say, can, by any device, be framed into a harmonious community. The root of all well-ordered social action is a sentiment of justice, which at once insists on personal freedom and is solicitous for the like freedom of others; and there at present exists but a very inadequate amount of this sentiment.

Hence the need for further long continuance of a social discipline which requires each man to carry on his activities with due regard to the like claims of others to carry on their activities; and which, while it insists that he shall have all the benefits his conduct naturally brings, insists also that he shall not saddle on others the evils his conduct naturally brings: unless they freely undertake to bear them. And hence the belief that endeavours to elude this discipline, will not only fail, but will bring worse evils than those to be escaped.

It is not, then, chiefly in the interests of the employing classes that socialism is to be resisted, but much more in the interests of the employed classes. In one way or other production must be regulated; and the regulators, in the nature of things, must always be a small class as compared with the actual producers. Under voluntary co-operation as at present carried on, the regulators, pursuing their personal interests, take as large a share of the produce as they can get; but, as we are daily shown by trades-union successes, are restrained in the selfish pursuit of their ends. Under that compulsory co-operation which socialism would necessitate, the regulators, pursuing their personal interests with no less selfishness, could not be met by the combined resistance of free workers; and their power, unchecked as now by refusals to work save on prescribed terms, would grow and ramify and consolidate till it became irresistible. The ultimate result, as I have before pointed out, must be a society like that of ancient Peru, dreadful to contemplate, in which the mass of the people, elaborately regimented in groups of 10, 50, 100, 500, and 1,000, ruled by officers of corresponding grades, and tied to their districts, were superintended in their private lives as well as in their industries, and toiled hopelessly for the support of the governmental organization.

17

Ignoble Utopias

Joseph Wood Krutch's Attack
on Behavioral Engineering

"I never have been, and am not now, any kind of utopian," wrote Joseph Wood Krutch (1893–1970) in a collection of his miscellaneous writing entitled *If You Don't Mind My Saying So*. Drama critic, biographer, professor of English, amateur naturalist as well as moral philosopher, Krutch often took the opportunity to deal critically with the assumptions underlying modern utopian thinking. In one of his earliest and most widely read books, *The Modern Temper* (1929), he discussed the disillusionment modern man experienced when he realized that science, while it had increased his knowledge and power over nature, had not necessarily increased his wisdom and happiness. Utopianism based upon uncritical confidence in science ends in pessimism, his analysis suggested. Communistic utopianism is also mistaken, Krutch claimed, in holding that the perfecting of man's social and material environment will bring human happiness. In his later books, notably in *The Condition of Man* (1953) and *Human Nature and the Human Condition* (1959), Krutch continued to criticize the assumptions from which, he believed, much modern thinking and acting proceeds.

Krutch presented an alternate way for thought and action which, if followed, would avoid many of the contradictions and dilemmas arising in everyday experience. This was the way of the humanist, who rejects the image of man presented in merely behavioristic and mechanistic terms and believes in the reality of reason, will, and purpose. Good and evil, for Krutch's ideal humanist, refer to universally valid human norms, not merely to customs and mores. Consciousness will not be dismissed as an epiphenomenon but will be considered an essential creative force. Only from this perspective, Krutch claimed, can man find his way beyond the confused and troubled contemporary "human condition" to genuinely valuable human conduct.

From this humanistic perspective Krutch criticized the "economy of abundance" which, he believed, impoverishes rather than enriches man. When man is viewed as primarily a consumer to be exploited, a product to be

216

reproduced, or an animal to be conditioned, his unique human endowments are distorted if not destroyed, Krutch held, and eventually a dystopia rather than a utopia will be the result.

Krutch would undoubtedly have agreed with Aldous Huxley that one of the most pressing problems facing men is that of finding a way of avoiding the community, identity, and stability which were the ideals of *Brave New World*. We will never find this way, Krutch contended, so long as we are willing to accept contentment instead of challange, indoctrination instead of education, technological power instead of human wisdom, and allow ourselves to drift rapidly toward a welfare state which will be to everyone's (and thus to no one's) best interest. In his works, Krutch criticized stringently the mentality and morality of the contemporary utilitarians and behavioral engineers who would welcome this kind of utopia and who would probably not object to quite radical and dictatorial measures to bring it about. His point of view is in agreement with Samuel Johnson's statement that "the remedy for the ills of life is palliative rather than radical" and with Thoreau's that our "first business is to live in this world be it good or bad."

The following selection from *Measure of Man* illustrates Krutch's criticism of supposedly scientific approaches to the planning of an ideal society. In the chapter prior to the one from which the selection is taken, Krutch attacked the deterministic assumption from which such planning proceeds. He also rejected the currently popular view that antisocial behavior is merely the result of determining or conditioning factors over which the individual has no control. This view, he argued, would either make the concept of personal responsibility meaningless or at least would reduce it to a mere socially useful illusion. Since it would be absurd to argue that a man is guilty of doing wrong if he can not help doing what he does, the exponent of "today's thinking" cannot (except by faulty logic) make sense of moral judgments of the rightness or wrongness of human conduct. He may have to accept these judgments as pragmatically necessary, but he cannot, according to Krutch, rationally explain or support them.

The focus of Krutch's attention in the selection given here is B. F. Skinner's behavioristic utopia, *Walden Two*. After considering the criticisms brought against Skinner's views, the reader may wish to turn immediately to Skinner's defense of his approach which is given in Part 4.

That exponent of "today's thinking" whose opinion was quoted in the preceding chapter had not carried his own thought beyond the point where it was still possible to accomplish a simple *reductio ad absurdum* and to declare that his premises lead to principles pragmatically absurd.

Other social scientists and experimental psychologists, operating on a different level, have proceeded further. Some, like Professor Thomas D. Eliot of Northwestern University, undertake the difficult task of explaining how a man may be in some sense *responsible* for what he does without actually being free to do anything else. In a paper called "Social Control of International Aggressions" published recently in the *American Journal of Sociology* Professor Eliot says: "The basic fallacy lies in imputing to offenders spontaneous, 'willing' evil and hatred and therefore treating them not merely *as accountable for their acts,* but as personally guilty. Blame and guilt are very actual feelings, *but they derive from false premises.* An enlarged perspective would show the offense and the offender emerging as parts of a larger situation-process, in which the offended community also provides the essential milieu and both are injured parties." (Italics mine)

Now this is a version of "today's thinking" considerably subtler than that previously quoted. But it poses a dilemma of its own. In former days those who revolted against the logic of Calvinism refused to accept the conclusion that an individual was responsible and punishable for doing what God had predestined him to do. Professor Eliot appears to have embraced a secular version of this same theology when he distinguishes between what men may be *held accountable for* and what they may be *blamed with*.

Other thinkers concerned less with such immediate matters as national or individual criminality adopt even more radical attitudes toward the question of man's nature and the kind of future to be hoped for him. Many of them are well aware that their convictions imply changes in both man and society far more radical than any assumed or even desired by the mere reformists, who might be al-

218

most as horrified as Mr. Churchill himself at the radical newness of
the new world which a more relentless pursuit of implications has led
bolder thinkers to regard as inevitable.

Such bolder thinkers, far from accepting the contention that some
belief, justified or illusory, in some degree of individual autonomy is a
pragmatic necessity, would dismiss that contention as contemptu-
ously as the present writer dismissed his example of "today's thinking."
Man, they would say, is almost limitlessly plastic. He may be conditioned to almost anything—certainly to an acceptance of the belief
that he is nothing but the product of his conditioning. In a world
dominated by that conviction he would, they say, be as successful
and as happy as his predecessor, conditioned to a belief in moral
responsibility, would no doubt be unsuccessful and miserable.

Many who share the conviction of that Dean of the Humanities
who announced "our approaching scientific ability to control men's
thoughts with precision" are therefore not appalled by the prospect.
Among them may be included B. F. Skinner, Professor of Psychology
at Harvard, one of the most able and esteemed leaders in his field,
and author of a fantasy called *Walden Two* which describes the contented life led by the inmates of an institution—though Professor
Skinner might dislike this designation—to which they have voluntarily committed themselves and where they are conditioned to like
being conditioned. An analysis of Professor Skinner's thought will reveal very clearly in what direction some believe that the Science of
Man is moving.

Walden Two is a utopian community created by an experimental
psychologist named Frazier who has learned the techniques for controlling thought with precision and who has conditioned his subjects
to be happy, obedient and incapable of antisocial behavior. Universal
benevolence and large tolerance of individual differences reign—not
because it is assumed, as the founders of such utopias generally do
assume, that they are natural to all innocent men uncorrupted by
society—but because an experimental scientist, having at last mastered the "scientific ability to control men's thoughts with precision,"
has caused them to think benevolently and tolerantly.

An appeal to reason in contradistinction to passion, habit, or mere
custom has been the usual basis of utopias from Plato to Sir Thomas
More and even down to Samuel Butler. Mr. Skinner's is, on the other
hand, distinctly modern in that it puts its faith in the conditioned
reflex instead, and proposes to perfect mankind by making individual
men incapable of anything except habit and prejudice. At Walden
Two men behave in a fashion we are accustomed to call "reasonable,"
not because they reason, but because they do not; because "right

responses" are automatic. At the very beginning of the story we are shown a flock of sheep confined to the area reserved for them by a single thread which long ago replaced the electric fence once employed to condition them not to wander. As predicted in official Communist theory, the State—represented here by electricity—has "withered away" and no actual restraint is necessary to control creatures in whom obedience has become automatic. Obviously the assumption is that what will work with sheep will work with men.

Now though men can reason, they are not exclusively reasoning creatures. None, therefore, of the classic utopias could be realized because each is based on the assumption that reason alone can be made to guide human behavior. Moreover—and what is perhaps more important—few people have ever seriously wished to be exclusively rational. The good life which most desire is a life warmed by passions and touched with that ceremonial grace which is impossible without some affectionate loyalty to traditional forms and ceremonies. Many have, nevertheless, been very willing to grant that a little more reason in the conduct of private and public affairs would not be amiss. That is why, as fantasies, the utopias of Plato and Sir Thomas More have seemed interesting, instructive, even inspiring. But who really wants, even in fancy, to be, as Walden Two would make him, more unthinking, more nearly automatic than he now is? Who, even in his imagination, would like to live in a community where, instead of thinking part of the time, one never found it possible to think at all?

Is it not meaningful to say that whereas Plato's Republic and More's Utopia are noble absurdities, Walden Two is an ignoble one; that the first two ask men to be more than human, while the second urges them to be less? When, in the present world, men behave well, that is no doubt sometimes because they are creatures of habit as well as, sometimes, because they are reasonable. But if one proposes to change Man as Professor Skinner and so many other cheerful mechanists propose, is it really so evident that he should be changed in the direction they advocate? Is he something which, in Nietzsche's phrase, "must be surpassed," or is he a creature to whom the best advice one can give is the advice to retreat—away from such reasoned behavior as he may be capable of and toward that automatism of which he is also capable.

Obviously Walden Two represents—glorified, perfected, and curiously modernized—that ideal of a "cloistered virtue" which European man has tended to find not only unsatisfactory as an ideal but almost meaningless in terms of his doubtless conflicting aspirations. Nevertheless it must be admitted that Thomas Henry Huxley, a proto-modern, once admitted in an often quoted passage that "if some great power would agree to make me always think what is true and do what is right, on condition of being turned into a sort of clock and wound up every morning before I got out of bed, I should instantly close with the offer." And what a Huxley would have agreed to, prospective candidates for admission into Walden Two might also find acceptable.

Frazier himself is compelled to make a significant confession: the motives which led him to undertake his successful experiment included a certain desire to exercise power over his fellows. That is not admirable in itself and is obviously not without its dangers. But he insists that the danger will disappear with him because those who succeed to his authority and inherit his techniques will have enjoyed, as he did not, the advantages of a scientific conditioning process and that therefore such potentially antisocial impulses as his will no longer exist. In other words, though the benevolent dictator is a rare phenomenon today, the happy chance which produced this one will not have to be relied on in the future. Walden Two will automatically produce the dictators necessary to carry it on.

Nevertheless and even if the skeptical reader will grant for the sake of argument that automatic virtue represents an ideal completely satisfactory, a multitude of other doubts and fears are likely to arise in his mind. He will remember of course that Brook Farm and the rest failed promptly and decisively. Perhaps he will remember also that Russian communism achieved at least some degree of permanence only by rejecting, more and more completely, everything which in any way parallels the mildness, the gentleness, and the avoidance of all direct restraints and pressures which is characteristic of Walden Two; that the makers of Soviet policy came to denounce and repress even that somewhat paradoxical enthusiasm for the culture of a different world which was as much encouraged in the earliest days of the experiment as it is at Walden Two.

Hence, if a Walden Two is possible it obviously has become so only because—and this is a point which presumably Mr. Skinner himself wishes to emphasize—it differs in several respects from all superficially similar projects. Like the Russian experiment it assumes that, for all practical purposes, man is merely the product of society; but it also assumes a situation which did not exist when the Communist state was set up: namely one in which "the scientific ability to control men's thoughts with precision" has fully matured.

Thus if the man upon whom the experiment is performed is nothing but the limitlessly plastic product of external processes operating upon him and is, by definition, incapable of any significant autonomous activity, he is also, in this case, a creature who has fallen into the hands of an ideally competent dictator. His desires, tastes, convictions and ideals are precisely what the experimenter wants to make them. He is the repository of no potentialities which can ever develop except as they are called forth by circumstances over which he has no control. Finally, of course, his happy condition is the result of the fortunate accident which determined that the "engineer" who created him and, indirectly, will create all of his progeny, was an experimenter whose own random conditioning happened to produce, not the monster who might just as likely have been the first to seize the power that science offered, but a genuinely benevolent dictator instead.

A propos this last premise it might, in passing, be remarked as a curious fact that though scientific method abhors the accidental, the uncontrollable and the unpredicted; though Mr. Skinner's own ideal seems to be to remove forever any possible future intrusion of it into human affairs; yet the successful establishment of the first utopia depended ultimately on the decisive effect of just such an accident as will henceforth be impossible.

Critics of the assumption that technological advance is the true key to human progress have often urged that new powers are dangerous rather than beneficial unless the question of how they should be used is at least opened before the powers become available. With more than usual anxiety they might contemplate the situation in which we are now placed if it is true that only chance will answer the question by whom and in the interest of what "our approaching scientific ability to control men's thoughts with precision" is to be used. But this is only one of several desperate questions which the premises of *Walden Two* provoke. Most of them can also be related to points made by Mr. Skinner in less fanciful contexts and to one or two of them we may turn in connection with a more general consideration of problems raised if we are ready to assume that we actually do stand at the threshold of a world in which men's thoughts will be controlled scientifically and as a matter of course.

18

From Utopia to Nightmare

CHAD WALSH'S REFORMULATION OF
THE DYSTOPIAN CASE

In a book entitled *From Utopia to Nightmare* (1962), Chad Walsh, poet, teacher, and social and literary critic, explored the problem of why in our century the dystopia or anti-utopia has replaced the utopia as the dominant type of literary speculation about the future. While there have been numerous nightmarish visions of imaginary societies such as Zamiatin's *We*, Huxley's *Brave New World*, and Orwell's *1984*, positive utopian visions have been few and far between. And, except for B. F. Skinner's *Walden Two* (1948), few of the positive utopias have stirred extensive discussion or inspired utopian efforts. Gone apparently are the days when a utopian novel could become the focus of the hopes of thousands of utopian colonists (as did Cabet's *Icaria*), or could furnish a political party with attractive ideals and the promise of imaginative leadership (as did Bellamy's *Looking Backward*).

Is the waning of utopia and the waxing of anti-utopias in literature a symptom of widespread pessimism over present world conditions and of the inability of contemporary man to find a positive vision of the future to support his hopes and guide his efforts? What does the popularity of inverted utopias reveal about the present human and social predicament? In this latter half of the twentieth century, does the shift from utopia to dystopia augur good or evil for humanity? By surveying the dystopian scene Walsh hoped to discover at least some tentative answers to these large and compelling questions.

Throughout his discussion, Walsh encourages his readers to share his conviction of the importance of the recent shift from utopian to dystopian fiction. This shift of perspective from optimism to pessimism, from confident prediction of a happy future to forecasts of coming social disasters could well foreshadow a radical shift in the basic beliefs and attitudes of our culture. To dismiss the dystopia either as the product of a diseased literary minority, as some critics do, or as the telling expression of a decadent social system, as do others, is to oversimplify and distort.

Dystopias have replaced utopias, Walsh believes, because utopianism has from one point of view already succeeded in the world while from another it has already failed. Utopianism has failed even while apparently succeeding in that a number of its proposed improvements, for example, the welfare state, have already become realities without making much difference in the overall happiness of mankind. At the same time, utopianism has failed in that some of its highest goals such as peace and individual freedom seem further from realization today than ever before. Two world wars have been fought in this century and another, which conceivably could destroy civilization and life on earth may soon be in the offing. And in face of the tremendous military, political, and technological power which confronts the individual man in the contemporary world it has become increasingly difficult for the individual to make his own choices freely or to play any significant role in determining the conditions under which he may wish to live.

In addition to the setbacks utopianism has experienced by its paradoxical success and failure, there are several other historical factors which Walsh thinks have contributed to the eclipse of utopia by dystopia: the impact of Freudian psychology, which with its emphasis on unconscious motivation and irrational impulse seems to rule out the possibility (or desirability) of a perfectly rational society; the decline of the optimistic social gospel theology which was so favorable to utopian efforts (unlike the recently developed austere theology of Neo-Orthodoxy with its gloomy appraisal of the sinful human predicament); and the widespread disenchantment with the competing efforts of the United States and the Soviet Union to create ideal societies for their citizens.

Whatever causes may have brought about the literary shift from utopian dream to dystopian nightmare, Walsh believes that those who give dystopias the critical appreciation they deserve have much to gain. Dystopian fiction is, in his view, "the prophetic form of our age." Like Old Testament prophets, dystopian writers expose the evils of their times, propose cures for them, and predict dire consequences if their words of warning go unheeded. Unlike the traditional prophets, however, the dystopians express their messages not in sermons and moral exhortations but through works of fiction in which they present, in Kingsley Amis' phrase, "new maps of hell." For contemporary man, the dystopian form can be far more effective than moral discourse and pulpit preaching, Walsh holds, in awakening moral conscience and in calling for the regeneration of the social order.

Yet despite Walsh's appreciation of the values of dystopian fiction, or perhaps because of it, he himself is no anti-utopian. From his Christian humanist perspective, he believes that "if the utopian dream dies, something profoundly human and perhaps profoundly Christian dies with it."[1] Without utopias we might stop dreaming of a better society, and unless we continue to plan for it in our imagination, we will never succeed in bringing it about. But while we should not relinquish our utopian dreams, we should learn "to

---

[1] Chad Walsh, *From Utopia to Nightmare* (New York: Harper & Row, 1962), p. 172.

dream more intelligently and profoundly."[2] Because it can help us to achieve this end, dystopian fiction, Walsh concludes, should be contemplated as well as enjoyed.

In the following selection Walsh summarizes the dystopian arguments against the basic tenets of the utopian faith as he defines it.

[2] Ibid., p. 178.

I have taken you on a guided tour, highly selective, of dystopia, and have pointed out some of the recurrent themes. I should like now to backtrack. Earlier I mentioned nine assumptions, many of which at least are likely to be held by any utopian dreamer. Let me now list them again and indicate what the dystopian would say in reply.

1. *Man is basically good.* The dystopian says No. He doesn't deny that there is goodness in man, but he says it isn't strong and constant enough to be depended on too far. Even the most elaborate system of education, character training and conditioning will not make goodness a reliable trait in either the masses or the *élite*. Man is and will remain a mixture. The savage and the sadist and the plain schemer and the importunate ego are always lurking within him, sometimes hidden from sight, but ready to spring.

2. *Man is exceedingly plastic.* Here the dystopian comes closer to agreeing. He is impressed by the advances of practical psychology and brainwashing. Man can be moulded so that his heart beats faster at the likeness of Big Brother, so that a sexual orgy becomes his communion with God and the Social Whole. He can be trained to go through the motions of subordinating his selfish interests to those of society. He is a clever dog; he can be taught a great repertoire of tricks. But when man is radically reshaped it is at a price. He acquires, perhaps, a pseudo-altruism, a pseudo-goodness. He is like a person in a hypnotic trance, obeying the hypnotist. Those who are thoroughly conditioned and brainwashed are something less than real human beings henceforth; they are more akin to the wretches who have submitted to an actual lobotomy. If real goodness and altruism are to exist, rather than the benign motions of puppets, men must be left free to choose between good and evil. The dystopian might also add or imply that, though the newborn child is something of a *tabula rasa,* some messages can be written on the blank slate more easily than others.

3. *There is no need to set up a dichotomy between the happiness of the individual and that of society.* The dystopian says this is true in

heaven, but not here. When men submerge themselves in the social whole they are engulfed in a magnification and multiplication of self. Society is man writ large, sometimes the worst of man. Also, the goals of society have to be of a broad and impersonal kind: survival, maintenance of order, etc. Society as such is little concerned with immortal longings, delicate raptures, obscure agonies. Society regulates mating and marriage; society does not fall in love with this girl or that. Society is by its nature more coarse-grained than many of its members. The individual who seeks his fulfilment by being a bee in the hive must give up the nuances of his nature. He may be rewarded by a kind of secular beatific vision as he 'dies to self', but it is a false fulfilment, not good for him, not good for society. The dystopian also asserts that too much emphasis on the well-being of society can lead to a world in which the collective whole is flourishing but not a single one of the automata inhabiting it is capable of happiness.

4. *Man is a rational being, and can become more so. His powers of reason can be harnessed to the task of creating a society that makes better sense than any existing society. There is nothing sacred about the social institutions that have so haphazardly evolved. Just as real science has supplanted a great mass of half-scientific, half-superstitious folklore, so a real science of society can create something much better than the accidental society now existing.*

To take these points up one by one, the dystopian says two things about reason. First, that man is intermittently and partially a rational animal, and secondly, that reason itself must not be equated with the benevolent will. The devils may have a purer power of reason than we do, but you would not engage them to build your utopia. Reason, like science, is two-edged. And even reason submitted to goodwill is subject to self-deception, rationalisation, and the myriad tricks by which we find good reasons for our special biases and interests.

About the further clause, the dystopian does not deny that existing societies have grown like Topsy, though he might insist that many apparently absurd customs and attitudes reflect an age-long process of trial and error, and serve a real but obscure purpose. He would say that planners who wish to start with a clean slate don't reckon with the complexities. Actual societies, as the anthropologists have taught us, have an internal logic. Can a society be created from scratch and have a sufficient internal logic? Isn't it better to work from within the existing societies, lovingly and cautiously making changes where it seems they are needed?

There is an analogy. When the calorie was first discovered as a unit of energy, it seemed sensible to devise prison diets that would guarantee an adequate number of calories per day. With a clear con science, society fed its criminals on calories. But the prisoners began to get scurvy and other afflictions. The trouble was not that they had too few calories but that no one yet knew about vitamins. The dystopian would be inclined to say that any society, in an intuitive or trial-and-error way, discovers the social vitamins needed for its well-being, and that a utopian planner, dreaming grand thoughts, is likely to construct a society strong in calories but weak in vitamins.

Public housing projects in both Britain and America often demonstrate the same knowledge of calories and ignorance of vitamins. The planner forgets, for example, that young married couples have parents and sometimes like to have them living less than an hour's journey away in another project. Or the planner is so intent on 'cleaning up the streets' that he makes them dull; the result is that few of the local people choose to stroll around of an evening, and hoodlums can come in and have the streets to themselves. Many old-style slums have a better morale and sense of neighbourliness than communities that spring complete from the planning board. This does not mean that public housing is bad, but that the planner needs to deal with more than the 'calories' of life.

5. *The future holds a finite number of possibilities, which can be sufficiently foreseen for practical purposes.* The dystopian says No. Outrageous novelties may upset the most careful plans. The insect you import to get rid of some other bug may eat up your garden. The Law of Reverse Effect may turn the planner's work upside down. The dystopian is more inclined to bumble along, feeling his way and hedging his bets, rather than assuming that he can feed all the relevant facts into a computer and thereby anticipate the multiple consequences of every decision and act.

6. *The purpose of utopias is man's earthly welfare.* Utopians and dystopians alike differ greatly in their attention to any transcendent goal, such as salvation or heaven. In general, they are both more concerned with having a tolerable order of things here on earth. One world at a time, if there is more than one world. So the disagreement is over methods. The utopian would create earthly beatitude by rational planning; the dystopian wants to make sure that the planning doesn't engender worse evils than it cures.

7. *People don't get tired of happiness.* Utopias have a way of depicting their inhabitants in a state of sustained contentment, if happiness is too strong a word. They go about their pleasant and useful tasks, conscious that they are serving the social whole. Little is usually said about private satisfactions or personal griefs. Dystopia emphasizes the perverseness of men, their restlessness, their ability to grow weary of a flat and virtuous contentment. Perhaps the utopian

has a 'classical' cast of mind, and would like to see the world a formal garden of well-laid-out paths and proper statues available to public gaze. The dystopian is more of a 'romanticist', and considerably more of a psychologist. He knows that man is obsessed with finitude, time and death, and that a little neurosis is part of our heritage. He is not so sure that the bland happiness of utopia is enough. If he had to choose, he might opt for more agony and more ecstasy.

8. *Rulers can be found who will rule justly, or men can be picked and trained so that they will rule justly.* The dystopian agrees with Lord Acton's famous *mot*—the more power a man has, the greater the danger of corruption. In a utopia, where the rulers are convinced that they are the selfless servants of the public good, the danger of corruption would be heightened. Power is habit-forming; too much of it in anyone's hands is an invitation to danger. The dystopian would argue that the American Constitution, with its fussy system of checks and balances, is a practical recognition of this important fact.

9. *Utopia is not opposed to freedom. It will lead to 'true freedom', as individual men and women find their own destiny fulfilled by co-operating freely with the purposes of society.* This is closely related to point 3, and the dystopian would make a similar rejoinder. Please define 'true freedom', he requests. He seems to recall that the nazis and communists alike have been fond of the phrase. Does 'true freedom' really mean a flowering of the individual as part of the social whole, or does it merely signify that he has been so brainwashed he is incapable of thinking any thoughts or having any longings of his own? In that event, the dystopian would settle for plain freedom. He knows what *that* means.

QUESTIONS ON PART III

Utopia Under Scrutiny (Aristotle)

1. Summarize Aristotle's main objections to Plato's utopian scheme. Do you think any of these objections would apply generally to utopian planning? Why or why not?
2. Even if you are not yet familiar with Plato's *Republic*, you can select several generalizations made by Aristotle in the course of his argument against Plato's utopianism and react critically to them. Comment upon this statement: "That which is common to the greatest number has the least care bestowed upon it."
3. Aristotle has been called one of the greatest precursors of conservatism. What evidence do you find in the present selection to support this view?

Nonconformity and Utopia (Dostoyevsky)

4. What are the major objections against utopian planning raised by the underground man?
5. What is the conception of human nature set forth and defended by the underground man? How might a utopian socialist attack this view of man?
6. Do you agree with the underground man's view that "once you have mathematical certainty there is nothing left to do or to understand?" Why or why not? Of what relevance to utopian planning is this issue?

Overorganization and Dystopia (Huxley)

7. Formulate Huxley's conception of human nature in so far as it is suggested or stated in this selection.
8. Explain why Huxley believes that overorganization is incompatible with self-realization.
9. What solution, if any, does Huxley suggest to the problem of overorganization? What solution would you suggest?

UTOPIA AND THE COMING SLAVERY (SPENCER)

10. Summarize Spencer's account of the evolution of the regimented industrial system. Why, in his view, would the end result of this evolution necessarily be a "despotic bureacracy"?

11. What argument might a utopian socialist give against Spencer's view that "the working of institutions is determined by men's characters?" ·

12. What solution, if any, does Spencer suggest to the problem of over-regimentation?

IGNOBLE UTOPIAS (KRUTCH)

13. Explain briefly the behavioristic conception of utopian planning which Krutch attacks. Why does he so vehemently reject this conception?

14. What seems to be Krutch's own conception of the good life as it might be inferred from this selection?

15. Do you agree with the following statement by T. H. Huxley quoted by Krutch? "If some great power would agree to make me always think what is true and do what is right, on condition of being turned into a sort of clock and wound up every morning before I got out of bed, I should instantly close with the offer."

FROM UTOPIA TO NIGHTMARE (WALSH)

16. After considering the arguments which can be given for and against each of the tenets of the utopian faith as Walsh formulates them, what are your own conclusions?

SUPPLEMENTARY READINGS

(Works marked * are available in paperbound editions.)

Dahrendorf, Ralf. "Out of Utopia: Toward a Reorientation of Sociological Analysis," *The American Journal of Sociology* LXIV (September 1958): 115–27.

Dostoyevsky, Feodor. *Notes from Underground and The Grand Inquisitor,* edited by Ralph E. Matlaw. New York: E. P. Dutton, 1960.

Hacker, Andrew. *Political Theory: Philosophy, Ideology, Science.* New York: Macmillan Co., 1961. Chaps. 2 and 3.

———. "Dostoevsky's Disciples: Man and Sheep in Political Theory," *The Journal of Politics* XVII (1955): 590–613.

———. "The Specter of Predictable Man," *The Antioch Review* XIV (1954): 195–207.

Hayek, Friedrich A. *The Road to Serfdom.* Chicago: University of Chicago Press, 1944.

Hillegas, Mark R. *The Future as Nightmare: H. G. Wells and the Anti-Utopians.* New York: Oxford University Press, 1967.

———. "Dystopian Science Fiction: New Index to the Human Situation," *New Mexico Quarterly* XXXI (1961): 238–49.

Huxley, Aldous. *Brave New World Revisited.* New York: Harper & Brothers, 1958.

Jarrett, James. "Dostoyevsky: Philosopher of Freedom, Love, and Life," *Review of Religion* XXI (November 1956): 17–30.

Kateb, George. *Utopia and its Enemies.* New York: The Free Press of Glencoe, 1963.

Kessler, Martin. "Power and the Perfect State", *Political Science Quarterly* LXXII (1957): 565–77.

Krutch, Joseph Wood. *The Measure of Man: On Freedom, Human Values, Survival and the Modern Temper.* Indianapolis: Bobbs-Merrill Co., 1953.

Leshinsky, Tania. "Dostoevsky—Revolutionary or Reactionary?", *American Slavic and East European Review* IV (December 1945): 98–106.

Mises, Ludwig von. *Bureaucracy.* New Haven: Yale University Press, 1944.

Molnar, Thomas. *Utopia, the Perennial Heresy.* New York: Sheed and Ward, 1967.

Oates, Whitney J. "The Ideal States of Plato and Aristotle" in *The Greek Political Experience: Studies in Honor of William Kelly Prentice*. Princeton: Princeton University Press, 1941, pp. 187–213.

Popper, Karl. *The Open Society and its Enemies*. Princeton: Princeton University Press, 1950.

———. "Utopia and Violence," *Hibbert Journal* XLVI (1947–1948): 109–16.

Rand, Ayn. **Capitalism, the Unknown Ideal*. New York: New American Library, 1966.

———. **For the New Intellectual*. New York: New American Library, 1963.

Shklar, Judith. *After Utopia*. Princeton: Princeton University Press, 1957.

Spencer, Herbert. *The Man versus the State*. New York: D. Appleton & Co., 1884.

Walsh, Chad. *From Utopia to Nightmare*. New York: Harper & Row, 1962.

Webber, Eugen. "The Anti-Utopia of the Twentieth Century," *The South Atlantic Quarterly* LVIII (Summer 1959): 440–47.

Wellek, René. *Dostoevsky: A Collection of Critical Essays, Twentieth Century Views*. Englewood Cliffs, N. J.: Prentice-Hall, 1962.

Woodcock, George. "Utopias in Negative," *Sewanee Review* LXIV (1956): 81–97.

IV

Utopian Rejoinders

Go back again, now that you have seen us, and your outward eyes have learned that in spite of all the infallible maxims of your day there is yet a time of rest in store for the world, when mastery has changed into fellowship—but not before. Go back again, then, and while you live you will see all round you people engaged in making others live lives which are not their own, while they themselves care nothing for their own real lives—men who hate life though they fear death. Go back and be happier for having seen us, for having added a little hope to your struggle. Go on living while you may, striving, with whatsoever pain and labour needs must be, to build up little by little the new days of fellowship, and rest, and happiness.

William Morris

19

The Eternal Idea of Utopia

PLATO'S JUSTIFICATION OF UTOPIAN SPECULATION

We have no way of knowing what Plato thought of Aristotle's criticisms of his utopian schemes; in fact there is no evidence to indicate even that Aristotle criticized his teacher Plato while he was still alive. There is evidence, however, that Plato was aware of the shortcomings of his own utopian planning, and, more specifically, of his first attempt to conceive of an ideal society, his *Republic*. A careful reading of the following selection from the *Republic* will reveal that like every great teacher, Plato was capable of being critical of his own views. In addition, he was aware that the case for utopian thinking should not be allowed to rest on its supposed practicality or impracticality. Utopian thinking is, he recognized, speculation about ends. This kind of speculation is not only unavoidable in legislation but is absolutely necessary if the legislator is to perform his essential function. Philosophers are, in Plato's view, the only men capable of such high-minded and difficult speculation; thus only they are able to be at once the formulators of the ends of the best kind of state and the guides to their realization.

In our time Plato's utopian views have been vigorously attacked as totalitarian in intent and consequence; his *Republic* has been criticized severely by thinkers such as Karl Popper in *The Open Society and Its Enemies*. If totalitarianism is the control of every phase of human existence—economic, political, sexual, artistic, etc.—then certainly, Popper contends, Plato's utopia, with its state control of production and distribution of goods, its dictatorship of an intellectual elite, its abolition of the family and its regulation of reproduction, and its strict censorship of art, is a totalitarian state *par excellence.* To be sure, Plato claims his ideal state will be one in which justice prevails, but by justice, Popper points out, Plato does not mean what we generally mean or include what any liberal humanitarian would in its conception. Justice to Plato, his critic Popper continues, means "that which is in the best interest of the state." It is that which arrests all change and keeps the dominant class, the philosopher rulers, in power and the others in their place

237

doing their assigned thing under benevolent but all-powerful rulers. From this point of view (which itself has been subject to attack), Plato is the archenemy of democratic freedom and individual responsibility; he is instead a rigid authoritarian and absolutist whose completely planned utopia would turn out to be a dystopia to liberal thinkers and enemies of a closed society.

This is not the place to attempt to evaluate the charges which have been leveled against Plato's utopianism—the reader can pursue at his leisure the pros and cons by consulting some of the appropriate books listed at the end of this part—but it should be stressed that the *Republic* was not Plato's last word on utopia. Although Aristotle, realizing that Plato in his old age had written another utopia, the *Laws*, also proceeded, after his strictures on the *Republic*, to criticize the latter work as well, some of Plato's modern critics have attacked the philosopher's views on utopia as though the final formulation of them had been given in the *Republic*, not in the *Laws*.

The reader who goes to this last and longest of Plato's works will find much of interest and much that will cause him to revise his conception of Plato as a utopian thinker. After reading Plato's lengthy and detailed presentation of the elaborate system of laws which he deemed necessary to the proper administration of an ideal city-state, and after reflecting on his fully-developed treatment of education, theology, and politics, no one could fairly say that Plato's speculation lacked sufficient and continuous reference to the everyday world of political experience. Not that one will necessarily be convinced of the feasibility or the desirability of establishing a city-state such as Plato envisages in the *Laws*; many would prefer the scheme presented previously in the *Republic*; others (including Aristotle) would reject both of the Platonic utopias. Gone in the *Laws* are the dictatorship of philosopher-rulers and the common possession of mates, children, and property. Plato proposes instead a "mixed constitution" which would combine, he believes, the best features of monarchy and democracy. The ultimate sanction of the laws of this constitution is considered by Plato to be God Himself, the supreme sovereign. Thus religious reverence must be instilled and perpetuated in the citizens of the utopia. Art, education, and marriage (which in Plato's new society is now quite conventionally treated) are still strictly supervised by the state, but Plato seems far less interested in these institutions than he is in elaborating a criminal and penal code and in developing a rational theology. Although under his new system of government, with its provision for representation, the society would undoubtedly be far less "closed" than that envisaged in the *Republic*, the authoritarian elements are strikingly present in the censorship of art, the fines imposed on bachelors, the restrictions on travel, the penalties for heresy, and the provision for a "Nocturnal Council," a kind of committee on public safety which would perform some of the functions of a secret police. Plato's second version of utopia is far less idealistic and inspired than his first and takes more into account, so he claims, the realities of human nature. Nevertheless, the philosopher, in writing both the *Republic* and the *Laws*, was continuing his search for justice and truth and attempting to help mankind to be guided by these ideals. In both of his utopias he argues for the same basic thesis: justice is to be preferred to injustice.

Plato, Republic, *bk. 5, secs. 472–73; bk. 9, secs. 588–92 from* The Dialogues of Plato, *translated by Benjamin Jowett, 3rd ed. (New York: Oxford University Press, 1892), vol. 3, 169–71; 301–6.*

Let me begin by reminding you that we found our way hither in the search after justice and injustice.

True, he replied; but what of that?

I was only going to ask whether, if we have discovered them, we are to require that the just man should in nothing fail of absolute justice; or may we be satisfied with an approximation, and the attainment in him of a higher degree of justice than is to be found in other men?

The approximation will be enough.

We are enquiring into the nature of absolute justice and into the character of the perfectly just, and into injustice and the perfectly unjust, that we might have an ideal. We were to look at these in order that we might judge of our own happiness and unhappiness according to the standard which they exhibited and the degree in which we resembled them, but not with any view of showing that they could exist in fact.

True, he said.

Would a painter be any the worse because, after having delineated with consummate art an ideal of a perfectly beautiful man, he was unable to show that any such man could ever have existed?

He would be none the worse.

Well, and were we not creating an ideal of a perfect State?

To be sure.

And is our theory a worse theory because we are unable to prove the possibility of a city being ordered in the manner described?

Surely not, he replied.

That is the truth, I said. But if, at your request, I am to try and show how and under what conditions the possibility is highest, I must ask you, having this in view, to repeat your former admissions.

What admissions?

I want to know whether ideals are ever fully realized in language? Does not the word express more than the fact, and must not the actual, whatever a man may think, always, in the nature of things, fall short of the truth? What do you say?

I agree.

Then you must not insist on my proving that the actual State will in every respect coincide with the ideal: if we are only able to discover how a city may be governed nearly as we proposed, you will admit that we have discovered the possibility which you demand; and will be contented. I am sure that I should be contented—will not you?

Yes, I will.

Let me next endeavour to show what is that fault in States which is the cause of their present maladministration, and what is the least change which will enable a State to pass into the truer form; and let the change, if possible, be of one thing only, or, if not, of two; at any rate, let the changes be as few and slight as possible.

Certainly, he replied.

I think, I said, that there might be a reform of the State if only one change were made, which is not a slight or easy though still a possible one.

What is it? he said.

Now then, I said, I go to meet that which I liken to the greatest of the waves; yet shall the word be spoken, even though the wave break and drown me in laughter and dishonour; and do you mark my words.

Proceed.

I said: *Until philosophers are kings, or the kings and princes of this world have the spirit and power of philosophy, and political greatness and wisdom meet in one, and those commoner natures who pursue either to the exclusion of the other are compelled to stand aside, cities will never have rest from their evils,—no, nor the human race, as I believe,—and then only will this our State have a possibility of life and behold the light of day.* Such was the thought, my dear Glaucon, which I would fain have uttered if it had not seemed too extravagant; for to be convinced that in no other State can there be happiness private or public is indeed a hard thing. . . .

Well, I said, and now having arrived at this stage of the argument, we may revert to the words which brought us hither: Was not some one saying that injustice was a gain to the perfectly unjust who was reputed to be just?

Yes, that was said.

Now then, having determined the power and quality of justice and injustice, let us have a little conversation with him.

What shall we say to him?

Let us make an image of the soul, that he may have his own words presented before his eyes.

Of what sort?

An ideal image of the soul, like the composite creations of ancient mythology, such as the Chimera or Scylla or Cerberus, and there are many others in which two or more different natures are said to grow into one.

There are said to have been such unions.

Then do you now model the form of a multitudinous, many-headed monster, having a ring of heads of all manner of beasts, tame and wild, which he is able to generate and metamorphose at will.

You suppose marvellous powers in the artist; but, as language is more pliable than wax or any similar substance, let there be such a model as you propose.

Suppose now that you make a second form as of a lion, and a third of a man, the second smaller than the first, and the third smaller than the second.

That, he said, is an easier task; and I have made them as you say.

And now join them, and let the three grow into one.

That has been accomplished.

Next fashion the outside of them into a single image, as of a man, so that he who is not able to look within, and sees only the outer hull, may believe the beast to be a single human creature.

I have done so, he said.

And now, to him who maintains that it is profitable for the human creature to be unjust, and unprofitable to be just, let us reply that, if he be right, it is profitable for this creature to feast the multitudinous monster and strengthen the lion and the lion-like qualities, but to starve and weaken the man, who is consequently liable to be dragged about at the mercy of either of the other two; and he is not to attempt to familiarize or harmonize them with one another—he ought rather to suffer them to fight and bite and devour one another.

Certainly, he said; that is what the approver of injustice says.

To him the supporter of justice makes answer that he should ever so speak and act as to give the man within him in some way or other the most complete mastery over the entire human creature. He should watch over the many-headed monster like a good husbandman, fostering and cultivating the gentle qualities, and preventing the wild ones from growing; he should be making the lion-heart his ally, and in common care of them all should be uniting the several parts with one another and with himself.

Yes, he said, that is quite what the maintainer of justice will say.

And so from every point of view, whether of pleasure, honour, or advantage, the approver of justice is right and speaks the truth, and the disapprover is wrong and false and ignorant?

Yes, from every point of view.

Come, now, and let us gently reason with the unjust, who is not intentionally in error. 'Sweet Sir,' we will say to him, 'what think you of things esteemed noble and ignoble? Is not the noble that which subjects the beast to the man, or rather to the god in man; and the ignoble that which subjects the man to the beast?' He can hardly avoid saying Yes—can he now?

Not if he has any regard for my opinion.

But, if he agree so far, we may ask him to answer another question: 'Then how would a man profit if he received gold and silver on the condition that he was to enslave the noblest part of him to the worst? Who can imagine that a man who sold his son or daughter into slavery for money, especially if he sold them into the hands of fierce and evil men, would be the gainer, however large might be the sum which he received? And will any one say that he is not a miserable caitiff who remorselessly sells his own divine being to that which is most godless and detestable? Eriphyle took the necklace at the price of her husband's life, but he is taking a bride in order to compass a worse ruin.'

Yes, said Glaucon, far worse—I will answer for him.

Has not the intemperate been censured of old, because in him the huge multiform monster is allowed to be too much at large?

Clearly.

And men are blamed for pride and bad temper when the lion and serpent element in them disproportionately grows and gains strength?

Yes.

And luxury and softness are blamed, because they relax and weaken this same creature, and make a coward of him?

Very true.

And is not a man reproached for flattery and meanness who subordinates the spirited animal to the unruly monster, and, for the sake of money, of which he can never have enough, habituates him in the days of his youth to be trampled in the mire, and from being a lion to become a monkey?

True, he said.

And why are mean employments and manual arts a reproach? Only because they imply a natural weakness of the higher principle; the individual is unable to control the creatures within him, but has to court them, and his great study is how to flatter them.

Such appears to be the reason.

And therefore, being desirous of placing him under a rule like that of the best, we say that he ought to be the servant of the best, in whom the Divine rules; not, as Thrasymachus supposed, to the injury of the servant, but because every one had better be ruled by divine wisdom dwelling within him; or, if this be impossible, then by an external authority, in order that we may be all, as far as possible, under the same government, friends and equals.

True, he said.

And this is clearly seen to be the intention of the law, which is the ally of the whole city; and is seen also in the authority which we exercise over children, and the refusal to let them be free until we have established in them a principle analogous to the constitution of a state, and by cultivation of this higher element have set up in their hearts a guardian and ruler like our own, and when this is done they may go their ways.

Yes, he said, the purpose of the law is manifest.

From what point of view, then, and on what ground can we say that a man is profited by injustice or intemperance or other baseness, which will make him a worse man, even though he acquire money or power by his wickedness?

From no point of view at all.

What shall he profit, if his injustice be undetected and unpunished? He who is undetected only gets worse, whereas he who is detected and punished has the brutal part of his nature silenced and humanized; the gentler element in him is liberated, and his whole soul is perfected and ennobled by the acquirement of justice and temperance and wisdom, more than the body ever is by receiving gifts of beauty, strength and health, in proportion as the soul is more honourable than the body.

Certainly, he said.

To this nobler purpose the man of understanding will devote the energies of his life. And in the first place, he will honour studies which impress these qualities on his soul, and will disregard others?

Clearly, he said.

In the next place, he will regulate his bodily habit and training, and so far will he be from yielding to brutal and irrational pleasures, that he will regard even health as quite a secondary matter; his first object will be not that he may be fair or strong or well, unless he is likely thereby to gain temperance, but he will always desire so to attemper the body as to preserve the harmony of the soul?

Certainly he will, if he has true music in him.

And in the acquisition of wealth there is a principle of order and harmony which he will also observe; he will not allow himself to be dazzled by the foolish applause of the world, and heap up riches to his own infinite harm?

Certainly not, he said.

He will look at the city which is within him, and take heed that no disorder occur in it, such as might arise either from superfluity or from want; and upon this principle he will regulate his property and gain or spend according to his means.

Very true.

And, for the same reason, he will gladly accept and enjoy such honours as he deems likely to make him a better man; but those, whether private or public, which are likely to disorder his life, he will avoid?

Then, if that is his motive, he will not be a statesman.

By the dog of Egypt, he will! in the city which is his own he certainly will, though in the land of his birth perhaps not, unless he have a divine call.

I understand; you mean that he will be a ruler in the city of which we are the founders, and which exists in idea only; for I do not believe that there is such an one anywhere on earth?

In heaven, I replied, there is laid up a pattern of it, methinks, which he who desires may behold, and beholding, may set his own house in order. But whether such an one exists, or ever will exist in fact, is no matter; for he will live after the manner of that city, having nothing to do with any other.

I think so, he said.

20

The Commonwealth
of the Golden Rule

EDWARD BELLAMY'S DEFENSE OF THE
IDEAL OF ECONOMIC EQUALITY

Edward Bellamy (1850–1898), one of America's best known and most influential utopians, was a Baptist minister's son from the mill town of Chicopee
Falls, Massachusetts. He had studied law, done newspaper work, and written
a number of short-story fantasies before winning national and international
acclaim for his best-selling utopian novel, *Looking Backward* (1888).

Inspired by its author's humanistic religious idealism and his firm conviction that socialism would inevitably triumph in the United States during the
twentieth century, *Looking Backward* recounts the experiences of Julian
West, a wealthy young Bostonian, who goes into a hypnotically induced
sleep in 1887 and wakes up in the new Boston 113 years later. Julian's hosts
are the sympathetic Dr. and Mrs. Leete and their beautiful daughter, Edith.
As Julian becomes acquainted with twentieth century America, he is aston-
ished at what amounts to an overall social reconstruction. All of the nation's
citizens cooperate to promote the general welfare; peace and prosperity have
been achieved permanently; and the golden rule is no longer a mere ideal
but a consistently and universally practiced moral maxim. These and other
social changes with which Julian becomes acquainted—the liberation of
women; the reform of education; the elimination of poverty, disease, and
crime; the curtailment of economic waste; the radical simplification of government—are the result of the replacement of private capitalism by public
capitalism.

Social regimentation and economic equality are the twin foundations of
the new social order envisaged by Bellamy. Smooth functioning of the machinery of production and distribution is achieved by a vast and highly regimented Industrial Army in which citizens serve from the ages of twenty-one
to forty-five. The wage system has been abolished and credit cards have
replaced money. All citizens receive exactly the same amount of credit. Self-
support and individual responsibility have been replaced by mutual support
and collective responsibility. Egoism and competition have disappeared along

with individual ownership, and altruistic incentives rather than egoistic incentives spur citizens to do their best for the happiness of the whole society. Although Bellamy's hero only becomes directly acquainted with the new American society in the Boston area, he is told that the industrial evolution which transformed the United States into a utopia has been world-wide. The federal system of autonomous nations which has already been achieved will, in all probability, Julian is told, eventually lead to a unification of all nations into one nation. Bellamy, like Wells, thus argues that a modern utopia can be nothing less than a world utopia.

At the conclusion of *Looking Backward*, Julian West, after a nightmare in which he had dreamed he had returned to the far-from-utopian old Boston, has fallen in love with the new society and with Edith Leete, who, incidentally, turns out to be the great-granddaughter of Julian's original nineteenth-century fiancée, Edith Bartlett.

But *Looking Backward* was not Bellamy's last word on utopia any more that the *Republic* was Plato's or *A Modern Utopia* was Wells's. The year before his death, he attempted to amplify his utopian views and to answer criticisms of them in *Equality*. Although *Equality* fails as a novel—the sugar-coating of romance on the bitter pill of economics has worn too thin—Bellamy's final work throws light on his earlier utopian ideas and social philosophy. In *Equality* he explains in greater detail the nature of the economic reorganization and how the new order came about through the revolutionary "Great Revival." The new religion, the new role of women, the new style of living and thinking and other topics only briefly touched on in *Looking Backward* are given fuller attention in *Equality*. Also, a number of topics not considered in the earlier work such as the agricultural life of the nation, the new code of sexual ethics, the status of Negroes in the new society, conservation of natural resources, the development of a world language, and population control are given coverage by Bellamy in his last work. Further, having changed his mind on a few points since writing *Looking Backward*, Bellamy expounded his new views in *Equality*. For example, he replaced credit cards with individual checking accounts; he introduced initiative, referendum, and recall to protect the democratic system; and he replaced solitary confinement of "atavistic" persons or social deviants with temporary exile in national parks. Finally, and most important, Bellamy concluded his last work by attempting to meet the major overall objections to the central doctrine on which his utopian thinking depended; economic equality. In the course of defending his own utopia against attack, the ailing utopian was also engaged in a larger task, the defense of utopianism itself against its enemies.

In the following selection taken from the concluding chapter of *Equality*, Dr. Leete is presenting to Julian West the objections to economic equality raised by Julian's nineteenth-century apologists for private capitalism. These objections Dr. Leete has taken from "Kenloe's Book of the Blind," a work which supposedly had been written a hundred years before when the "Revolution" had swept away the old capitalistic society and had established a new society based on economic equality and public ownership of the means of production. A supporter of the new order, Kenloe had taken the trouble to record for posterity the objections which he believed would seem completely incredible were they not fully recorded and documented. "Thus," says Dr. Leete, "he proposed to pillory for all time the blind guides who had done their best to lead the nation and the world into the ditch." The doctor then proceeds as follows.

From Edward Bellamy, Equality *(New York: D. Appleton-Century Company, 1897), chap. 38, pp. 383–412 (with omissions).*

THE PULPIT OBJECTION

"The clergy in your day assumed to be the leaders of the people, and it is but respectful to their pretensions to take up first what seems to have been the main pulpit argument against the proposed system of economic equality collectively guaranteed. It appears to have been rather in the nature of an excuse for not espousing the new social ideal than a direct attack on it, which indeed it would have been rather difficult for nominal Christians to make, seeing that it was merely the proposal to carry out the golden rule.

"The clergy reasoned that the fundamental cause of social misery was human sin and depravity, and that it was vain to expect any great improvement in the social condition through mere improvements in social forms and institutions unless there was a corresponding moral improvement in men. Until that improvement took place it was therefore of no use to introduce improved social systems, for they would work as badly as the old ones if those who were to operate them were not themselves better men and women.

"The element of truth in this argument is the admitted fact that the use which individuals or communities are able to make of any idea, instrument, or institution depends on the degree to which they have been educated up to the point of understanding and appreciating it.

"On the other hand, however, it is equally true, as the clergy must at once have admitted, that from the time a people begins to be morally and intellectually educated up to the point of understanding and appreciating better institutions, their adoption is likely to be of the greatest benefit to them. Take, for example, the ideas of religious liberty and of democracy. There was a time when the race could not understand or fitly use either, and their adoption as formal institutions would have done no good. Afterward there came a time when the world was ready for the ideas, and then their realization by means of new social institutions constituted great forward steps in civilization.

"That is to say, if, on the one hand, it is of no use to introduce an improved institution before people begin to be ready for it, on the other hand great loss results if there be a delay or refusal to adopt the better institution as soon as the readiness begins to manifest itself.

"This being the general law of progress, the practical question is, How are we to determine as to any particular proposed improvement in institutions whether the world is yet ready to make a good use of it or whether it is premature?

"The testimony of history is that the only test of the fitness of people at any time for a new institution is the volume and earnestness of the popular demand for the change. When the peoples began in earnest to cry out for religious liberty and freedom of conscience, it was evident that they were ready for them. When nations began strongly to demand popular government, it was proof that they were ready for that. It did not follow that they were entirely able at once to make the best possible use of the new institution; that they could only learn to do by experience, and the further development which they would attain through the use of the better institution and could not otherwise attain at all. What was certain was that after the people had reached this state of mind the old institution had ceased to be serviceable, and that however badly for a time the new one might work, the interest of the race demanded its adoption, and resistance to the change was resistance to progress. . . .

"If the clergymen who objected to the Revolution on the ground that better institutions would be of no utility without a better spirit had been sincere in that objection, they would have found in a survey of the state and tendencies of popular feeling the most striking proof of the presence of the very conditions in extraordinary measure which they demanded as necessary to insure the success of the experiment.

"But indeed it is to be greatly feared that they were not sincere. They pretended to hold Christ's doctrine that hatred of the old life and a desire to lead a better one is the only vocation necessary to enter upon such a life. If they had been sincere in professing this doctrine, they would have hailed with exultation the appeal of the masses to be delivered from their bondage to a wicked social order and to be permitted to live together on better, kinder, juster terms. But what they actually said to the people was in substance this: It is true, as you complain, that the present social and economic system is morally abominable and thoroughly antichristian, and that it destroys men's souls and bodies. Nevertheless, you must not think of trying to change it for a better system, because you are not yet good enough to try to be better. It is necessary that you should wait until you are more righteous before you attempt to leave off doing evil. You must go on stealing and fighting until you shall become fully sanctified.

"How would the clergy have been scandalized to hear that a Christian minister had in like terms attempted to discourage an individual penitent who professed loathing for his former life and a desire to lead a better! What language shall we find then that is strong enough fitly to characterize the attitude of these so-called ministers of Christ, who in his name rebuked and derided the aspirations of a world weary of social wrong and seeking for a better way?"

THE LACK OF INCENTIVE OBJECTION

"But, after all," pursued the doctor, turning the pages of Kenloe, "Let us not be too hard on these unfortunate clergymen, as if they were more blinded or bigoted in their opposition to progress than were other classes of the learned men of the day, as, for example, the economists. One of the main arguments—perhaps the leading one—of the nineteenth-century economists against the programme of economic equality under a nationalized economic system was that the people would not prove efficient workers owing to the lack of sufficiently sharp personal incentives to diligence.

"Now, let us look at this objection. Under the old system there were two main incentives to economic exertion: the one chiefly operative on the masses, who lived from hand to mouth, with no hope of more than a bare subsistence; the other operating to stimulate the well-to-do and rich to continue their efforts to accumulate wealth. The first of these motives, the lash that drove the masses to their tasks, was the actual pressure or imminent fear of want. The second of the motives, that which spurred the already rich, was the desire to be ever richer, a passion which we know increased with what it fed on. Under the new system every one on easy conditions would be sure of as good a maintenance as any one else and be quite relieved from the pressure or fear of want. No one, on the other hand, by any amount of effort, could hope to become the economic superior of another. Moreover, it was said, since every one looked to his share in the general result rather than to his personal product, the nerve of zeal would be cut. It was argued that the result would be that everybody would do as little as he could and keep within the minimum requirement of the law, and that therefore, while the system might barely support itself, it could never be an economic success."

"That sounds very natural," I said. "I imagine it is just the sort of argument that I should have thought very powerful."

"So your friends the capitalists seem to have regarded it, and yet the very statement of the argument contains a confession of the economic imbecility of private capitalism which really leaves nothing to be desired as to completeness. Consider, Julian, what is implied as to an economic system by the admission that under it the people never escape the actual pressure of want or the immediate dread of it. What more could the worst enemy of private capitalism allege against it, or what stronger reason could he give for demanding that some radically new system be at least given a trial, than the fact which its defenders stated in this argument for retaining it—namely, that under it the masses were always hungry? Surely no possible new system could work any worse than one which confessedly depended upon the perpetual famine of the people to keep it going."

"It was a pretty bad giving away of their case," I said, "when you come to think of it that way. And yet at first statement it really had a formidable sound."

"Manifestly," said the doctor, "the incentives to wealth-production under a system confessedly resulting in perpetual famine must be ineffectual, and we really need consider them no further; but your economists praised so highly the ambition to get rich as an economic motive and objected so strongly to economic equality because it would shut it off, that a word may be well as to the real value of the lust of wealth as an economic motive. Did the individual pursuit of riches under your system necessarily tend to increase the aggregate wealth of the community? The answer is significant. It tended to increase the aggregate wealth only when it prompted the production of new wealth. When, on the other hand, it merely prompted individuals to get possession of wealth already produced and in the hands of others, it tended only to change the distribution without at all increasing the total of wealth. Not only, indeed, did the pursuit of wealth by acquisition, as distinguished from production, not tend to increase the total, but greatly to decrease it by wasteful strife. Now, I will leave it to you, Julian, whether the successful pursuers of wealth, those who illustrated most strikingly the force of this motive of accumulation, usually sought their wealth by themselves producing it or by getting hold of what other people had produced or supplanting other people's enterprises and reaping the field others had sown."

"By the latter processes, of course," I replied. "Production was slow and hard work. Great wealth could not be gained that way, and everybody knew it. The acquisition of other people's product and the supplanting of their enterprises were the easy and speedy and royal ways to riches for those who were clever enough, and were the basis of all large and rapid accumulations."

"So we read," said the doctor; "but the desire of getting rich also stimulated capitalists to more or less productive activity which was the source of what little wealth you had. This was called production for profit, but the political economy class the other morning showed us that production for profit was economic suicide, tending inevitably, by limiting the consuming power of a community, to a fractional part of its productive power to cripple production in turn, and so to keep the mass of mankind in perpetual poverty. And surely this is enough to say about the incentives to wealth-making which the world lost in abandoning private capitalism, first general poverty, and second the profit system, which caused that poverty. Decidedly we can dispense with those incentives.

"Under the modern system it is indeed true that no one ever imagined such a thing as coming to want unless he deliberately chose to, but we think that fear is on the whole the weakest as well as certainly the cruelest of incentives. We would not have it on any terms were it merely for gain's sake. Even in your day your capitalists knew that the best man was not he who was working for his next dinner, but he who was so well off that no immediate concern for his living affected his mind. Self-respect and pride in achievement made him a far better workman than he who was thinking of his day's pay. But if those motives were as strong then, think how much more powerful they are now! In your day when two men worked side by side for an employer it was no concern of the one, however the other might cheat or loaf. It was not his loss, but the employer's. But now that all work for the common fund, the one who evades or scamps his work robs every one of his fellows. A man had better hang himself nowadays than get the reputation of a shirk.

"As to the notion of these objectors that economic equality would cut the nerve of zeal by denying the individual the reward of his personal achievements, it was a complete misconception of the effects of the system. The assumption that there would be no incentives to impel individuals to excel one another in industry merely because these incentives would not take a money form was absurd. Every one is as directly and far more certainly the beneficiary of his own merits as in your day, save only that the reward is not in what you called 'cash'. As you know, the whole system of social and official rank and headship, together with the special honors of the state, are determined by the relative value of the economic and other services of individuals to the community. Compared with the emulation aroused by this system of nobility by merit, the incentives to effort offered under the old order of things must have been slight indeed.

"The whole of this subject of incentive taken by your contem-

poraries seems, in fact, to have been based upon the crude and child-
ish theory that the main factor in diligence or execution of any kind is
external, whereas it is wholly internal. A person is congenitally sloth-
ful or energetic. In the one case no opportunity and no incentive can
make him work beyond a certain minimum of efficiency, while in the
other case he will make his opportunity and find his incentives, and
nothing but superior force can prevent his doing the utmost possible.
If the motive force is not in the man to start with, it can not be supplied from without, and there is no substitute for it. If a man's main-
spring is not wound up when he is born, it never can be wound up
afterward. The most that any industrial system can do to promote
diligence is to establish such absolutely fair conditions as shall promise sure recognition for all merit in its measure. This fairness, which
your system, utterly unjust in all respects, wholly failed to secure, ours
absolutely provides. As to the unfortunates who are born lazy, our system has certainly no miraculous power to make them energetic, but it
does see to it with absolute certainty that every able-bodied person
who receives economic maintenance of the nation shall render at least
the minimum of service. The laziest is sure to pay his cost. In your
day, on the other hand, society supported millions of able-bodied
loafers in idleness, a dead weight on the world's industry. From the
hour of the consummation of the great Revolution this burden ceased
to be borne."

"Doctor," I said, "I am sure my old friends could do better than
that. Let us have another of their objections."

AFRAID THAT EQUALITY WOULD MAKE
EVERYBODY ALIKE

"Here, then, is one which they seem to have thought a great deal of.
They argued that the effect of economic equality would be to make
everybody just alike, as if they had been sawed off to one measure,
and that consequently life would become so monotonous that people
would all hang themselves at the end of a month. This objection is
beautifully typical of an age when everything and everybody had
been reduced to a money valuation. It having been proposed to equalize everybody's supply of money, it was at once assumed, as a matter
of course, that there would be left no points of difference between
individuals that would be worth considering. How perfectly does this
conclusion express the philosophy of life held by a generation in
which it was the custom to sum up men as respectively 'worth' so
many thousands, hundred thousands, or millions of dollars! Naturally

enough, to such people it seemed that human beings would become well-nigh indistinguishable if their bank accounts were the same.

"But let us be entirely fair to your contemporaries. Possibly those who used this argument against economic equality would have felt aggrieved to have it made out the baldly sordid proposition it seems to be. They appear, to judge from the excerpts collected in this book, to have had a vague but sincere apprehension that in some quite undefined way economic equality would really tend to make people monotonously alike, tediously similar, not merely as to bank accounts, but as to qualities in general, with the result of obscuring the differences in natural endowments, the interaction of which lends all the zest to social intercourse. It seems almost incredible that the obvious and necessary effect of economic equality could be apprehended in a sense so absolutely opposed to the truth. How could your contemporaries look about them without seeing that it is always inequality which prompts the suppression of individuality by putting a premium on servile imitation of superiors, and, on the other hand, that it is always among equals that one finds independence? Suppose, Julian, you had a squad of recruits and wanted to ascertain at a glance their difference in height, what sort of ground would you select to line them up on?"

"The levelest piece I could find, of course."

"Evidently; and no doubt these very objectors would have done the same in a like case, and yet they wholly failed to see that this was precisely what economic equality would mean for the community at large. Economic equality with the equalities of education and opportunity implied in it was the level standing ground, the even floor, on which the new order proposed to range all alike, that they might be known for what they were, and all their natural inequalities be brought fully out. The charge of abolishing and obscuring the natural differences between men lay justly not against the new order, but against the old, which, by a thousand artificial conditions and opportunities arising from economic inequality, made it impossible to know how far the apparent differences in individuals were natural, and how far they were the result of artificial conditions. Those who voiced the objection to economic equality as tending to make men all alike were fond of calling it a leveling process. So it was, but it was not men whom the process leveled, but the ground they stood on. From its introduction dates the first full and clear revelation of the natural and inherent varieties in human endowments. Economic equality, with all it implies, is the first condition of any true anthropometric or man-measuring system."

"Really," I said, "all these objections seem to be of the boomerang pattern, doing more damage to the side that used them than to the enemy."

"For that matter," replied the doctor, "the revolutionists would have been well off for ammunition if they had used only that furnished by their opponents' arguments. Take, for example, another specimen, which we may call the aesthetic objection to economic equality, and might regard as a development of the one just considered. It was asserted that the picturesqueness and amusement of the human spectacle would suffer without the contrast of conditions between the rich and poor. The question first suggested by this statement is: "To whom, to what class did these contrasts tend to make life more amusing? Certainly not to the poor, who made up the mass of the race. To them, they must have been maddening. It was then in the interest of the mere handful of rich and fortunate that this argument for retaining poverty was urged. Indeed this appears to have been quite a fine ladies' argument. Kenloe puts it in the mouths of leaders of polite society. As coolly as if it had been a question of parlor decoration, they appear to have argued that the black background of the general misery was a desirable foil to set off the pomp of the rich. But, after all, this objection was not more brutal than it was stupid. If here and there might be found some perverted being who relished his luxuries the more keenly for the sight of others' want, yet the general and universal rule is that happiness is stimulated by the sight of the happiness of others. As a matter of fact, far from desiring to see or be even reminded of squalor and poverty, the rich seem to have tried to get as far as possible from sight or sound of them, and to wish to forget their existence. . . .

OBJECTION THAT EQUALITY WOULD END THE COMPETITIVE SYSTEM

"The theory of Kenloe," continued the doctor, "that unless he carefully recorded and authenticated these objections to economic equality, posterity would refuse to believe that they had ever been seriously offered, is specially justified by the next one on the list. This is an argument against the new order because it would abolish the competitive system and put an end to the struggle for existence. According to the objectors, this would be to destroy an invaluable school of character and testing process for the weeding out of inferiority, and the development and survival as leaders of the best types of humanity. Now, if your contemporaries had excused themselves for tolerating the competitive system on the ground that, bad and cruel as it was, the world was not ripe for any other, the attitude would have been intelligible, if not rational; but that they should defend it as a desirable institution in itself, on account of its moral results, and therefore not to be dispensed with even if it could be, seems hard to believe. For what was the competitive system but a pitiless, all-involving combat for the means of life, the whole zest of which depended on the fact that there was not enough to go round, and the losers must perish or purchase bare existence by becoming the bondmen of the successful? Between a fight for the necessary means of life like this and a fight for life itself with sword and gun, it is impossible to make any real distinction. However, let us give the objection a fair hearing.

"In the first place, let us admit that, however dreadful were the incidents of the fight for the means of life called competition, yet, if it were such a school of character and testing process for developing the best types of the race as these objectors claimed, there would be something to have been said in favor of its retention. But the first condition of any competition or test, the results of which are to command respect or possess any value, is the fairness and equality of the struggle. Did this first and essential condition of any true competitive struggle characterize the competitive system of your day?"

"On the contrary," I replied, "the vast majority of the contestants were hopelessly handicapped at the start by ignorance and lack of early advantages, and never had even the ghost of a chance from the word go. Differences in economic advantages and backing, moreover gave half the race at the beginning to some, leaving the others at a distance which only extraordinary endowments might overcome. Finally, in the race for wealth all the greatest prizes were not subject to competition at all, but were awarded without any contest according to the accident of birth."

"On the whole, then, it would appear," resumed the doctor, "that of all the utterly unequal, unfair, fraudulent, sham contests, whether in sport or earnest, that were ever engaged in, the so-called competitive system was the ghastliest farce. It was called the competitive system apparently for no other reason than that there was not a particle of genuine competition in it, nothing but brutal and cowardly slaughter of the unarmed and overmatched by bullies in armor; for, although we have compared the competitive struggle to a foot race, it was no such harmless sport as that, but a struggle to the death for life and liberty, which, mind you, the contestants did not even choose to risk, but were forced to undertake, whatever their chances. The old Romans used to enjoy the spectacle of seeing men fight for their lives, but they at least were careful to pair their gladiators as nearly as possible.

The most hardened attendants at the Coliseum would have hissed from the arena a performance in which the combatants were matched with such utter disregard of fairness as were those who fought for their lives in the so-called competitive struggle of your day."

"Even you, doctor," I said, "though you know these things so well through the written record, can not realize how terribly true your words are."

"Very good. Now tell me what it would have been necessary to do by way of equalizing the conditions of the competitive struggle in order that it might be called, without mockery, a fair test of the qualities of the contestants."

"It would have been necessary, at least," I said, "to equalize their educational equipment, early advantages, and economic or money backing."

"Precisely so; and that is just what economic equality proposed to do. Your extraordinary contemporaries objected to economic equality because it would destroy the competitive system, when, in fact, it promised the world the first and only genuine competitive system it ever had." . . .

"It strikes me," I said, "so far as you have gone, that if some one had been employed to draw up a list of the worst and weakest aspects of private capitalism, he could not have done better than to select the features of the system on which its champions seem to have based their objections to a change."

OBJECTION THAT EQUALITY WOULD DISCOURAGE INDEPENDENCE AND ORIGINALITY

"That is an impression," said the doctor, "which you will find confirmed as we take up the next of the arguments on our list against economic equality. It was asserted that to have an economic maintenance on simple and easy terms guaranteed to all by the nation would tend to discourage originality and independence of thought and conduct on the part of the people, and hinder the development of character and individuality. This objection might be regarded as a branch of the former one that economic equality would make everybody just alike, or it might be considered a corollary of the argument we have just disposed of about the value of competition as a school of character. But so much seems to have been made of it by the opponents of the Revolution that I have set it down separately.

"The objection is one which, by the very terms necessary to state it, seems to answer itself, for it amounts to saying that a person will be in danger of losing independence of feeling by gaining independence of position. If I were to ask you what economic condition was regarded as most favorable to moral and intellectual independence in your day, and most likely to encourage a man to act out himself without fear or favor, what would you say?"

"I should say, of course, that a secure and independent basis of livelihood was that condition."

"Of course. Now, what the new order promised to give and guarantee everybody was precisely this absolute independence and security of livelihood. And yet it was argued that the arrangement would be objectionable, as tending to discourage independence of character. It seems to us that if there is any one particular in which the influence upon humanity of economic equality has been more beneficent than any other, it has been the effect which security of economic position has had to make every one absolute lord of himself and answerable for his opinions, speech, and conduct to his own conscience only.

"That is perhaps enough to say in answer to an objection which, as I remarked, really confutes itself, but the monumental audacity of the defenders of private capitalism in arguing that any other possible system could be more unfavorable than itself to human dignity and independence tempts a little comment, especially as this is an aspect of the old order on which I do not remember that we have had much talk. As it seems to us, perhaps the most offensive feature of private capitalism, if one may select among so many offensive features, was its effect to make cowardly, time-serving, abject creatures of human beings, as a consequence of the dependence for a living, or pretty nearly everybody upon some individual or group. . . .

"Worse and worse," I exclaimed. "What is the use of going further?"

"Patience," said the doctor. "Let us complete the subject while we are on it. There are only a couple more of the objections that have shape enough to admit of being stated."

OBJECTION THAT A NATIONALIZED INDUSTRIAL SYSTEM WOULD THREATEN LIBERTY

"The first of them," pursued the doctor, "was the argument that such an extension of the functions of public administration as nationalized industries involved would lodge a power in the hand of the Government, even though it were the people's own government, that would be dangerous to their liberties.

"All the plausibility there was to this objection rested on the tacit assumption that the people in their industrial relations had under capitalism been free and unconstrained and subject to no form of authority. But what assumption could have been more regardless of facts than this? Under private capitalism the entire scheme of industry and commerce, involving the employment and livelihood of everybody, was subject to the despotic and irresponsible government of private masters. The very demand for nationalizing industry has resulted wholly from the sufferings of the people under the yoke of the capitalists.

"In 1776 the Americans overthrew the British royal government in the colonies and established their own in its place. Suppose at that time the king had sent an embassy to warn the American people that by assuming these new functions of government which formerly had been performed for them by him they were endangering their liberty. Such an embassy would, of course, have been laughed at. If any reply had been thought needful, it would have been pointed out that the Americans were not establishing over themselves any new government, but were substituting a government of their own, acting in their own interests, for the government of others conducted in an indifferent or hostile interest. Now, that was precisely what nationalizing industry meant. The question was, Given the necessity of some sort of regulation and direction of the industrial system, whether it would tend more to liberty for the people to leave that power to irresponsible persons with hostile interests, or to exercise it themselves through responsible agents? Could there conceivably be but one answer to that question?

"And yet it seems that a noted philosopher of the period, in a tract which has come down to us, undertook to demonstrate that if the people perfected the democratic system by assuming control of industry in the public interest, they would presently fall into a state of slavery which would cause them to sigh for the days of Nero and Caligula. I wish we had that philosopher here, that we might ask him how, in accordance with any observed laws of human nature, slavery was going to come about as the result of a system aiming to establish and perpetuate a more perfect degree of equality, intellectual as well as material, than had ever been known. Did he fancy that the people would deliberately and maliciously impose a yoke upon themselves, or did he apprehend that some usurper would get hold of the social machinery and use it to reduce the people to servitude? But what usurper from the beginning ever essayed a task so hopeless as the subversion of a state in which there were no classes or interests to set against one another, a state the stability of which represented the equal and entire stake in life of every human being in it? Truly it would seem that people who conceived the subversion of such a republic possible ought to have lost no time in chaining down the Pyramids, lest they, too, defying ordinary laws of Nature, should incontinently turn upon their tops.

"But let us leave the dead to bury their dead, and consider how the nationalization of industry actually did affect the bearing of government upon the people. If the amount of governmental machinery— that is, the amount of regulating, controlling, assigning, and directing under the public management of industry—had continued to be just the same it was under the private administration of the capitalists, the fact that it was now the people's government, managing everything in the people's interest under responsibility to the people, instead of an irresponsible tyranny seeking its own interest, would of course make an absolute difference in the whole character and effect of the system and make it vastly more tolerable. But not merely did the nationalization of industry give a wholly new character and purpose to the economic administration, but it also greatly diminished the net amount of governing necessary to carry it on. This resulted naturally from the unity of system with the consequent co-ordination and interworking of all the parts which took the place of the former thousand-headed management following as many different and conflicting lines of interest, each a law to itself. To the workers the difference was as if they had passed out from under the capricious personal domination of innumerable petty despots to a government of laws and principles so simple and systematic that the sense of being subject to personal authority was gone.

"But to fully realize how strongly this argument of too much government directed against the system of nationalized industry partook of the boomerang quality of the previous objections, we must look on the later effects which the social justice of the new order would naturally have to render superfluous well-nigh the whole machinery of government as previously conducted. The main, often almost sole, business of governments in your day was the protection of property and person against criminals, a system involving a vast amount of interference with the innocent. This function of the state has now become almost obsolete. There are no more any disputes about property, any thefts of property, or any need of protecting property. Everybody has all he needs and as much as anybody else. In former ages a great number of crimes have resulted from the passions of love and jealousy. There were consequences of the idea derived from immemorial barbarism that men and women might acquire sexual proprietorship in one another, to be maintained and asserted against the will of the person. Such crimes ceased to be known after the first generation had grown up under the absolute sexual autonomy and independence which followed from economic equality. There being no lower classes now which upper classes feel it their duty to bring up in the way they should go, in spite of themselves, all sorts of attempts to regulate personal behavior in self-regarding matters by sumptuary legislation have long ago ceased. A government in the sense of a co-ordinating directory of our associated industries we shall always need, but that is practically all the government we have now. It used to be a dream of philosophers that the world would some time enjoy such a reign of reason and justice that men would be able to live to-gether without laws. That condition, so far as concerns punitive and coercive regulations, we have practically attained. As to compulsory laws, we might be said to live almost in a state of anarchy.

"There is, as I explained to you in the Labor Exchange the other morning, no compulsion, in the end, even as to the performance of the universal duty of public service. We only insist that those who finally refuse to do their part toward maintaining the social welfare shall not be partakers of it, but shall resort by themselves and provide for themselves.

THE MALTHUSIAN OBJECTION

"And now we come to the last objection on my list. It is entirely different in character from any of the others. It does not deny that economic equality would be practicable or desirable, or assert that the machinery would work badly. It admits that the system would prove a triumphant success in raising human welfare to an unprece-dented point and making the world an incomparably more agreeable place to live in. It was indeed the conceded success of the plan which was made the basis of this objection to it."

"That must be a curious sort of objection," I said. "Let us hear about it."

"The objectors put it in this way: 'Let us suppose,' they said, 'that poverty and all the baneful influences upon life and health that follow in its train are abolished and all live out their natural span of life. Everybody being assured of maintenance for self and children, no motive of prudence would be operative to restrict the number of off-spring. Other things being equal, these conditions would mean a much faster increase of population than ever before known, and ultimately an overcrowding of the earth and a pressure on the food supply, unless indeed we suppose new and indefinite food sources to be found."

"I do not see why it might not be reasonable to anticipate such a result," I observed, "other things being equal."

"Other things being equal," replied the doctor, "such a result might be anticipated. But other things would not be equal, but so different that their influence could be depended on to prevent any such result."

"What are the other things that would not be equal?"

"Well, the first would be the diffusion of education, culture, and general refinement. Tell me, were the families of the well-to-do and cultured class in the America of your day, as a whole, large?"

"Quite the contrary. They did not, as a rule, more than replace themselves."

"Still, they were not prevented by any motive of prudence from increasing their numbers. They occupied in this respect as independent a position as families do under the present order of economic equality and guaranteed maintenance. Did it never occur to you why the families of the well-to-do and cultured in your day were not larger?"

"Doubtless," I said, "it was on account of the fact that in proportion as culture and refinement opened intellectual and aesthetic fields of interest, the impulses of crude animalism played less important parts in life. Then, too, in proportion as families were refined the woman ceased to be the mere sexual slave of the husband, and her wishes as to such matters were considered."

"Quite so. The reflection you have suggested is enough to indicate the fallacy of the whole Malthusian theory of the increase of population on which this objection to better social conditions was founded. Malthus, as you know, held that population tended to increase faster than means of subsistence, and therefore that poverty and the tremendous wastes of life it stood for were absolutely necessary in order to prevent the world from starving to death by over-crowding. Of course, this doctrine was enormously popular with the rich and learned class, who were responsible for the world's misery. They naturally were delighted to be assured that their indifference to the woes of the poor, and even their positive agency in multiplying those woes, were providentially overruled for good, so as to be really rather praiseworthy than otherwise. The Malthus doctrine also was very convenient as a means of turning the tables on reformers who proposed to abolish poverty by proving that, instead of benefiting mankind, their reforms would only make matters worse in the end by overcrowding the earth and starving everybody. By means of the Malthus doctrine, the meanest man who ever ground the face of the poor had no difficulty in showing that he was really a slightly disguised benefactor of the race, while the philanthropist was an injurious fellow.

"This prodigious convenience of Malthusianism has an excuse for things as they were, furnishes the explanation for the otherwise incomprehensible vogue of so absurd a theory. That absurdity consists in the fact that, while laying such stress on the direct effects of poverty and all the ills it stands for to destroy life, it utterly failed to allow for the far greater influence which the brutalizing circumstances of poverty exerted to promote the reckless multiplication of the species. Poverty, with all its deadly consequences, slew its millions, but only after having, by means of its brutalizing conditions, promoted the reckless reproduction of tens of millions—that is to say, the Malthus doctrine recognized only the secondary effects of misery and degradation in reducing population, and wholly overlooked their far more important primary effect in multiplying it. That was its fatal fallacy.

"It was a fallacy the more inexcusable because Malthus and all his followers were surrounded by a society the conditions of which absolutely refuted their theory. They had only to open their eyes to see that wherever the poverty and squalor chiefly abounded, which they vaunted as such valuable checks to population, humankind multiplied like rabbits, while in proportion as the economic level of a class was raised its proliferousness declined. What corollary from this fact of universal observation could be more obvious than that the way to prevent reckless overpopulation was to raise, not to depress, the economic status of the mass, with all the general improvement in well-being which that implied? How long do you suppose such an absurdly fundamental fallacy as underlay the Malthus theory would have remained unexposed if Malthus had been a revolutionist instead of a champion and defender of capitalism?

"But let Malthus go. While the low birth-rate among the cultured classes—whose condition was the prototype of the general condition under economic equality—was refutation enough of the overpopulation objection, yet there is another and far more conclusive answer, the full force of which remains to be brought out. You said a few moments ago that one reason why the birth-rate was so moderate among the cultured classes was the fact that in that class the wishes of women were more considered than in the lower classes. The necessary effect of economic equality between the sexes would mean, however, that, instead of being more or less considered, the wishes of women in all matters touching the subject we are discussing would be final and absolute. Previous to the establishment of economic equality by the great Revolution the non-child-bearing sex was the sex which determined the question of child-bearing, and the natural consequence was the possibility of a Malthus and his doctrine. Nature has provided in the distress and inconvenience of the maternal function a sufficient check upon its abuse, just as she has in regard to all the other natural functions. But, in order that Nature's check should be properly operative, it is necessary that the women through whose wills it must operate, if at all, should be absolutely free agents in the disposition of themselves, and the necessary condition of that free agency is economic independence. That secured, while we may be sure that the maternal instinct will forever prevent the race from dying out, the world will be equally little in danger of being recklessly overcrowded."

21

A Modern Utopia

H. G. WELLS'S CONCEPTION OF UTOPIAN FREEDOM

Although H. G. Wells (1866–1946) is rightfully considered one of the greatest utopian thinkers of the twentieth century, he was not always as optimistic about humanity's prospects as most utopians have been. Wells began his brilliant literary career late in the nineteenth century with the publication of *The Time Machine* (1895), a captivating but extremely pessimistic projection into man's ultimate future; he ended that career fifty years later with the publication of a brief essay entitled "Mind at the End of its Tether," in which he relinquished all hope for man's future, gave vent to the gloomiest pessimism imaginable, and declared utopian visions and efforts to be completely futile. Before he reached the end of his tether and bade bitter farewell to the human race in his last essay, Wells had written over a hundred books including scientific romances, short stories, novels, essays, and encyclopedic outlines of several fields of knowledge. He was one of the most influential writers of this century, incredibly prolific and energetic and filled with a seemingly inexhaustible enthusiasm for melioristic efforts, supported by an unshakable confidence in science, technology, and socialism.

In addition to works which today would be called dystopias such as *The Time Machine, The Island of Doctor Moreau*, and *The War of the Worlds*, Wells wrote two major utopian novels, *A Modern Utopia* (1905) and *Men Like Gods* (1923). In these he described social life at different stages of development on an imaginary planet whose topography is very similar to the earth's. From these and his other books it is possible to formulate an outline of Wells's utopianism.

First, Wells is convinced that human beings must look forward and learn to use their best "creative or future-regarding minds" rather than mere "legal or past-regarding minds" if they are to anticipate, prepare for, and take advantage of "the shape of things to come." Life should be regarded not as "a system of consequences" but as a "system of constructive effort." Utopian reforms can never be achieved until people have the courage to release themselves from "the stranglehold of past things." Wells believes that while the future may not be foretellable, the conditions which shall determine it can for the most part be ascertained and studied and used as a basis for making predictions. Recent futurists such as Arthur C. Clarke (in *Profiles of the Future*) are following the trail blazed by Wells.

Second, Wells, like his utopian English predecessor Sir Francis Bacon, believed that science could provide the knowledge and technology by which mankind could conquer nature and transform the world. Properly controlled, scientific discoveries and technological advances should promote rather than threaten moral values. The suspicion and fear of machines prevalent in the modern writers of science fiction dystopias is foreign to Wells. Machines are the only genuine and morally justifiable slaves by nature.

The third tenet of Wells's utopianism is practically identical with a belief of Plato's: that an intellectual élite, a "voluntary nobility" as Wells calls his order of *samurai*, must govern the ideal society. The best educated, most talented, and highly disciplined members of society composing this select group of men and women would provide the leadership and control for the state. This would make possible, Wells believes, the combination of political stability with progress for the first time in history. In presenting his views on leadership, Wells (again like Plato) argues that all men are not by nature equal. He proposes a division of human beings according to four basic types of character: the poietic, the kinetic, the dull, and the base. Only the base, persons of strong antisocial disposition, could never be associated with the order of *samurai*.

As Wells became convinced that only such a governing order as the *samurai* could bring into existence the socialistic world state which he imagined would fulfill the hopes and needs of mankind in the future, he attempted to establish in fact an Order of Samurai. Meeting with no success—he even failed to convince his friends the Fabian socialists that they should be the initial "voluntary nobility"—Wells turned his last efforts to promoting a peaceful revolution. He hoped this "open conspiracy" would lead eventually to the establishment of a supernational World State. Not until the end of his life, after he had come through two world wars only to face the frightening dawn of the Atomic Age, did Wells have his faith shaken in the possibility of a modern world utopia. As he envisaged it in *Men Like Gods*, this would be "a world fairly and righteously at peace, its resources husbanded and exploited for the common good, its every citizen freed not only from servitude but from ignorance, and its surplus energies directed steadfastly to the increase of knowledge and beauty."[1]

[1] H. G. Wells, *Men Like Gods* (New York: Grosset & Dunlap, 1922), p. 314.

H. G. Wells, A Modern Utopia *(London: Chapman & Hall, 1905), pp. 5–12; 31–43. Reprinted by permission of The Estate of H. G. Wells.*

The Utopia of a modern dreamer must needs differ in one funda-mental aspect from the Nowheres and Utopias men planned before Darwin quickened the thought of the world. Those were all perfect and static States, a balance of happiness won for ever against the forces of unrest and disorder that inhere in things. One beheld a healthy and simple generation enjoying the fruits of the earth in an atmosphere of virtue and happiness, to be followed by other virtuous, happy, and entirely similar generations, until the Gods grew weary. Change and development were dammed back by invincible dams for ever. But the Modern Utopia must be not static but kinetic, must shape not as a permanent state but as a hopeful stage, leading to a long ascent of stages. Nowadays we do not resist and overcome the great stream of things, but rather float upon it. We build now not citadels, but ships of state. For one ordered arrangement of citizens rejoicing in an equality of happiness safe and assured to them and their children for ever, we have to plan "a flexible common com-promise, in which a perpetually novel succession of individualities may converge most effectually upon a comprehensive onward develop-ment." That is the first, most generalised difference between a Utopia based upon modern conceptions and all the Utopias that were written in the former time.

Our business here is to be Utopian, to make vivid and credible, if we can, first this facet and then that, of an imaginary whole and happy world. Our deliberate intention is to be not, indeed, impossible, but most distinctly impracticable, by every scale that reaches only between to-day and to-morrow. We are to turn our backs for a space upon the insistent examination of the thing that is, and face towards the freer air, the ampler spaces of the thing that perhaps might be, to the projection of a State or city "worth while," to designing upon the sheet of our imaginations the picture of a life conceivably possible, and yet better worth living than our own. That is our present enter-prise. We are going to lay down certain necessary starting propositions, and then we shall proceed to explore the sort of world these propositions give us. . . .

It is no doubt an optimistic enterprise. But it is good for awhile to be free from the carping note that must needs be audible when we discuss our present imperfections, to release ourselves from practical difficulties and the tangle of ways and means. It is good to stop by the track for a space, put aside the knapsack, wipe the brows, and talk a little of the upper slopes of the mountain we think we are climbing, would but the trees let us see it.

There is to be no inquiry here of policy and method. This is to be a holiday from politics and movements and methods. But, for all that, we must needs define certain limitations. Were we free to have our untrammelled desire, I suppose we should follow Morris to his Nowhere, we should change the nature of man and the nature of things together; we should make the whole race wise, tolerant, noble, perfect —wave our hands to a splendid anarchy, every man doing as it pleases him, and none pleased to do evil, in a world as good in its essential nature, as ripe and sunny, as the world before the Fall. But that golden age, that perfect world, comes out into the possibilities of space and time. In space and time the pervading Will to Live sustains for evermore a perpetuity of aggressions. Our proposal here is upon a more practical plane at least than that. We are to restrict ourselves first to the limitations of human possibility as we know them in the men and women of this world to-day, and then to all the inhumanity, all the insubordination of nature. We are to shape our state in a world of uncertain seasons, sudden catastrophes, antagonistic diseases, and inimical beasts and vermin, out of men and women with like passions, like uncertainties of mood and desire to our own. And, moreover, we are going to accept this world of conflict, to adopt no attitude of renunciation towards it, to face it in no ascetic spirit, but in the mood of the Western peoples, whose purpose is to survive and overcome. So much we adopt in common with those who deal not in Utopias, but in the world of Here and Now.

Certain liberties, however, following the best Utopian precedents, we may take with existing fact. We assume that the tone of public thought may be entirely different from what it is in the present world. We permit ourselves a free hand with the mental conflict of life, within the possibilities of the human mind as we know it. We permit ourselves also a free hand with all the apparatus of existence that man has, so to speak, made for himself, with houses, roads, clothing, canals, machinery, with laws, boundaries, conventions, and traditions, with schools, with literature and religious organisation, with creeds and customs, with everything, in fact, that it lies within man's power to alter. That, indeed, is the cardinal assumption of all Utopian speculations old and new; the Republic and Laws of Plato, and More's Utopia, Howells' implicit Altruria, and Bellamy's future Boston, Comte's great Western Republic, Hertzka's Freeland, Cabet's Icaria, and Campanella's City of the Sun, are built, just as we shall build, upon that, upon the hypothesis of the complete emancipation of a community of men from tradition, from habits, from legal bonds, and that subtler servitude possessions entail. And much of the essential value of all such speculations lies in this assumption of emancipation, lies in that regard towards human freedom, in the undying interest of the human power of self-escape, the power to resist the causation of the past, and to evade, initiate, endeavour, and overcome. . . .

There are very definite artistic limitations also.

There must always be a certain effect of hardness and thinness about Utopian speculations. Their common fault is to be comprehensively jejune. That which is the blood and warmth and reality of life is largely absent; there are no individualities, but only generalised people. In almost every Utopia—except, perhaps, Morris's "News from Nowhere"—one sees handsome but characterless buildings, symmetrical and perfect cultivations, and a multitude of people, healthy, happy, beautifully dressed, but without any personal distinction whatever. Too often the prospect resembles the key to one of those large pictures of coronations, royal weddings, parliaments, conferences, and gatherings so popular in Victorian times, in which, instead of a face, each figure bears a neat oval with its index number legibly inscribed. This burthens us with an incurable effect of unreality, and I do not see how it is altogether to be escaped. It is a disadvantage that has to be accepted. Whatever institution has existed or exists, however irrational, however preposterous, has, by virtue of its contact with individualities, an effect of realness and rightness no untried thing may share. It has ripened, it has been christened with blood, it has been stained and mellowed by handling, it has been rounded and dented to the softened contours that we associate with life; it has been salted, maybe, in a brine of tears. But the thing that is merely proposed, the thing that is merely suggested, however rational, however necessary, seems strange and inhuman in its clear, hard, uncompromising lines, its unqualified angles and surfaces.

There is no help for it, there it is! The Master suffers with the last and least of his successors. For all the humanity he wins to, through his dramatic device of dialogue, I doubt if anyone has ever been warmed to desire himself a citizen in the Republic of Plato; I doubt if anyone could stand a month of the relentless publicity of virtue planned by More. . . . No one wants to live in any community of intercourse really, save for the sake of the individualities he would meet there. The fertilising conflict of individualities is the ultimate meaning of the personal life, and all our Utopias no more than schemes for bettering that interplay. At least, that is how life shapes itself more and more to modern perceptions. Until you bring in individualities, nothing comes into being, and a Universe ceases when you shiver the mirror of the least of individual minds. . . .

No less than a planet will serve the purpose of a modern Utopia. Time was when a mountain valley or an island seemed to promise sufficient isolation for a polity to maintain itself intact from outward force; the Republic of Plato stood armed ready for defensive war, and the New Atlantis and the Utopia of More in theory, like China and Japan through many centuries of effectual practice, held themselves isolated from intruders. Such late instances as Butler's satirical "Erewhon," and Mr. Stead's queendom of inverted sexual conditions in Central Africa, found the Tibetan method of slaughtering the inquiring visitor a simple, sufficient rule. But the whole trend of modern thought is against the permanence of any such enclosures. We are acutely aware nowadays that, however subtly contrived a State may be, outside your boundary lines the epidemic, the breeding barbarian or the economic power, will gather its strength to overcome you. The swift march of invention is all for the invader. Now, perhaps you might still guard a rocky coast or a narrow pass; but what of that near to-morrow when the flying machine soars overhead, free to descend at this point or that? A state powerful enough to keep isolated under modern conditions would be powerful enough to rule the world, would be, indeed, if not actively ruling, yet passively acquiescent in all other human organizations, and so responsible for them altogether. World-state, therefore, it must be. . . .

Now what sort of question would first occur to two men descending upon the planet of a Modern Utopia? Probably grave solicitude about their personal freedom. Towards the Stranger, as I have already remarked, the Utopias of the past displayed their least amiable aspect. Would this new sort of Utopian State, spread to the dimensions of a world, be any less forbidding?

We should take comfort in the thought that universal Toleration is certainly a modern idea, and it is upon modern ideas that this World State rests. But even suppose we are tolerated and admitted to this unavoidable citizenship, there will still remain a wide range of possibility. . . . I think we should try to work the problem out from an inquiry into first principles, and that we should follow the trend of our time and kind by taking up the question as one of "Man *versus* the State," and discussing the compromise of Liberty.

The idea of individual liberty is one that has grown in importance and grows with every development of modern thought. To the classical Utopists freedom was relatively trivial. Clearly they considered virtue and happiness as entirely separable from liberty, and as being altogether more important things. But the modern view, with its deepening insistence upon individuality and upon the significance of its uniqueness, steadily intensifies the value of freedom, until at last we begin to see liberty as the very substance of life, that indeed it is life, and that only the dead things, the choiceless things, live in absolute obedience to law. To have free play for one's individuality is, in the modern view, the subjective triumph of existence, as survival in creative work and offspring is its objective triumph. But for all men, since man is a social creature, the play of will must fall short of absolute freedom. Perfect human liberty is possible only to a despot who is absolutely and universally obeyed. Then to will would be to command and achieve, and within the limits of natural law we could at any moment do exactly as it pleased us to do. All other liberty is a compromise between our own freedom of will and the wills of those with whom we come in contact. In an organised state each one of us has a more or less elaborate code of what he may do to others and to himself, and what others may do to him. He limits others by his rights, and is limited by the rights of others, and by considerations affecting the welfare of the community as a whole.

Individual liberty in a community is not, as mathematicians would say, always of the same sign. To ignore this is the essential fallacy of the cult called Individualism. But in truth, a general prohibition in a state may increase the sum of liberty, and a general permission may diminish it. It does not follow, as these people would have us believe, that a man is more free where there is least law and more restricted where there is most law. A socialism or a communism is not necessarily a slavery, and there is no freedom under Anarchy. Consider how much liberty we gain by the loss of the common liberty to kill. Thereby one may go to and fro in all the ordered parts of the earth, unencumbered by arms or armour, free of the fear of playful poison, whimsical barbers, or hotel trap-doors. Indeed, it means freedom from a thousand fears and precautions. Suppose there existed even the limited freedom to kill in vendetta, and think what would happen in our suburbs. Consider the inconvenience of two households in a modern suburb estranged and provided with modern weapons of precision, the inconvenience not only to each other, but to the neutral pedestrian, the practical loss of freedoms all about them. The butcher, if he came at all, would have to come round in an armoured cart. . . .

It follows, therefore, in a modern Utopia, which finds the final hope of the world in the evolving interplay of unique individualities, that the State will have effectually chipped away just all those spendthrift liberties that waste liberty, and not one liberty more, and so have attained the maximum general freedom.

There are two distinct and contrasting methods of limiting liberty; the first is Prohibition, "thou shalt not," and the second Command, "thou shalt." There is, however, a sort of prohibition that takes the form of a conditional command, and this one needs to bear in mind. It says if you do so-and-so, you must also do so-and-so; if, for example, you go to sea with men you employ, you must go in a seaworthy vessel. But the pure command is unconditional; it says, whatever you have done or are doing or want to do, you are to do this, as when the social system, working through the base necessities of base parents and bad laws, sends a child of thirteen into a factory. Prohibition takes one definite thing from the indefinite liberty of a man, but it still leaves him an unbounded choice of actions. He remains free, and you have merely taken a bucketful from the sea of his freedom. But compulsion destroys freedom altogether. In this Utopia of ours there may be many prohibitions, but no indirect compulsions—if one may so contrive it—and few or no commands. As far as I see it now, in this present discussion, I think, indeed, there should be no positive compulsions at all in Utopia, at any rate for the adult Utopian—unless they fall upon him as penalties incurred. . . .

What prohibitions should we be under, we two Uitlanders in this Utopian world? We should certainly not be free to kill, assault, or threaten anyone we met, and in that we earth-trained men would not be likely to offend. And until we knew more exactly the Utopian idea of property we should be very chary of touching anything that might conceivably be appropriated. If it was not the property of individuals it might be the property of the State. But beyond that we might have our doubts. . . .

I submit that to the modern minded man it can be no sort of Utopia worth desiring that does not give the utmost freedom of going to and fro. Free movement is to many people one of the greatest of life's privileges—to go wherever the spirit moves them, to wander and see— and though they have every comfort, every security, every virtuous discipline, they will still be unhappy if that is denied them. Short of damage to things cherished and made, the Utopians will surely have this right, so we may expect no unclimbable walls and fences, nor the discovery of any laws we may transgress in coming down these mountain places.

And yet, just as civil liberty itself is a compromise defended by

prohibitions, so this particular sort of liberty must also have its qualifications. Carried to the absolute pitch the right of free movement
ceases to be distinguishable from the right of free intrusion. We have
already, in a comment on More's Utopia, hinted at an agreement with
Aristotle's argument against communism, that it flings people into an
intolerable continuity of contact. Schopenhauer carried out Aristotle
in the vein of his own bitterness and with the truest of images when
he likened human society to hedgehogs clustering for warmth, and unhappy when either too closely packed or two widely separated. Empedocles found no significance in life whatever except as an unsteady
play of love and hate, of attraction and repulsion, of assimilation and
the assertion of difference. So long as we ignore difference, so long as
we ignore individuality, and that I hold has been the common sin of
all Utopias hitherto, we can make absolute statements, prescribe com-
munisms or individualisms, and all sorts of hard theoretic arrangements. But in the world of reality, which—to modernise Heraclitus
and Empedocles—is nothing more nor less than the world of individuality, there are no absolute rights and wrongs, there are no qualita-
tive questions at all, but only quantitative adjustments. Equally strong
in the normal civilised man is the desire for freedom of movement
and the desire for a certain privacy, for a corner definitely his, and
we have to consider where the line of reconciliation comes.

The desire for absolute personal privacy is perhaps never a very
strong or persistent craving. In the great majority of human beings,
the gregarious instinct is sufficiently powerful to render any but the
most temporary isolations not simply disagreeable, but painful. The
savage has all the privacy he needs within the compass of his skull;
like dogs and timid women, he prefers ill-treatment to desertion, and
it is only a scarce and complex modern type that finds comfort and
refreshment in quite lonely places and quiet solitary occupations. Yet
such there are, men who can neither sleep well nor think well, nor attain to a full perception of beautiful objects, who do not savour the
best of existence until they are securely alone, and for the sake of
these even it would be reasonable to draw some limits to the general
right of free movement. But their particular need is only a special
and exceptional aspect of an almost universal claim to privacy among
modern people, not so much for the sake of isolation as for congenial
companionship. We want to go apart from the great crowd, not so
much to be alone as to be with those who appeal to us particularly
and to whom we particularly appeal; we want to form households
and societies with them, to give our individualities play in intercourse with them, and in the appointments and furnishings of that
intercourse. We want gardens and enclosures and exclusive freedoms

for our like and our choice, just as spacious as we can get them—and it is only the multitudinous uncongenial, anxious also for similar developments in some opposite direction, that checks this expansive movement of personal selection and necessitates a compromise on privacy.

Glancing back from our Utopian mountain side down which this discourse marches, to the confusions of old earth, we may remark that the need and desire for privacies there is exceptionally great at the present time, that it was less in the past, that in the future it may be less again, and that under the Utopian conditions to which we shall come when presently we strike yonder road, it may be reduced to quite manageable dimensions. But this is to be effected not by the suppression of individualities to some common pattern, . . . but by the broadening of public charity and the general amelioration of mind and manners. It is not by assimilation, that is to say, but by understanding that the modern Utopia achieves itself. The ideal community of man's past was one with a common belief, with common customs and common ceremonies, common manners and common formulae; men of the same society dressed in the same fashion, each according to his defined and understood grade, behaved in the same fashion, loved, worshipped, and died in the same fashion. They did or felt little that did not find a sympathetic publicity. The natural disposition of all peoples, white, black, or brown, a natural disposition that education seeks to destroy, is to insist upon uniformity, to make publicity extremely unsympathetic to even the most harmless departures from the code. To be dressed "odd," to behave "oddly," to eat in a different manner or of different food, to commit, indeed, any breach of the established convention is to give offence and to incur hostility among unsophisticated men. But the disposition of the more original and enterprising minds at all times has been to make such innovations.

This is particularly in evidence in this present age. The almost cataclysmal development of new machinery, the discovery of new materials, and the appearance of new social possibilities though the organised pursuit of material science, has given enormous and unprecedented facilities to the spirit of innovation. The old local order has been broken up or is now being broken up all over the earth, and everywhere societies deliquesce, everywhere men are afloat amidst the wreckage of their flooded conventions, and still tremendously unaware of the thing that has happened. The old local orthodoxies of behaviour, of precedence, the old accepted amusements and employments, the old ritual of conduct in the important small things of the daily life and the old ritual of thought in the things that make discussion, are smashed up and scattered and mixed discordantly together, one use with another, and no world-wide culture of toleration, no courteous admission of differences, no wider understanding has yet replaced them. And so publicity in the modern earth has become confusedly unsympathetic for everyone. Classes are intolerable to classes and sets to sets, contact provokes aggressions, comparisons, persecutions and discomforts, and the subtler people are excessively tormented by a sense of observation, unsympathetic always and often hostile. To live without some sort of segregation from the general mass is impossible in exact proportion to one's individual distinction.

Of course things will be very different in Utopia. Utopia will be saturated with consideration. . . . And Utopian manners will not only be tolerant, but almost universally tolerable. Endless things will be understood perfectly and universally that on earth are understood only by a scattered few; baseness of bearing, grossness of manner, will be the distinctive mark of no section of the community whatever. The coarser reasons for privacy, therefore, will not exist here. And that savage sort of shyness, too, that makes so many half-educated people on earth recluse and defensive, that too the Utopians will have escaped by their more liberal breeding. In the cultivated State we are assuming it will be ever so much easier for people to eat in public, rest and amuse themselves in public, and even work in public. Our present need for privacy in many things marks, indeed, a phase of transition from an ease in public in the past due to homogeneity, to an ease in public in the future due to intelligence and good breeding, and in Utopia that transition will be complete. We must bear that in mind throughout the consideration of this question.

Yet, after this allowance has been made, there still remains a considerable claim for privacy in Utopia. The room, or apartments, or home, or mansion, whatever it may be a man or woman maintains, must be private, and under his or her complete dominion; it seems harsh and intrusive to forbid a central garden plot or peristyle, such as one sees in Pompeii, within the house walls, and it is almost as difficult to deny a little private territory beyond the house. Yet if we concede that, it is clear that without some further provision we concede the possibility that the poorer townsman (if there are to be rich and poor in the world) will be forced to walk through endless miles of high fenced villa gardens before he may expand in his little scrap of reserved open country. Such is already the poor Londoner's miserable fate. . . . Our Utopia will have of course, faultless roads and beautifully arranged inter-urban communications, swift trains or motor services or what not, to diffuse its population, and without anticipatory provisions, the prospect of the residential areas becoming a vast area of defensively walled villa Edens is all too possible.

This is a quantitative question, be it remembered, and not to be dismissed by any statement of principle. Our Utopians will meet it, I presume, by detailed regulations, very probably varying locally with local conditions. Privacy beyond the house might be made a privilege to be paid for in proportion to the area occupied, and the tax on these licences of privacy might increase as the square of the area affected. A maximum fraction of private enclosure for each urban and suburban square mile could be fixed. A distinction could be drawn between an absolutely private garden and a garden private and closed only for a day or a couple of days a week, and at other times open to the well-behaved public. Who, in a really civilised community, would grudge that measure of invasion? Walls could be taxed by height and length, and the enclosure of really natural beauties, of rapids, cascades, gorges, viewpoints, and so forth made impossible. So a reasonable compromise between the vital and conflicting claims of the freedom of movement and the freedom of seclusion might be attained.

22

The Utopian Element
in Socialism

MARTIN BUBER'S RE-EVALUATION
OF UTOPIAN SOCIALISM

The Jewish religious philosopher Martin Buber (1878–1965) was strongly opposed to those who would stereotype utopian thought as shallow, irresponsible fantasying which had little practicality or relation to reality. In his little book *Paths to Utopia* (1949), he attempts to rescue one kind of utopian thought, utopian socialism, from the misinterpretations, accusations, and injustices that had been fostered upon it since it was developed in the early nineteenth century.

Buber is particularly concerned to correct the misinterpretations of this kind of socialism given by the Marxists who had, he believed, intentionally denigrated and rejected it dogmatically and unfairly. After carefully tracing the origin and development of utopian socialism, beginning with Saint-Simon, Fourier, and Owen, and continuing with Proudhon, Kropotkin, and Landauer, Buber compares this kind of socialism with that of Marx, Engels, and Lenin in order to show that the so-called "scientific socialism" of the latter is not necessarily more scientific or empirically based than the former. Further, he points out that not only are there several unacknowledged similarities between the Marxists and the utopian socialists, but also that the end of Marx's dialectical materialism—the ultimate withering away of the state—is an article of utopian eschatology rather than an article of scientific faith.

But Buber's chief objection to Marxist socialism, especially as it has been applied in the Soviet Union, is that it has not made possible the achievement of genuine community, authentic association. "The most valuable of all goods —the life between man and man" (what Buber calls elsewhere the "I and Thou relationship") becomes impossible when collective relationships are involuntary, living is strictly regimented, and technology serves the end of a centralized political power. Buber believes that utopian socialism offers an alternative, one variation of which has been dramatically and successfully exemplified in the Kibbutz or Collectivist Movement in Israel. If no alternative such as this is taken, Buber, like Huxley and Orwell and the more recent dystopians, sees little hope that humanity can overcome the greatest danger it faces today: the danger of a world-wide, totalitarian regime in which political power is centralized and freedom destroyed.

In restructuring society, Buber would restore the supremacy of the social principle over the political principles, encouraging the development of "socialist pluralism" rather than "socialist unitarianism." His utopian ideal is "a league of leagues," a "community of communities" in each of which individuals can experience "a living togetherness, constantly renewing itself." Centralization there will have to be, but not to the degree that the economic and political autonomy of each community will be destroyed.

Finally, as many of the utopian socialists before him, Buber refuses to separate socialism from religion. His own religious perspective arises out of his profound existential encounter with God and man. One becomes genuinely religious and socialistic, he holds, not as a result of rational inquiry but from learning to communicate, to be responsive and responsible, and to welcome personal confrontation with that which is immediately and ultimately real. As he put it succinctly in *I and Thou*, "All real living is meeting."

What, at first sight, seems common to the Utopias that have passed into the spiritual history of mankind, is the fact that they are pictures, and pictures moreover of something not actually present but only represented. Such pictures are generally called fantasy-pictures, but that tells us little enough. This "fantasy" does not float vaguely in the air, it is not driven hither and thither by the wind of caprice, it centres with architectonic firmness on something primary and original which it is its destiny to build; and this primary thing is a wish. The utopian picture is a picture of what "should be", and the visionary is one who wishes it to be. Therefore some call the Utopias wish-pictures, but that again does not tell us enough. A "wish-picture" makes us think of something that rises out of the depths of the Unconscious and, in the form of a dream, a reverie, a "seizure", overpowers the defenceless soul, or may, at a later stage, even be invoked, called forth, hatched out by the soul itself. In the history of the human spirit the image-creating wish—although it, too, like all image-making is rooted deep down in us—has nothing instinctive about it and nothing of self-gratification. It is bound up with something suprapersonal that communes with the soul but is not governed by it. What is at work here is the longing for that *rightness* which, in religious or philosophical vision, is experienced as revelation or idea, and which of its very nature cannot be realized in the individual, but only in human community. The vision of "what should be"—independent though it may sometimes appear of personal will—is yet inseparable from a critical and fundamental relationship to the existing condition of humanity. All suffering under a social order that is senseless prepares the soul for vision, and what the soul receives in this vision strengthens and deepens its insight into the perversity of what is perverted. The longing for the realization of "the seen" fashions the picture.

The vision of rightness in Revelation is realized in the picture of a perfect time—as messianic eschatology; the vision of rightness in the Ideal is realized in the picture of a perfect space—as Utopia. The first necessarily goes beyond the social and borders on the creational, the cosmic; the second necessarily remains bounded by the circumference of society, even if the picture it presents sometimes implies an inner transformation of man. Eschatology means perfection of creation; Utopia the unfolding of the possibilities, latent in mankind's communal life, of a "right" order. Another difference is still more important. For eschatology the decisive act happens from above, even when the elemental or prophetic form of it gives man a significant and active share in the coming redemption; for Utopia everything is subordinated to conscious human will, indeed we can characterize it outright as a picture of society designed as though there were no other factors at work than conscious human will. But they are neither of them mere cloud castles: if they seek to stimulate or intensify in the reader or listener his critical relationship to the present, they also seek to show him perfection—in the light of the Absolute, but at the same time as something towards which an active path leads from the present. And what may seem impossible as a concept arouses, as an image, the whole might of faith, ordains purpose and plan. It does this because it is in league with powers latent in the depths of reality. Eschatology, in so far as it is prophetic, Utopia, in so far as it is philosophical, both have the character of realism.

The Age of Enlightenment and its aftermath robbed religious eschatology in increasing measure of its sphere of action: in the course of ten generations it has become more and more difficult for man to believe that at some point in the future an act from above will redeem the human world, i.e. transform it from a senseless one into one full of meaning, from disharmony into harmony. This incapacity has become an actual physical incapacity, in avowedly religious no less than in areligious people, save that in the former it is concealed from consciousness by the fixed nexus of tradition. On the other hand, the age of technology with its growing social contradictions has influenced Utopia profoundly. Under the influence of pan-technical trends Utopia has become wholly technical; conscious human will, its foundation hitherto, is now understood as technics, and society like Nature is to be mastered by technological calculation and construction. Society, however, with its present contradictions poses a question that cannot be dismissed; all thinking and planning for the future must seek the answer to it, and where Utopia is concerned the political and cultural formulations necessarily give way before the task of contriving a "right" order of society. But here social thinking shows its superiority over technical thinking. Utopias which revel in technical fantasias mostly find foothold nowadays only in the feebler species of novel, in which little or none of the imagination that went into the grand Utopias of old can be discovered. Those, on the contrary, which undertake to deliver a blueprint of the perfect social structure, turn into systems. But into these "utopian" social systems there enters all the force of dispossessed Messianism. The social system of modern socialism or communism has, like eschatology, the character of annunciation or of a proclamation. It is true that Plato was moved by the desire to establish a reality proportioned to the Idea, and it is true that he also sought, to the end of his days and with unflagging passion, for the human tools of its realization; but only with the modern social systems did there arise this fierce interplay of doctrine and action, planning and experiment. For Thomas More it was still possible to mingle serious instruction with incongruous jesting, and, with supercilious irony, to allow a picture of "very absurd" institutions to rub shoulders with such as he "wishes rather than hopes" to see copied. For Fourier that was no longer possible; here everything is practical inference and logical resolve, for the point with him is "to emerge at last from a civilization which, far from being man's social destiny, is only mankind's childhood sickness."

The polemics of Marx and Engels have resulted in the term "utopian" becoming used, both within Marxism and without, for a socialism which appeals to reason, to justice, to the will of man to remedy the maladjustments of society, instead of his merely acquiring an active awareness of what is "dialectically" brewing in the womb of industrialism. All voluntaristic socialism is rated "utopian." Yet it is by no means the case that the socialism diametrically opposed to it—which we may call necessitarian because it professes to demand nothing more than the setting in motion of the necessary evolutionary machinery—is free of utopianism. The utopian elements in it are of another kind and stand in a different context.

I have already indicated that the whole force of dispossessed eschatology was converted into Utopia at the time of the French Revolution. But, as I have intimated, there are two basic forms of eschatology: the prophetic, which at any given moment sees every person addressed by it as endowed, in a degree not to be determined beforehand, with the power to participate by his decisions and deeds in the preparing of Redemption: and the apocalyptic, in which the redemptive process in all its details, its very hour and course, has been fixed from everlasting and for whose accomplishment human beings are only used as tools, though what is immutably fixed may yet be "unveiled" to them, revealed, and they be assigned their function. The first of these forms derives from Israel, the second from ancient Persia. The differences and agreements between the two, their combinations and separations, play an important part in the inner history of Christianity. In the socialist secularization of eschatology they

work out separately: the prophetic form in some of the systems of the
so-called Utopians, the apocalyptic one above all in Marxism (which
is not to say that no prophetic element is operative here—it has only
been overpowered by the apocalyptic). With Marx, belief in humanity's road through contradiction to the overcoming of the same, takes
the form of Hegelian dialectic, since he makes use of a scientific inquiry into the changing processes of production; but the vision of
upheavals past or to come "in the chain of absolute necessity," as
Hegel says, does not derive from Hegel. Marx's apocalyptic position is
purer and stronger than Hegel's, which lacked any real driving power
for the future; Franz Rosenzweig has pointed out, and rightly, that
Marx remained truer to Hegel's belief in historical determinism than
Hegel himself. "No one else has seen so directly where and how and
in what form the last day would dawn on the horizon of history."
The point at which, in Marx, the utopian apocalypse breaks out and
the whole topic of economics and science is transformed into pure
"utopics," is the convulsion of all things *after* the social revolution.
The Utopia of the so-called Utopians is pre-revolutionary, the Marxist
one post-revolutionary. The "withering away" of the state, "the leap
of humanity out of the realm of necessity into the realm of freedom"
may be well-founded dialectically, but it is no longer so scientifically.
As a Marxist thinker, Paul Tillich, says, these things "can in no way
be made intelligible in terms of existing reality," "between reality and
expectation there is a gulf," "for this reason Marxism has never, despite its animosity to Utopias, been able to clear itself of the suspicion
of a hidden belief in Utopia." Or in the words of another Marxist
sociologist, Eduard Heimann: "With men as they are, a withering
away of the State is inconceivable. In speculating on a radical and
inmost change of human nature, we pass beyond the borders of
empirical research and enter the realm of prophetic vision where the
true significance and providential destination of man are circum-
scribed in stammering metaphors." But what is of decisive significance
for us is the difference between this Utopianism and that of the non-
marxist socialists. We shall have to observe this difference more closely.

When we examine what Marxist criticism calls the utopian element
in the non-marxist systems we find that it is by no means simple or
uniform. Two distinct elements are to be distinguished. The essence of
one is schematic fiction, the essence of the other is organic planning.
The first, as we encounter it particularly in Fourier, originates in a
kind of abstract imagination which, starting from a theory of the nature of man, his capacities and needs, deduces a social order that shall
employ all his capacities and satisfy all his needs. Although in Fourier
the theory is supported by a mass of observational material, every

observation becomes unreal and untrustworthy as soon as it enters this sphere; and in his social order, which pretends to be social architecture but is in reality formless schematism, all problems (as Fourier himself says) have the same "solution", that is, from real problems in the life of human beings they become artificial problems in the life of instinctive robots—artificial problems which all allow of the same solution because they all proceed from the same mechanistic set-up. Wholly different, indeed of a directly contrary nature, is the second element. Here the dominant purpose is to inaugurate, from an impartial and undogmatic understanding of contemporary man and his condition, a transformation of both, so as to overcome the contradictions which make up the essence of our social order.

Starting with no reservations from the condition of society as it is, this view gazes into the depths of reality with a clarity of vision unclouded by any dogmatic pre-occupation, discerning those still hidden tendencies which, although obscured by more obvious and more powerful forces, are yet moving towards that transformation. It has justly been said that in a positive sense every planning intellect is utopian. But we must add that the planning intellect of the socialist "Utopians" under consideration, proves the positive character of its utopianism by being at every point aware, or at least having an inkling, of the diversity, indeed the contrariety, of the trends discernible in every age; by not failing to discover, despite its insight into the dominant trends, those others which these trends conceal; and by asking whether and to what extent those and those alone are aiming at an order in which the contradictions of existing society will truly be overcome.

Here, then, we have one or two motives which require further explanation and amplification both in themselves and in order to mark them off from Marxism.

In the course of the development of so-called utopian socialism its leading representatives have become more and more persuaded that neither the social problem nor its solution can be reduced to a lowest common denominator, and that every simplification—even the most intellectually important—exerts an unfavourable influence both on knowledge and action. When in 1846, some six months before he started his controversy with Proudhon, Marx invited the latter to collaborate with him in a "correspondence" which should subserve "an exchange of ideas and impartial criticism," and for which—so Marx writes—"as regards France we all believe that we could find no better correspondent than yourself," he received the answer: "Let us, if you wish, look together for the laws of society, the manner in which they are realized, but after we have cleared away all these a priori dogma-

tisms, let us not, for God's sake, think of tangling people up in doctrines in our turn! Let us not fall into the contradiction of your
countryman Martin Luther who, after having overthrown the catholic
theology, immediately set about founding a protestant theology of his
own amid a great clamour of excommunications and anathemas. . . .
Because we stand in the van of a new movement let us not make
ourselves the protagonists of a new intolerance, let us not act like
apostles of a new religion, even if it be a religion of logic, a religion of
reason." Here it is chiefly a question of political means, but from many
of Proudhon's utterances it is evident that he saw the ends as well
in the light of the same freedom and diversity. And fifty years after
that letter Kropotkin summed up the basic view of the ends in a single
sentence: the fullest development of individuality "will combine with
the highest development of voluntary association in all its aspects, in
all possible degrees and for all possible purposes; an association that
is always changing, that bears in itself the elements of its own dura-
tion, that takes on the forms which best correspond at any given moment to the manifold strivings of all." This is precisely what Proudhon
had wanted in the maturity of his thought. It may be contended that
the Marxist objective is not essentially different in constitution; but at
this point a yawning chasm opens out before us which can only be
bridged by that special form of Marxist utopics, a chasm between, on
the one side, the transformation to be consummated sometime in the
future—no one knows how long after the final victory of the Revolution—and, on the other, the road to the Revolution and beyond it,
which road is characterized by a far-reaching centralization that per-
mits no individual features and no individual initiative. Uniformity as
a means is to change miraculously into multiplicity as an end; compulsion into freedom. As against this the "utopian" or non-marxist
socialist desires a means commensurate with his ends; he refused to
believe that in our reliance on the future "leap" we have to do now
the direct opposite of what we are striving for; he believes rather
that we must create here and now the space *now* possible for the
thing for which we are striving, so that it may come to fulfilment *then;*
he does not believe in the post-revolutionary leap, but he does believe
in revolutionary continuity. To put it more precisely: he believes in
a continuity within which revolution is only the accomplishment, the
setting free and extension of a reality that has already grown to its
true possibilties.

Seen from another angle this difference may be clarified still further.
When we examine the capitalist society which has given birth to
socialism, *as a society*, we see that it is a society inherently poor in
structure and growing visibly poorer every day. By the structure of a

society is to be understood its social content or community-content: a society can be called structurally rich to the extent that it is built up of genuine societies, that is, local communes and trade communes and their step by step association. What Gierke says of the Co-operative Movement in the Middle Ages is true of every structurally rich society: it is "marked by a tendency to expand and extend the unions, to produce larger associations over and above the smaller association, confederations over and above individual unions, all-embracing confederations over and above particular confederations." At whatever point we examine the structure of such a society we find the cell-tissue "Society" everywhere, i.e. a living and life-giving collaboration, an essentially autonomous consociation of human beings, shaping and re-shaping itself from within. Society is naturally composed not of disparate individuals but of associative units and the associations between them. Under capitalist economy and the State peculiar to it the constitution of society was being continually hollowed out, so that the modern individualizing process finished up as a process of atomization. At the same time the old organic forms retained their outer stability, for the most part, but they became hollow in sense and in spirit—a tissue of decay. Not merely what we generally call the masses but the whole of society is in essence amorphous, unarticulated, poor in structure. Neither do those associations help which spring from the meeting of economic or spiritual interests—the strongest of which is the party: what there is of human intercourse in them is no longer a living thing, and the compensation for the lost community-forms we seek in them can be found in none. In the face of all this, which makes "society" a contradiction in terms, the "utopian" socialists have aspired more and more to a restructuring of society; not, as the Marxist critic thinks, in any romantic attempt to revive the stages of development that are over and done with, but rather in alliance with the decentralist counter-tendencies which can be perceived underlying all economic and social evolution, and in alliance with something that is slowly evolving in the human soul: the most intimate of all resistances—resistance to mass or collective loneliness.

Victor Hugo called Utopia "the truth of to-morrow." Those efforts of the spirit, condemned as inopportune and derided as "utopian socialism," may well be clearing the way for the structure of society-to-be. (There is, of course, no historical process that is necessary in itself and independent of human resolve.) It is obvious that here, too, it is a matter of preserving the community-forms that remain and filling them anew with spirit, and a new spirit. Over the gateway to Marxist centralization stands—for who knows how long?—the inscription in which Engels summed up the tyrannical character of the automatism in a great factory: "Lasciate ogni autonomia voi ch'entrate." Utopian socialism fights for the maximum degree of communal autonomy possible in a "restructured" society.

In that socialist meeting of 1928, I said: "There can be pseudo-realization of socialism, where the real life of man to man is but little changed. The real living together of man with man can only thrive where people have the real things of their common life in common; where they can experience, discuss and administer them together; where real fellowships and real work Guilds exist. We see more or less from the Russian attempt at realization that human relationships remain essentially unchanged when they are geared to a socialist-centralist hegemony which rules the life of individuals and the life of the natural social groups. Needless to say we cannot and do not want to go back to primitive agrarian communism or to the corporate State of the Christian Middle Ages. We must be quite unromantic, and, living wholly in the present, out of the recalcitrant material of our own day in history, fashion a true community."

23

Freedom, Control, and Utopia

B. F. Skinner's Defense of Behavioral Engineering

B. F. Skinner's novel *Walden Two* (1948) describes an imaginary community in which the traditional problems facing utopian planners have been solved by the application of the principles of "behavioral engineering." Psychological conditioning or "positive reinforcement" has been used instead of political action to build a better social environment. Frazier, the chief behavioral engineer in Walden Two, advocates "a constantly experimental attitude toward everything," whether it be child rearing or creative use of leisure. As in Bellamy's utopia, labor-credits have been substituted for money, and altruistic incentives have replaced those based on egoism and competition. As in Plato's ideal city-state, democracy has been abandoned in favor of rule by experts, the community controls the moral training of its citizens, and there is common ownership of property. Although individual marriages still exist in Walden Two, the family structure has been weakened by having the community take over several of its functions, and eventually experimental breeding will probably be undertaken. "Free love" is not practiced, but there is plenty of "free affection." These are some of the features of Skinner's ideal community in which peace and prosperity, harmony and happiness have been achieved primarily by the application of "positive reinforcement."

Skinner's belief in the possibility of a utopia thus rests upon his faith in a behavioral engineering based upon a science of human nature and undertaken by scientifically trained "men of good will." As the following selection shows, he is well aware of the dangers mankind faces when scientists are misled and science is misused: when it is used to make war more destructive or when it is used by men of evil will, for example; but he believes this is not the fault of science but of its misapplication. Properly applied scientific methods have been enormously successful in controlling nature; we must now, Skinner urges, learn to apply them as successfully to society in order to control human affairs. A science of human nature coequal to the science of nature needs to be developed. We must learn to observe human behavior

287

before we can describe and understand it, and we must learn to describe and understand it before we can predict it. Most important, we must learn to predict it before we can control it.

Presupposed throughout the study of human behavior must be, Skinner holds, the assumption of scientific determinism: that such behavior is the result of lawful relations rather than chance, of uniformity rather than spontaneity; that there is no such thing as "uncaused behavior" or unconditioned chance. To be sure, human behavior is highly complex and difficult to observe objectively, but this does not mean, Skinner points out, that such behavior necessarily presents problems which are insoluble to the scientist. With sufficient ingenuity and skill, the scientific student of human behavior can discover the "causes" of human behavior and explain why men behave as they do. Then, and only then, can he manipulate these "causes" and control human behavior.

As a neo-behaviorist, Skinner does not expect to discover the causes of human behavior within individuals, for in his view there are no "psychic causes." Instead he holds that behavior can only be explained by independent variables or "causes" lying outside the organism. It is the human being's relations to his external physical environment rather than his relations to some sort of inner psychic environment that accounts for his characteristic behavior patterns.

In Skinner's major work, *Science and Human Behavior* (1953), he classified the variables involved in human behavior, surveyed the processes of behavioral change, analyzed "self-control" from a neo-behavioristic standpoint, discussed the behavior of people in groups, considered controlling agents such as government, law, religion, psychotherapy, economic factors, and education, and, finally, presented a view of the total culture as a controlling social environment. It is within this context that his approach to the problem of designing an intentional community or a utopia can be best understood.

In *Science and Human Behavior*, as in *Walden Two*, Skinner expresses his conviction that the design of a culture, in that it determines human behavior, is far too important a matter to be left largely to accident. Why should we not, Skinner asks, deliberately design social environments and perform experiments in controlling human behavior which would eventually allow us to overcome the shortcomings of previous cultures? If we refuse to because we fear control and loss of freedom, we are, he believes, under an illusion. A man or a group of men who refuse to accept control in the name of freedom is, Skinner suggests, only relinquishing control to others who may be far less skilled, and far less hesitant to manipulate and to use the social system for their own selfish ends.

From B. F. Skinner, "Freedom and the Control of Men," The American Scholar 25 (Winter 1955–56): 47–65. Reprinted by permission of B. F. Skinner.

The second half of the twentieth century may be remembered for its solution of a curious problem. Although Western democracy created the conditions responsible for the rise of modern science, it is now evident that it may never fully profit from that achievement. The so-called "democratic philosophy" of human behavior to which it also gave rise is increasingly in conflict with the application of the methods of science to human affairs. Unless this conflict is somehow resolved, the ultimate goals of democracy may be long deferred.

I

Just as biographers and critics look for external influences to account for the traits and achievements of the men they study, so science ultimately explains behavior in terms of "causes" or conditions which lie beyond the individual himself. As more and more causal relations are demonstrated, a practical corollary becomes difficult to resist: it should be possible to *produce* behavior according to plan simply by arranging the proper conditions. Now, among the specifications which might reasonably be submitted to a behavioral technology are these: Let men be happy, informed, skillful, well behaved and productive.

This immediate practical implication of a science of behavior has a familiar ring, for it recalls the doctrine of human perfectibility of eighteenth- and nineteenth-century humanism. A science of man shares the optimism of that philosophy and supplies striking support for the working faith that men can build a better world and through it, better men. The support comes just in time, for there has been little optimism of late among those who speak from the traditional point of view. Democracy has become "realistic," and it is only with some embarrassment that one admits today to perfectionistic or utopian thinking.

The earlier temper is worth considering, however. History records many foolish and unworkable schemes for human betterment, but al most all the great changes in our culture which we now regard as worthwhile can be traced to perfectionistic philosophies. Governmental, religious, educational, economic and social reforms follow a common pattern. Someone believes that a change in a cultural practice —for example, in the rules of evidence in a court of law, in the characterization of man's relation to God, in the way children are taught to read and write, in permitted rates of interest, or in minimal housing standards—will improve the condition of men: by promoting justice, permitting men to seek salvation more effectively, increasing the literacy of a people, checking an inflationary trend, or improving public health and family relations, respectively. The underlying hypothesis is always the same: that a different physical or cultural environment will make a different and better man.

The scientific study of behavior not only justifies the general pattern of such proposals; it promises new and better hypotheses. The earliest cultural practices must have originated in sheer accidents. Those which strengthened the group survived with the group in a sort of natural selection. As soon as men began to propose and carry out changes in practice for the sake of possible consequences, the evolutionary process must have accelerated. The simple practice of making changes must have had survival value. A further acceleration is now to be expected. As laws of behavior are more precisely stated, the changes in the environment required to bring about a given effect may be more clearly specified. Conditions which have been neglected because their effects were slight or unlooked for may be shown to be relevant. New conditions may actually be created, as in the discovery and synthesis of drugs which affect behavior.

This is no time, then, to abandon notions of progress, improvement or, indeed, human perfectibility. The simple fact is that man is able, and now as never before, to lift himself by his own bootstraps. In achieving control of the world of which he is a part, he may learn at last to control himself.

II

Timeworn objections to the planned improvement of cultural practices are already losing much of their force. Marcus Aurelius was probably right in advising his readers to be content with a haphazard amelioration of mankind. "Never hope to realize Plato's republic," he sighed, ". . . for who can change the opinions of men? And without a change of sentiments what can you make but reluctant slaves and hypocrites?" He was thinking, no doubt, of contemporary patterns of control based upon punishment or the threat of punishment which, as he correctly observed, breed only reluctant slaves of those who submit and hypocrites of those who discover modes of evasion. But we need not share his pessimism, for the opinions of men can be changed. The techniques of indoctrination which were being devised by the early Christian Church at the very time Marcus Aurelius was writing are relevant, as are some of the techniques of psychotherapy and of advertising and public relations. Other methods suggested by recent scientific analyses leave little doubt of the matter.

The study of human behavior also answers the cynical complaint that there is a plain "cussedness" in man which will always thwart efforts to improve him. We are often told that men do not want to be changed, even for the better. Try to help them, and they will outwit you and remain happily wretched. Dostoevsky claimed to see some plan in it. "Out of sheer ingratitude," he complained, or possibly boasted, "man will play you a dirty trick, just to prove that men are still men and not the keys of a piano. . . . And even if you could prove that a man is only a piano key, he would still do something out of sheer perversity—he would create destruction and chaos—just to gain his point. . . . And if all this could in turn be analyzed and prevented by predicting that it would occur, then man would deliberately go mad to prove his point." This is a conceivable neurotic reaction to inept control. A few men may have shown it, and many have enjoyed Dostoevsky's statement because they tend to show it. But that such perversity is a fundamental reaction of the human organism to controlling conditions is sheer nonsense.

So is the objection that we have no way of knowing what changes to make even though we have the necessary techniques. That is one of the great hoaxes of the century—a sort of booby trap left behind in the retreat before the advancing front of science. Scientists themselves have unsuspectingly agreed that there are two kinds of useful propositions about nature—facts and value judgments—and that science must confine itself to "what is," leaving "what ought to be" to others. But with what special sort of wisdom is the non-scientist endowed? Science is only effective knowing, no matter who engages in it. Verbal behavior proves upon analysis to be composed of many different types of utterances, from poetry and exhortation to logic and factual description, but these are not all equally useful in talking about cultural practices. We may classify useful propositions according to the degrees of confidence with which they may be asserted. Sentences about nature range from highly probable "facts" to sheer guesses. In general, future events are less likely to be correctly described than past. When a scientist talks about a projected experiment, for example, he must often resort to statements having only a moderate likelihood of being correct; he calls them hypotheses.

Designing a new cultural pattern is in many ways like designing an experiment. In drawing up a new constitution, outlining a new educational program, modifying a religious doctrine, or setting up a new fiscal policy, many statements must be quite tentative. We cannot be sure that the practices we specify will have the consequences we predict, or that the consequences will reward our efforts. This is in the nature of such proposals. They are not value judgments—they are guesses. To confuse and delay the improvement of cultural practices by quibbling about the word *improve* is itself not a useful practice. Let us agree, to start with, that health is better than illness, wisdom better than ignorance, love better than hate, and productive energy better than neurotic sloth.

Another familiar objection is the "political problem." Though we know what changes to make and how to make them, we still need to control certain relevant conditions, but these have long since fallen into the hands of selfish men who are not going to relinquish them for such purposes. Possibly we shall be permitted to develop areas which at the moment seem unimportant, but at the first signs of success the strong men will move in. This, it is said, has happened to Christianity, democracy and communism. There will always be men who are fundamentally selfish and evil, and in the long run innocent goodness cannot have its way. The only evidence here is historical, and it may be misleading. Because of the way in which physical science developed, history could until very recently have "proved" that the unleashing of the energy of the atom was quite unlikely, if not impossible. Similarly, because of the order in which processes in human behavior have become available for purposes of control, history may seem to prove that power will probably be appropriated for selfish purposes. The first techniques to be discovered fell almost always to strong, selfish men. History led Lord Acton to believe that power corrupts, but he had probably never encountered absolute power, certainly not in all its forms, and had no way of predicting its effect.

An optimistic historian could defend a different conclusion. The principle that if there are not enough men of good will in the world the first step is to create more seems to be gaining recognition. The Marshall Plan (as originally conceived), Point Four, the offer of atomic materials to power-starved countries—these may or may not be wholly new in the history of international relations, but they suggest an increasing awareness of the power of governmental good will. They are proposals to make certain changes in the environments of men for the sake of consequences which should be rewarding for all concerned. They do not exemplify a disinterested generosity, but an in terest which is the interest of everyone. We have not yet seen Plato's philosopher-king, and may not want to, but the gap between real and utopian government is closing.

III

But we are not yet in the clear, for a new and unexpected obstacle has arisen. With a world of their own making almost within reach, men of good will have been seized with distaste for their achievement. They have uneasily rejected opportunities to apply the techniques and findings of science in the service of men, and as the import of effective cultural design has come to be understood, many of them have voiced an outright refusal to have any part in it. Science has been challenged before when it has encroached upon institutions already engaged in the control of human behavior; but what are we to make of benevolent men, with no special interests of their own to defend, who nevertheless turn against the very means of reaching long-dreamed-of goals?

What is being rejected, of course, is the scientific conception of man and his place in nature. So long as the findings and methods of science are applied to human affairs only in a sort of remedial patchwork, we may continue to hold any view of human nature we like. But as the use of science increases, we are forced to accept the theoretical structure with which science represents its facts. The difficulty is that this structure is clearly at odds with the traditional democratic conception of man. Every discovery of an event which has a part in shaping a man's behavior seems to leave so much the less to be credited to the man himself; and as such explanations become more and more comprehensive, the contribution which may be claimed by the individual himself appears to approach zero. Man's vaunted creative powers, his original accomplishments in art, science and morals, his capacity to choose and our right to hold him responsible for the consequences of his choice—none of these is conspicuous in this new self-portrait. Man, we once believed, was free to express himself in art, music and literature, to inquire into nature, to seek salvation in his own way. He could initiate action and make spontaneous and capricious changes of course. Under the most extreme duress some sort of choice remained to him. He could resist any effort to control him, though it might cost him his life. But science insists that action is initiated by forces impinging upon the individual, and that caprice is only another name for behavior for which we have not yet found a cause.

In attempting to reconcile these views it is important to note that the traditional democratic conception was not designed as a description in the scientific sense but as a philosophy to be used in setting up and maintaining a governmental process. It arose under historical circumstances and served political purposes apart from which it cannot be properly understood. In rallying men against tyranny it was necessary that the individual be strengthened, that he be taught that he had rights and could govern himself. To give the common man a new conception of his worth, his dignity, and his power to save himself, both here and hereafter, was often the only resource of the revolutionist. When democratic principles were put into practice, the same doctrines were used as a working formula. This is exemplified by the notion of personal responsibility in Anglo-American law. All governments make certain forms of punishment contingent upon certain kinds of acts. In democratic countries these contingencies are expressed by the notion of responsible choice. But the notion may have no meaning under governmental practices formulated in other ways and would certainly have no place in systems which did not use punishment.

The democratic philosophy of human nature is determined by certain political exigencies and techniques, not by the goals of democracy. But exigencies and techniques change; and a conception which is not supported for its accuracy as a likeness—is not, indeed, rooted in fact at all—may be expected to change too. No matter how effective we judge current democratic practices to be, how highly we value them or how long we expect them to survive, they are almost certainly not the *final* form of government. The philosophy of human nature which has been useful in implementing them is also almost certainly not the last word. The ultimate achievement of democracy may be long deferred unless we emphasize the real aims rather than the verbal devices of democratic thinking. A philosophy which has been appropriate to one set of political exigencies will defeat its purpose if, under other circumstances, it prevents us from applying to human affairs the science of man which probably nothing but democracy itself could have produced.

IV

Perhaps the most crucial part of our democratic philosophy to be reconsidered is our attitude toward freedom—or its reciprocal, the control of human behavior. We do not oppose all forms of control because it is "human nature" to do so. The reaction is not characteristic of all men under all conditions of life. It is an attitude which has been carefully engineered, in large part by what we call the "literature" of democracy. With respect to some methods of control (for example, the threat of force), very little engineering is needed, for the techniques or their immediate consequences are objectionable. Society has suppressed these methods by branding them "wrong," "illegal" or "sinful." But to encourage these attitudes toward objectionable forms of control, it has been necessary to disguise the real nature of certain indispensable techniques, the commonest examples of which are education, moral discourse, and persuasion. The actual procedures appear harmless enough. They consist of supplying information, presenting opportunities for action, pointing out logical relationships, appealing to reason or "enlightened understanding," and so on. Through a masterful piece of misrepresentation, the illusion is fostered that these procedures do not involve the control of behavior; at most, they are simply ways of "getting someone to change his mind." But analysis not only reveals the presence of well-defined behavioral processes, it demonstrates a kind of control no less inexorable, though in some ways more acceptable, than the bully's threat of force.

Let us suppose that someone in whom we are interested is acting unwisely—he is careless in the way he deals with his friends, he drives too fast, or he holds his golf club the wrong way. We could probably help him by issuing a series of commands: don't nag, don't drive over sixty, don't hold your club that way. Much less objectionable would be "an appeal to reason." We could show him how people are affected by his treatment of them, how accident rates rise sharply at higher speeds, how a particular grip on the club alters the way the ball is struck and corrects a slice. In doing so we resort to verbal mediating devices which emphasize and support certain "contingencies of reinforcement"—that is, certain relations between behavior and its consequences—which strengthen the behavior we wish to set up. The same consequences would possibly set up the behavior without our help, and they eventually take control no matter which form of help we give. The appeal to reason has certain advantages over the authoritative command. A threat of punishment, no matter how subtle, generates emotional reactions and tendencies to escape or revolt. Perhaps the controllee merely "feels resentment" at being made to act in a given way, but even that is to be avoided. When we "appeal to reason," he "feels freer to do as he pleases." The fact is that we have exerted *less* control than in using a threat; since other conditions may contribute to the result, the effect may be delayed or, possibly in a given instance, lacking. But if we have worked a change in his behavior at all, it is because we have altered relevant environmental conditions, and the processes we have set in motion are just as real and just as inexorable, if not as comprehensive, as in the most authoritative coercion.

"Arranging an opportunity for action" is another example of disguised control. The power of the negative form has already been exposed in the analysis of censorship. Restriction of opportunity is recognized as far from harmless. As Ralph Barton Perry said in an article which appeared in the Spring, 1953, *Pacific Spectator*, "Whoever determines what alternatives shall be made known to man controls what that man shall choose *from*. He is deprived of freedom in proportion as he is denied access to *any* ideas, or is confined to any range of ideas short of the totality of relevant possibilities." But there is a positive side as well. When we present a relevant state of affairs, we increase the likelihood that a given form of behavior will be emitted. To the extent that the probability of action has changed, we have made a definite contribution. The teacher of history controls a student's behavior (or, if the reader prefers, "deprives him of freedom") just as much in *presenting* historical facts as in suppressing them. Other conditions will no doubt affect the student, but the contribution made to his behavior by the presentation of material is fixed and, within its range, irresistible.

The methods of education, moral discourse, and persuasion are acceptable not because they recognize the freedom of the individual or his right to dissent, but because they make only *partial* contributions to the control of his behavior. The freedom they recognize is freedom from a more coercive form of control. The dissent which they tolerate is the possible effect of other determiners of action. Since these sanctioned methods are frequently ineffective, we have been able to convince ourselves that they do not represent control at all. When they show too much strength to permit disguise, we give them other names and suppress them as energetically as we suppress the use of force. Education grown too powerful is rejected as propaganda or "brainwashing," while really effective persuasion is decried as "undue influence," "demagoguery," "seduction," and so on.

If we are not to rely solely upon accident for the innovations which give rise to cultural evolution, we must accept the fact that some kind of control of human behavior is inevitable. We cannot use good sense in human affairs unless someone engages in the design and construction of environmental conditions which affect the behavior of men. Environmental changes have always been the condition for the improvement of cultural patterns, and we can hardly use the more effective methods of science without making changes on a grander scale. We are all controlled by the world in which we live, and part of that world has been and will be constructed by men. The question is this: Are we to be controlled by accident, by tyrants, or by ourselves in effective cultural design?

The danger of the misuse of power is possibly greater than ever.

It is not allayed by disguising the facts. We cannot make wise decisions if we continue to pretend that human behavior is not controlled, or if we refuse to engage in control when valuable results might be forthcoming. Such measures weaken only ourselves, leaving the strength of science to others. The first step in a defense against tyranny is the fullest possible exposure of controlling techniques. A second step has already been taken successfully in restricting the use of physical force. Slowly, and yet imperfectly, we have worked out an ethical and governmental design in which the strong man is not allowed to use the power deriving from his strength to control his fellow men. He is restrained by a superior force created for that purpose— the ethical pressure of the group, or more explicit religious and governmental measures. We tend to distrust superior forces, as we currently hesitate to relinquish sovereignty in order to set up an international police force. But it is only through such counter-control that we have achieved what we call peace—a condition in which men are not permitted to control each other through force. In other words, control itself must be controlled.

Science has turned up dangerous processes and materials before. To use the facts and techniques of a science of man to the fullest extent without making some monstrous mistake will be difficult and obviously perilous. It is no time for self-deception, emotional indulgence, or the assumption of attitudes which are no longer useful. Man is facing a difficult test. He must keep his head now, or he must start again—a long way back.

V

Those who reject the scientific conception of man must, to be logical, oppose the methods of science as well. The position is often supported by predicting a series of dire consequences which are to follow if science is not checked. A recent book by Joseph Wood Krutch, *The Measure of Man*, is in this vein. Mr. Krutch sees in the growing science of man the threat of an unexampled tryanny over men's minds. If science is permitted to have its way, he insists, "we may never be able really to think again." A controlled culture will, for example, lack some virtue inherent in disorder. We have emerged from chaos through a series of happy accidents, but in an engineered culture it will be "impossible for the unplanned to erupt again." But there is no virtue in the accidental character of an accident, and the diversity which arises from disorder can not only be duplicated by design but vastly extended. The experimental method is superior to simple observation just because it multiplies "accidents" in a systematic coverage of the possibilities. Technology offers many familiar examples. We no longer wait for immunity to disease to develop from a series of accidental exposures, nor do we wait for natural mutations in sheep and cotton to produce better fibers; but we continue to make use of such accidents when they occur, and we certainly do not prevent them. Many of the things we value have emerged from the clash of ignorant armies on darkling plains, but it is not therefore wise to encourage ignorance and darkness.

It is not always disorder itself which we are told we shall miss but certain admirable qualities in men which flourish only in the presence of disorder. A man rises above an unpropitious childhood to a position of eminence, and since we cannot give a plausible account of the action of so complex an environment, we attribute the achievement to some admirable faculty in the man himself. But such "faculties" are suspiciously like the explanatory fictions against which the history of science warns us. We admire Lincoln for rising above a deficient school system, but it was not necessarily something *in him* which permitted him to become an educated man in spite of it. His educational environment was certainly unplanned, but it could nevertheless have made a full contribution to his mature behavior. He was a rare man, but the circumstances of his childhood were rare too. We do not give Franklin Delano Roosevelt the same credit for becoming an educated man with the help of Groton and Harvard, although the same behavioral processes may have been involved. The founding of Groton and Harvard somewhat reduced the possibility that fortuitous combinations of circumstances would erupt to produce other Lincolns. Yet the founders can hardly be condemned for attacking an admirable human quality.

Another predicted consequence of a science of man is an excessive uniformity. We are told that effective control—whether governmental, religious, educational, economic or social—will produce a race of men who differ from each other only through relatively refractory genetic differences. That would probably be bad design, but we must admit that we are not now pursuing another course from choice. In a modern school, for example, there is usually a syllabus which specifies what every student is to learn by the end of each year. This would be flagrant regimentation if anyone expected every student to comply. But some will be poor in particular subjects, others will not study, others will not remember what they have been taught, and diversity is assured. Suppose, however, that we someday possess such effective educational techniques that every student will in fact be put in possession of all the behavior specified in a syllabus. At the end of the year, all students will correctly answer all questions on the final examination and "must all have prizes." Should we reject such a system on the grounds that in making all students excellent it has made them all alike? Advocates of the theory of a special faculty might contend that an important advantage of the present system is that the good student learns *in spite of* a system which is so defective that it is currently producing bad students as well. But if really effective techniques are available, we cannot avoid the problem of design simply by preferring the status quo. At what point should education be deliberately inefficient?

Such predictions of the havoc to be wreaked by the application of science to human affairs are usually made with surprising confidence. They not only show a faith in the orderliness of human behavior; they presuppose an established body of knowledge with the help of which it can be positively asserted that the changes which scientists propose to make will have quite specific results—albeit not the results they foresee. But the predictions made by the critics of science must be held to be equally fallible and subject also to empirical test. We may be sure that many steps in the scientific design of cultural patterns will produce unforeseen consequences. But there is only one way to find out. And the test must be made, for if we cannot advance in the design of cultural patterns with absolute certainty, neither can we rest completely confident of the superiority of the status quo.

VI

Apart from their possibly objectionable consequences, scientific methods seem to make no provision for certain admirable qualities and faculties which seem to have flourished in less explicitly planned cultures; hence they are called "degrading" or "lacking in dignity." (Mr. Krutch has called the author's *Walden Two* an "ignoble Utopia.") The conditioned reflex is the current whipping boy. Because conditioned reflexes may be demonstrated in animals, they are spoken of as though they were exclusively subhuman. It is implied, as we have seen, that no behavioral processes are involved in education and moral discourse or, at least, that the processes are exclusively human. But men do show conditioned reflexes (for example, when they are frightened by all instances of the control of human behavior because some instances engender fear), and animals do show processes similar to the human behavior involved in instruction and moral discourse. When Mr. Krutch asserts that " 'Conditioning' is achieved by methods which by-pass or, as it were, short-circuit those very reasoning faculties which education proposes to cultivate and exercise," he is making a technical statement which needs a definition of terms and a great deal of supporting evidence.

If such methods are called "ignoble" simply because they leave no room for certain admirable attributes, then perhaps the practice of admiration needs to be examined. We might say that the child whose education has been skillfully planned has been deprived of the right to intellectual heroism. Nothing has been left to be admired in the way he acquires an education. Similarly, we can conceive of moral training which is so adequate to the demands of the culture that men will be good practically automatically, but to that extent they will be deprived of the right to moral heroism, since we seldom admire automatic goodness. Yet if we consider the end of morals rather than certain virtuous means, is not "automatic goodness" a desirable state of affairs? Is it not, for example, the avowed goal of religious education? T. H. Huxley answered the question unambiguously: "If some great power would agree to make me always think what is true and do what is right, on condition of being a sort of clock and wound up every morning before I got out of bed, I should close instantly with the offer." Yet Mr. Krutch quotes this as the scarcely credible point of view of a "proto-modern" and seems himself to share T. S. Eliot's contempt for ". . . systems so perfect/That no one will need to be good."

"Having to be good" is an excellent example of an expendable honorific. It is inseparable from a particular form of ethical and moral control. We distinguish between the things we *have* to do to avoid punishment and those we *want* to do for rewarding consequences. In a culture which did not resort to punishment we should never "have" to do anything except with respect to the punishing contingencies which arise directly in the physical environment. And we are moving toward such a culture, because the neurotic, not to say psychotic, by-products of control through punishment have long since led compassionate men to seek alternative techniques. Recent research had explained some of the objectionable results of punishment and has revealed resources of at least equal power in "positive reinforcement." It is reasonable to look forward to a time when man will seldom "have" to do anything, although he may show interest, energy, imagination and productivity far beyond the level seen under the present system (except for rare eruptions of the unplanned).

What we have to do we do with *effort*. We call it "work." There is no other way to distinguish between exhausting labor and the possibly equally energetic but rewarding activity of play. It is presumably good cultural design to replace the former with the latter. But an adjustment in attitudes is needed. We are much more practiced in admiring the heroic labor of a Hercules than the activity of one who works without having to. In a truly effective educational system the student might not "have to work" at all, but that possibility is likely to be received by the contemporary teacher with an emotion little short of rage.

We cannot reconcile traditional and scientific views by agreeing upon *what* is to be admired or condemned. The question is whether anything is to be so treated. Praise and blame are cultural practices which have been adjuncts of the prevailing system of control in Western democracy. All peoples do not engage in them for the same purposes or to the same extent, nor, of course, are the same behaviors always classified in the same way as subject to praise or blame. In admiring intellectual and moral heroism and unrewarding labor, and in rejecting a world in which these would be uncommon, we are simply demonstrating our own cultural conditioning. By promoting certain tendencies to admire and censure, the group of which we are a part has arranged for the social reinforcement and punishment needed to assure a high level of intellectual and moral industry. Under other and possibly better controlling systems, the behavior which we now admire would occur, but not under those conditions which make it admirable, and we should have no reason to admire it because the culture would have arranged for its maintenance in other ways.

To those who are stimulated by the glamorous heroism of the battlefield, a peaceful world may not be a better world. Others may reject a world without sorrow, longing or a sense of guilt because the relevance of deeply moving works of art would be lost. To many who have devoted their lives to the struggle to be wise and good, a world without confusion and evil might be an empty thing. A nostalgic concern for the decline of moral heroism has been a dominating theme in the work of Aldous Huxley. In *Brave New World* he could see in the application of science to human affairs only a travesty on the notion of the Good (just as George Orwell, in *1984*, could foresee nothing but horror). In a recent issue of *Esquire*, Huxley has expressed the point this way: "We have had religious revolutions, we have had political, industrial, economic and nationalistic revolutions. All of them, as our descendants will discover, were but ripples in an ocean of conservatism—trival by comparison with the psychological revolution toward which we are so rapidly moving. *That* will really be a revolution. When it is over, the human race will give no further trouble." (Footnote for the reader of the future: This was not meant as a happy ending. Up to 1956 men had been admired, if at all, either for causing trouble or alleviating it. Therefore—)

It will be a long time before the world can dispense with heroes and hence with the cultural practice of admiring heroism, but we move in that direction whenever we act to prevent war, famine, pestilence and disaster. It will be a long time before man will never need to submit to punishing environments or engage in exhausting labor, but we move in that direction whenever we make food, shelter, clothing and labor-saving devices more readily available. We may mourn the passing of heroes but not the conditions which make for heroism. We can spare the self-made saint or sage as we spare the laundress on the river's bank struggling against fearful odds to achieve cleanliness.

VII

The two great dangers in modern democratic thinking are illustrated in a paper by former Secretary of State Dean Acheson. "For a long time now," writes Mr. Acheson, "we have gone along with some well-tested principles of conduct: That it was better to tell the truth than falsehoods; . . . that duties were older than and as fundamental as rights; that, as Justice Holmes put it, the mode by which the inevitable came to pass was effort; that to perpetrate a harm was wrong no matter how many joined in it . . . and so on. . . . Our institutions are founded on the assumption that most people follow these principles most of the time because they want to, and the institutions work pretty well when this assumption is true. More recently, however, bright people have been fooling with the machinery in the human head and they have discovered quite a lot. . . . Hitler introduced new refinements [as the result of which] a whole people have been utterly confused and corrupted. Unhappily neither the possession of this knowledge nor the desire to use it was confined to Hitler . . . Others dip from this same devil's cauldron."

The first dangerous notion in this passage is that most people follow democratic principles of conduct "because they want to." This does not account for democracy or any other form of government if we have not explained why people *want* to behave in given ways. Although it is tempting to assume that it is human nature to believe in democratic principles, we must not overlook the "cultural engineering" which produced and continues to maintain democratic practices. If we neglect the conditions which produce democratic *behavior*, it is useless to try to maintain a democratic *form* of government. And we cannot expect to export a democratic form of government successfully if we do not also provide for the cultural practices which will sustain it. Our forebears did not discover the essential nature of man; they evolved a pattern of behavior which worked remarkably well under the circumstances. The "set of principles" expressed in that pattern is not the only true set or necessarily the best. Mr. Acheson has presumably listed the most unassailable items; some of them are probably beyond question, but others—concerning duty and effort—may need revision as the world changes.

The second—and greater—threat to the democracy which Mr. Acheson is defending is his assumption that knowledge is necessarily on the side of evil. All the admirable things he mentions are attributed to the innate goodness of man, all the detestable to "fooling with the machinery in the human head." This is reminiscent of the position, taken by other institutions engaged in the control of men, that certain forms of knowledge are in themselves evil. But how out of place in a democratic philosophy! Have we come this far only to conclude that well-intentioned people cannot study the behavior of men without becoming tyrants or that informed men cannot show good will? Let us for once have strength and good will on the same side.

VIII

Far from being a threat to the tradition of Western democracy, the growth of a science of man is a consistent and probably inevitable part of it. In turning to the external conditions which shape and maintain the behavior of men, while questioning the reality of inner qualities and faculties to which human achievements were once attributed, we turn from the ill-defined and remote to the observable and manipulable. Though it is a painful step, it has far-reaching consequences, for it not only sets higher standards of human welfare but shows us how to meet them. A change in a theory of human nature cannot change the facts. The achievements of man in science, art, literature, music and morals will survive any interpretation we place upon them. The uniqueness of the individual is unchallenged in the scientific view. Man, in short, will remain man. (There will be much to admire for those who are so inclined. Possibly the noblest achievement to which man can aspire, even according to present standards, is to accept himself for what he is, as that is revealed to him by the methods which he devised and tested on a part of the world in which he had only a small personal stake.)

If Western democracy does not lose sight of the aims of humanitarian action, it will welcome the almost fabulous support of its own science of man and will strengthen itself and play an important role in building a better world for everyone. But if it cannot put its "democratic philosophy" into proper historical perspective—if, under the control of attitudes and emotions which it generated for other purposes, it now rejects the help of science—then it must be prepared for defeat. For if we continue to insist that science has nothing to offer but a new and more horrible form of tyranny, we may produce just such a result by allowing the strength of science to fall into the hands of despots. And if, with luck, it were to fall instead to men of good will in other political communities, it would be perhaps a more ignominious defeat; for we should then, through a miscarriage of democratic principles, be forced to leave to others the next step in man's long struggle to control nature and himself.

24

In Defense of Utopia

ANDREW HACKER'S RESTATEMENT OF
THE UTOPIAN FAITH

One of the best short defenses of utopian thinking written in our day is the following by the American political scientist and social critic Andrew Hacker (b. 1929). Currently a professor of government at Cornell University, Hacker is the author of several books, including *Politics and the Corporation* (1958) and *Political Theory* (1961), and a wide variety of articles, both scholarly and popular, on such subjects as academic freedom, lawyers in Congress, Britain's political style, the new conservatism, State righters, the pill and morality, the welfare state, and utopia. His understanding of utopian thinking has allowed him to throw new light on the development of British socialism and the workings of the British Labour movement.[1] His insight into utopian planning has also given him an usual perspective from which to view the life of the modern corporation.

In his article "Utopia, Inc."[2] he points out the characteristics of some corporation planning which relate such planning to the grand tradition of radical and utopian thinking. Having discovered that happy workers are better, more productive thinkers, corporation planners have set out to build new utopias for workers complete with country clubs and psychiatrists.

While Hacker recognizes that the corporation communities are popular today because they can meet the felt needs of millions of Americans, and that they will probably be an important part of American life for some time to come, he points out their shortcomings. As static societies dedicated to peace and prosperity in the present, they will probably not be able to meet changing needs and challenges in the future. Furthermore, as products of community designs undertaken not by philosophers but by behavioral engineers with tremendous power to manipulate the "subjects" which they are making

[1] Andrew Hacker, "Original Sin vs. Utopia in British Socialism," *The Review of Politics* 18 (April 1956): 184–206.

[2] Andrew Hacker, "Utopia, Inc.," *The Commonweal* 65 (February 1957): 479–81.

happy, they present us with a rather frightening prospect, "the specter of predictable man" which we should probably wish to dispell at all costs if we value our freedom.[3] The dangers facing man which were pointed out by Dostoyevsky and Huxley should not, Hacker warns, go unheeded. Using modern techniques already available to social scientists, human beings can be adjusted and socialized until they are transformed into predictable entities with no individual capriciousness and no freedom of choice. Although Hacker would like to see the area of human autonomy preserved and extended, he accepts no easy refutation of determinism.[4] To attack deterministic approaches as Joseph Wood Krutch attacks B. F. Skinner's behavioral engineering can be merely the expression of "naive humanism." Utopian thinking, to be sure, can at times be terrifying—especially when it leads to the conception of the complete control of mankind—but this does not mean that this is its only possible outcome or that it should be eschewed.

[3] See Andrew Hacker, "The Specter of Predictable Man," *The Antioch Review* 14 (1954): 195–207. Also his "Dostoevsky's Disciples: Man and Sheep in Political Theory," *The Journal of Politics* 17 (1955): 590–613.

[4] For Hacker's most recent views see his *The End of the American Era* (New York: Atheneum, 1970).

From Andrew Hacker, "In Defense of Utopia," Ethics
65 *(January 1955): 135–38. Copyright 1955 by the
University of Chicago. Reprinted by permission of
the University of Chicago Press and Andrew Hacker.*

It is no secret that the Utopian is not a respectable member of the
company of political and social theorists. Of course, it must be ac-
knowledged that his breed never was numerous. In this country, since
Edward Bellamy published his *Looking Backward* in 1887, no significant writer has seen fit to pen a Utopia. There have, of course, been
Utopian murmurings in a variety of writings, ranging from Marxists
to current-day followers of Adam Smith. And a number of people, as I
shall indicate, are "Utopian" in their thinking on contemporary affairs.
But all have been roundly attacked: attacked on the seemingly self-
sufficient ground that the ideas and ideals which they ventured to
espouse were "Utopian."

I wish here, then, to speak in defense of the Utopia. Indeed, more
than that: I wish to persuade students of political theory that they
should create their own Utopias and commit them to paper. For
Utopias not only deserve a fair hearing: they should be one of the
main foundation stones of the body of theory now being created.
Utopianism need know no parties. It is quite true that most Utopians
have been collectivists of one sort or another. However, in England,
Tory Radicals such as Richard Oastler were bona fide Utopians. And
one can catch glimmers of the same mode of thinking in Benjamin
Disraeli's novels. The return to a pastoral medievalism which Oastler
and Disraeli advocated was quite respectable Utopianizing. In our
day Mr. Henry Luce's conception of a world built on the "American
Century" is a Utopian scheme, albeit dimly outlined. The World
Federalists, and the misty-eyed moralists at whom both George
Kennan and Reinhold Niebuhr lash out, are also Utopian in their
orientation. Many of them, of course, deny it. They should, it is my
contention, be proud of their way of thought. I do not happen to
agree with the grandiloquent Lucean or World Federalism schemes;
but one can still applaud their frankness despite the seeming ingenu-
ousness of their proponents.

A Utopia is a full-blooded animal. It is not at all subject to the current sociological contention of whether or not to introduce (or admit of possessing) values. It is *all* values. The Utopia is a model, conceived in the author's own mind's eye, of a perfect society. It contains all the possible facets of life that he can conceive of, ordered in the way he thinks they should be ordered. It can include aspects of life from art to zoölogy; the addition or omission of ingredients is purely the prerogative of its creator. I personally have such a Utopia of my own; but this is not the place to describe it. However, if the critics are to demolish Utopias, they must learn how to analyze Utopian language. But, more important, they must (at least while they have the subject under study) try to understand the Utopian rationale. If they do not do these things, their energetic demolition work will knock down many false gods; however, the Utopia itself will remain unscathed. One further point needs be made. To my mind a Utopia is not only all values: it is also all *desirable*. Until the introduction of *Brave New World* and *1984* this definition was usually granted. And we should continue to hold to the traditional view that a true Utopia is a society that the author wholeheartedly approves of The nightmares of Huxley and Orwell may be called many things But they ought not to be called Utopias.

The most recent critics of Utopian thinking can, I think, be divided into three main categories. For reasons both alliterative and economical I shall call them the Democrats, the Dialecticians, and the Devil-Hunters. The first set are mainly people who are concerned with the state of the world today. They are antiauthoritarian (which is admirable) and fearful of any dictatorial tendencies in our society. The second are *not* Hegelians or Marxists. They have, rather, read a trifle too much history and are impressed with the utility of historical "laws" and processes. The last are religiously minded for the most part and are much attracted with the newly resurrected vogue of the importance of original sin.

The critic who is most bothersome is the Democrat. He has read Karl Popper's *The Open Society and Its Enemies*. And he has been persuaded by the powerful condemnation of Plato which lies on those scholarly pages. He uses Popper to vanquish Utopia for once and for all. In the *Republic*, Popper says, Plato intends to make everyone do just what Plato wants him to do. Plato and his guardian-henchmen will tell lies, establish a caste system, wrench children from their mothers' breasts, and generally close the door on the open society. Through subtle devices and stratagems, they will eventually have herded everyone into Utopia. Hence, says the Democrat, Utopias are autocratic. The Utopian is, in reality, a ruthless would-be dictator who would compel everyone else to follow a set pattern of life, and to "enjoy" it whether he likes it or not. Plato, like his child Rousseau, would force us all to be free. Hence individual choice is out of the question. Utopia must mean the rankest compulsion: for has not the Utopian told us how people *must* behave?

Perhaps the best way to answer the Democrat is by way of analogy. Suppose the date to be 100 A.D. and that I have been invited to address the Imperial Society of Gladiators in Rome. I am seeking to convert them to a Utopian scheme called Parliamentarianism. In the course of my speech I say:

> In my Utopia—let us put the date arbitrarily at 1953 A.D.—people will not, as a method of settling disputes, want to pick up swords and slice their adversaries in two. They will prefer to sit in things called congresses and parliaments, to discuss and compromise in order to reach agreement. This is what most people in my Utopia will *want* to do. Strangely enough, they will prefer talk and persuasion to bloodshed.

Of course, however, being Popper-minded gladiators, they will immediately accuse me of being dictatorial. I will want, they would say, to *make* people prefer discussion to fighting. Nevertheless, it is true that in 1953 A.D. *most of us* do prefer debating and ompromise to fighting. And it is *not* because some sub e autocrat · s compelled us to abandon one value for the other. It s n his vein that the Utopian would say that his future society is descriptive rather than compulsive. All that he is doing is to *describe* a society in which people want to do some things and do not want to do others. The things that they want to do—of their own "free will"—may be quite alien to our culture. But there is no harm in this fairy-tale kind of description. And, considering what Roman gladiators would think of the genuine desires that a good number of us harbor today, there is no obstacle in the way of imagining even "stranger" (i.e., Utopian) desires on the part of members of a future Utopia. There is no wilful disobedience to Utopian norms in Utopia; and this is for the simple reason that it *is* a Utopia that is being described. Utopias do not need police forces; they only need some imagination.

The Dialectician is more scientific. He is worried about historical change. Things have always changed, he says, and they always will change. But a Utopia, he goes on to say, stands still. William Morris as much as admitted it when he subtitled his famous Utopia *An Epoch of Rest.* In the same way Marxists allow for social change *until* a Communist society comes into existence. Then "prehistory" ceases and "history" begins. But his "history" just stands still; the clock is made to stop. One need hold no brief for the Communist brand of Utopia (and I do not), but one should at least have the courtesy to give its proponents a hearing on their *methodology*. And I think that any Utopian (Marxist or otherwise) would reply as follows:

> I have put a good deal of time and effort into planning my Utopia. In fact I think that *I* have done quite enough work. Why do I have to tell you what comes *after* my Utopia? In point of fact, I don't know. I am not so ingenuous as to think that *something* will not follow it. But I have not had the time or inclination to imagine out that step. In fact, I am quite content to get *to* my Utopia. If you grant me that, I shall not complain.

What we must note, then, is that the Dialectician is not telling the Utopian something he does not know. He is really asking him to do a job that is not his. If the Dialectician wants to join the Utopian ranks and describe Utopia II which will follow Utopia I, then more power to him. (And these same arguments apply to the economist who asserts that there will *always* be "scarce goods." Of course, the reply to him depends on the particular Utopia. In some there won't be any scarce goods—you just pick what you want off the trees. In others people will not want things that are in short supply. And in still others they may want them, but they will be quite content with the kind of rationing system that the Utopian author has devised.)

"Human nature doesn't change," says the Devil-Hunter. Original sin was original, and that means it is eternal and everlasting. If Utopia is collectivistic, there will always be some individualists to throw a monkey wrench in the machinery. If it is individualistic, there will always be some obnoxious collectivists intent on sabotage. Human nature in society, the Devil-Hunter says, is diverse. And hence *some* people will always be bound to be perverse. A Utopia postulates universal and unanimous contentment. But this has never existed anywhere or anytime. Hence the Utopia will need a center of power that will coerce nonconformists and persuade dissidents who veer from Utopian standards. But despite these measures the sinners will continue to crop up. There is nothing you can do to thwart them.

This criticism, it will be noted, contains elements of the Democrat's argument in it. And to it the Utopian must reply:

> This is *my* Utopia. And in it "human nature" (which I consider to be infinitely malleable) is going to be just what I intend to make it. Everyone (bar none) will hold the same basic values, and such ancillary changes as have to be made will be mutually satisfactory to all. There will be no saboteurs because no one *wants* to harm the beautiful mechanism.

In saying this the Utopian disposes not only of original sin (which he doesn't believe in anyway) but also of the vexed problem of power.

For when people "naturally" do things in such ways that they do not irritate other people, then a coercive state is no longer necessary. So there is no point in trying to smear the Utopian with the label "anarchist." Utopias are all anarchies. They have to be.

Finally, a plaint common to all critics of Utopia is the simple question: Will not life be so very *dull* in Utopia? To this the Utopian must reply: "Not at all." It is just that the *kinds* of disputes that we have nowadays will be obsolete in Utopia. Politics and economics, armies and navies, diplomacy and wars—all of these as we now know them will be quite passé. But there may well be raging controversies on, say, the merits of sea-shell *vs.* butterfly collecting, surfboarding *vs.* mountain-climbing, or Bach *vs.* Britten. If we find it hard nowadays to understand why the gold standard advocates once got so annoyed at the silver standard people, the Utopians will find it equally difficult to see why the Democrats and Republicans are at sword's points in our time. Dullness springs from lack of variety and dearth of controversy. But there is no reason to suspect that *new kinds* of variety and controversy may not be most exhilarating in Utopian society.

But why be a Utopian? Three main reasons can, I think, be offered: frailty, simple-mindedness, and honesty. On the first count, many of us must have a star to guide us through our thinking: this is our Utopia. We cannot settle for patching a piece here and replacing a scrap there. The only *raison d'être* we can find for patching and replacing the pieces and scraps in a specific way is if we can conceive of them as leading to a far-flung goal. We are ardent in advocating a better water supply system for Chicago because Utopia will have a perfect water supply system. The "piecemeal engineering" that Professor Popper admires may be well and good for those who can see a water supply system as an end in itself. But many of us are too frail to be content with such a short-range target. It is only if we see all roads (water, electricity, fire service, ad infinitum) as leading to Utopia that we will have any spur to join in with day-to-day reforms.

In addition we are too simple-minded to derive much from abstract words like "freedom," "equality," "law," "rights," and so forth. But if we conjure up an image of a Utopia which is inhabited by real (real, at least, in our minds) people; and if we label these people as being free and equal, living under law, having rights, etc.; then and only then do these abstractions take on some body and some meaning. A philosophical word in politics cannot stir us without a picture to illustrate it. Non-Utopians usually have vague pictures for these words. But for the Utopian they are in sharp focus, and hence the definitions are that much more clear.

Lastly, we think we are being honest. A Utopian, at least, is making his ideals very explicit. In truth, everyone has ideals. Some people sneak them in through the back door. The Utopian makes them march up through the front gate. It is better to systematize them into a Utopian scheme rather than pretend to being "scientific" or "nonpartisan." These feats are often professed, but they are never accomplished. This is not to say that analytical and institutional studies should cease. Rather, it would be all to the good if every writer of political books sat down, after his second or third volume had appeared, and penned his own private Utopia. This would not only be a guide to the rest of us; it would also cause him to scrutinize his own assumptions more carefully.

No one can deny that Utopias may be abused. Unimaginative or unscrupulous politicians may set their course rigidly toward a Utopia, and everyone who stands between them and the final destination may be ground underfoot. But this is not an indictment of Utopianizing alone. Any general outlook can be abused, and all should be handled with care. It is not Utopias which are dangerous. They are usually written by mild and scholarly people. It is the wilful men who use Utopian slogans. And they do not need Utopian books to help them; if they want they will construct literary bedlams of their own. But there are all too many people who regard political life, in Professor Michael Oakeshott's words, as "a boundless and bottomless sea [with] neither starting-place nor appointed destination." Those of us who find such a prospect distasteful will seek refuge in our Utopias.

QUESTIONS ON PART IV

11. How does Wells propose to protect individual freedom in a utopian state? What limits would he be willing to impose upon such freedom? Do you agree or disagree with his treatment of freedom? Why?

THE UTOPIAN ELEMENT IN SOCIALISM (BUBER)

12. What is Buber's explanation of the origin and use of utopias?
13. What is the meaning of Buber's phrase, "the socialist secularization of eschatology"?
14. What disguised utopian elements does Buber find in Marxist socialism?
15. Why does Buber favor utopian socialism rather than Marxism?

FREEDOM, CONTROL, AND UTOPIA (SKINNER)

16. Why does Skinner think that the prospect of controlling human behavior is better today than ever before?
17. What are some of the objections to control of human behavior considered by Skinner? What arguments does he present to meet these objections?
18. What is Skinner's opinion of the views of human nature presented by Dostoyevsky's underground man and by Joseph Wood Krutch?
19. What is Skinner's view of the democratic form of government? Explain what he means by the statement that "the ultimate achievement of democracy may be long deferred unless we emphasize the real aims rather than the verbal devices of democratic thinking."
20. Explain why Skinner rejects the notion of freedom. Do you agree with his reasoning? Why or why not?

IN DEFENSE OF UTOPIA (HACKER)

21. What is Hacker's reply to the objection that utopias are autocratic?
22. Why does Hacker think that the dialectical critic is unjustified in his objection that utopias are too static?
23. How does Hacker defend the utopian against the objection that "human nature doesn't change"?
24. Why does Hacker think that life in utopia would not necessarily be dull? Do you agree?
25. Do you agree with Hacker's defense of utopia? Why or why not?

SUPPLEMENTARY READINGS

(Works marked * are available in paperbound editions.)

Barker, Ernest. *Political Thought of Plato and Aristotle.* New York: Dover Publications, 1959.

Becker, George J. "Edward Bellamy: Utopia, American Plan," *Antioch Review* XIV (1954): 181–94.

Bowman, Sylvia E. *The Year 2000; a Critical Biography of Edward Bellamy.* New York: Bookman Associates, 1958

Buber, Martin. *Paths in Utopia,* translated by R. F. C. Hull. Boston: Beacon Press, 1949.

Chase, Stuart. *The Most Probable World.* New York: Harper & Row, 1968.

Clarke, Arthur. *Profiles of the Future.* New York: Harper & Row, 1963.

Crossman, R. H. S. *Plato Today,* 2nd ed. New York: Oxford University Press, 1959.

Dubos, René. *The Dreams of Reason: Science and Utopia.* New York: Columbia University Press, 1961.

Ernst, Morris L. *Utopia 1976.* New York: Rinehart and Company, 1955.

Finer, Herman. *The Road to Reaction.* Boston: Little, Brown & Co., 1945. (An answer to Friedrich A. Hayek, *The Road to Serfdom.*)

Fromm, Erich. *The Revolution of Hope.* New York: Bantam Books, 1968.

———. *The Sane Society.* New York: Fawcett Publications, 1955.

Fisher, James A., and Peyton E. Richter. "Education for Citizenship: A Utopian Approach to General Education," *Journal of Higher Education* XXVIII (April 1957): 220–24.

Goodman, Paul. *Utopian Essays and Practical Proposals.* New York: Vintage Books, 1960.

Goodman, Percival, and Paul. *Communitas: Means of Livelihood and Ways of Life.* New York: Vintage Books, 1960.

Hacker, Andrew. "Utopia, Inc.," *Commonweal* 65 (8 February 1957): 479–81.

Hillegas, Mark R. *The Future as Nightmare: H. G. Wells and the Anti-Utopians.* New York: Oxford University Press, 1967.

Horsburgh, H. J. N. "The Relevance of the Utopian," *Ethics* 67 (1957): 127–38.

Infield, Henrik F. *The American Intentional Communities.* Glen Gardner, N. J.: Community Press, 1955.

———. *Utopia and Experiment: Essays in the Sociology of Cooperation*. New York: Frederick A. Praeger, 1955.

Kahn, Hermann, and Anthony J. Wiener. *The Year 2000: A Framework for Speculation on the Next Thirty-three Years*. New York: Macmillan Co., 1967.

Levi, Albert W. "Edward Bellamy: Utopian," *Ethics* LV (1945): 131–44.

Levinson, R. B. *In Defense of Plato*. Cambridge, Mass.: Harvard University Press, 1950.

Madison, Charles A. "Edward Bellamy, Social Dreamer," *New England Quarterly* XV (1942): 444–66.

Mead, Margaret. "Toward More Vivid Utopias," *Science* 126 (November 1957): 957–61.

Morgan, Arthur E. *Edward Bellamy*. New York: Columbia University Press, 1944.

Popper, Karl. *The Open Society and its Enemies*. Princeton: Princeton University Press, 1950.

Richter, Peyton E. "Utopian Speculation and Practical Thinking," *Improving College and University Teaching*, Autumn 1959, pp. 104–106.

Riesman, David. "Some Observations on Community Plans and Utopia," in *Selected Essays from Individualism Reconsidered*. New York: Doubleday and Co., 1955.

Rogers, Carl R., and B. F. Skinner. "Some Issues Concerning the Control of Human Behavior," *Science* CXXIV (1956): 1057–66.

Shonfield, Andrew. "Thinking about the Future," *Encounter* XXXII (February 1969).

Sibley, Mulford Q. "Apology for Utopia, II," *The Journal of Politics*, II (May 1940): 165–88.

Skinner, B. F. *Science and Human Behavior*. New York: Macmillan Co., 1953.

———. *Walden Two*. New York: Macmillan Co., 1948.

Sommer, Robert. "Planning 'Notplace' for Nobody," *Saturday Review* 52 (5 April 1969): 67–69.

Spiro, Melford E. *Kibbutz, Venture in Utopia*. New York: Schocken Books, 1956.

Todd, Richard. "Walden Two: Three? Many More?," *The New York Times Magazine*, 15 March 1970: pp. 24–126.

Wagar, W. Warren. *H. G. Wells and the World State*. New Haven: Yale University Press, 1961.

———. *The City of Man: Prophecies of a World Civilization in Twentieth Century Thought*. Baltimore: Penguin Books, 1963.

Williams, Donald C. "The Social Scientist as Philosopher and King," *Philosophical Review* LVIII (1949): 345–59.

Young, Michael, ed. *Forecasting and the Social Sciences*. London: William Heinemann, 1968.

Index

317